THE OTHER ISLANDS OF NEW YORK CITY

A HISTORY AND GUIDE

Sharon Seitz and Stuart Miller

Second Edition

THE COUNTRYMAN PRESS
Woodstock, Vermont

Library of Congress Cataloging-in-Publication Data
Seitz, Sharon.
The other islands of New York City : a history and guide / by
Sharon Seitz & Stuart Miller.--2nd ed.
  p. cm.
  Includes bibliographical references (p. 285) and index.
ISBN 0-88150-502-1 (alk. paper)
1. Islands—New York (State)—New York—History. 2. Islands—
New York (State)—New York—Guidebooks. 3. New York
(N.Y.)—Guidebooks. 4. New York (N.Y.)—History. I. Miller,
Stuart, 1966– II. Title.

Cover and text design by Julie Duquet
Cover photo by Catherine Steinmann
Maps by Paul Woodward, © 1996, 2001 The Countryman Press
Interior photographs by Sharon Seitz unless otherwise credited

Published by The Countryman Press
P.O. Box 748, Woodstock, VT 05091

Distributed by W. W. Norton & Company, Inc.
500 Fifth Avenue, New York, NY 10110

Printed in the United States
10 9 8 7 6 5 4 3 2

Dedications

For Mom and Dad—without your endless supply of love, encouragement, and inspiration, none of this would have been possible.

—Stuart

To all those who have encouraged me on my journey thus far . . . and to Rattsu.

—Sharon

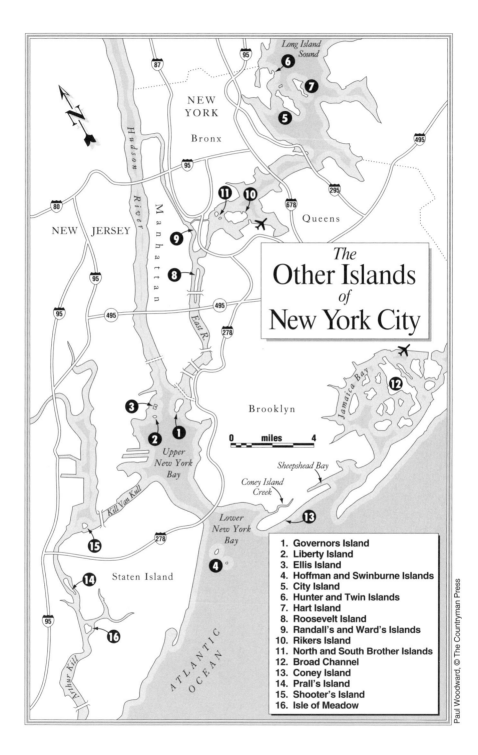

The
Other Islands
of
New York City

1. **Governors Island**
2. **Liberty Island**
3. **Ellis Island**
4. **Hoffman and Swinburne Islands**
5. **City Island**
6. **Hunter and Twin Islands**
7. **Hart Island**
8. **Roosevelt Island**
9. **Randall's and Ward's Islands**
10. **Rikers Island**
11. **North and South Brother Islands**
12. **Broad Channel**
13. **Coney Island**
14. **Prall's Island**
15. **Shooter's Island**
16. **Isle of Meadow**

Contents

Preface to the Second Edition

WHY NOW? That's the logical question when any new edition of a book is released. Of course, when a book is about New York City, updates can be justified nearly every month since the city changes so rapidly. In the five years since this book was first published, virtually all of the islands have experienced transformations large and small. Ellis Island's abandoned south side was wrested away by New Jersey, much to the shock of New Yorkers. City Island experienced a building boom, much to the chagrin of many residents. A new stadium went up in Coney Island, while one came down on Randall's Island. Roosevelt Island lost its state subsidies, and Prall's Island lost hundreds of nesting herons and egrets (many of which seem to have moved to Hoffman Island). In fact, this edition even features two previously overlooked islands—Hog Island, which was wiped out in 1902 and forgotten until 1997; and White Island, which is just now capturing attention as part of a new nature center in Brooklyn.

The timing was also perfect for another reason. We have been fortunate enough to realize a dream we have had since publishing the first edition—to transform this book into a documentary. Twice, eager but inexperienced producers approached us; both times the project went nowhere. But last year, Alan Glazen, who has produced numerous documentaries for WNET, New York's public television station, read our book and decided to bring it to life. Producing the television project with Alan brought us back to the islands, revealing new snippets and stories to tell, and reinforcing our belief that the islands play a unique and pivotal role in New York City's life and history. So this edition of the book will have a television companion on Channel 13, a sort of South Brother to its North Brother Island.

The islands have, quite naturally, become extremely significant to us. And so, when we got married in 1998, we chose the Morris Yacht Club on City Island for the big day. Our island adventures continue . . .

—SHARON SEITZ AND STUART MILLER

Introduction to the Island Empire

TAKE THE A TRAIN. And be sure to get a window seat, because after the train emerges from the dark subway tunnels of Manhattan and Brooklyn and onto the elevated lines of Queens, the hard-edged cityscape slowly vanishes. Outside your urban porthole, commercial strips beneath the tracks fade into private homes; then the entire landscape melts into an aquatic tableau dotted with boats out for a day of fishing. White-rumped sandpipers, American oystercatchers, and common snipes congregate in marshes and wetlands. Then the subway stops, and its double doors slide open, revealing a weathered fishing village where houses are built on stilts. For the price of a token, you've traveled worlds away from the steamy city in the distance.

You have just entered one of New York City's "other" islands.

Broad Channel, home of the Jamaica Bay Wildlife Refuge and a modest community, is one of dozens of islands within the confines of New York City, a metropolis where even the "mainland" is an island. Manhattan, Staten Island, Queens, and Brooklyn are all either islands or part of Long Island; only the Bronx is connected to the contiguous United States.

New York's true archipelago, however, resides in its rivers, bays, and other waterways. Some of its islands are famous, like Ellis Island, some obscure, like North Brother, and some, like Coney Island, are island has-beens. From Rat Island, a tiny two-acre speck in the Bronx, to Rikers Island, a sprawling mini-city in Queens with thirteen thousand prisoners, the islands of New York City are often overlooked pieces in the city's geographic jigsaw puzzle.

New York's islands were formed by glacial erosion, most of which occurred twelve to eighteen thousand years ago. As glaciers slowly flowed south, they carved channels in the region's rocky terrain; some sections were so hard that they weren't ground down. When the glaciers melted, they filled in the channels between the landmasses, leaving the hard knobs jutting out as islands.

The isolation unique to islands has endowed them with special purpose and an evocative aura throughout history: from Napoleon's banishment to St. Helena after Waterloo and Charles Darwin's evolutionary theories cultivated in the seclusion of the Galapagos Islands, to the swashbuckling drama of *Treasure Island* and the slapstick comedy of *Gilligan's Island.* Islands are at once forlorn, mysterious, seductive, and eccentric. "What's so fascinating about islands is that they're just out of reach," says New York historian Joyce Gold.

But the remoteness that fires the imagination also relegates many islands to the recesses of the mind—Woody Guthrie never looked beyond Manhattan when he composed his classic lines: "This land is your land, this land is my land, from California to the New York Island." Even with the benefit of growing up in New York, we were guilty of the same myopia, having overlooked the city's vast network of islands for years.

Finally, in 1990, while at Columbia University's Graduate School of Journalism, Sharon investigated the curious, often derogatory stories she'd heard as a child in Cypress Hills about the cloistered community of Broad Channel. Her award-winning master's thesis revealed a proud neighborhood of activists determined to safeguard their island hamlet in the face of continuous adversity.

After visiting Ellis Island two years later with Stuart's family—whose roots traced back through the immigrant depot—we chatted casually about the contrast between the Island of Hope and Broad Channel. Thinking we'd stumbled upon a magazine story, we explored further and discovered an entire galaxy of islands, many with a crucial role in New York City's development.

Born a great port city, New York gradually shed its maritime identity as it evolved into a sprawling megalopolis and center for manufacturing, finance, and culture. As New York embraced the modern era—building bridges and tunnels to speed the flow of commerce, and highways like the FDR Drive and the Belt Parkway that cut its citizenry off from the waterfront—its identity as a city of islands diminished.

Many of the city's islands also followed a general pattern of development: Family farms of wealthy merchants were replaced first by forts, then by oppressive government institutions and garbage dumps, and at last by recreational centers and wildlife preserves. According to Russell Gilmore, author of *Forts of New York City,* the islands' most critical role came during their "fort phase" as defenders of America's independence. In the years leading up to the War of 1812 with England, the U.S. government erected a comprehensive defense to protect New York. The outer bastions were on the Brooklyn and Staten Island shores and aimed at The Narrows, while the interior defense was constructed at Castle Clinton and Ellis, Bedloe's, and Governors Islands. While the English invaded and burned Washington, D.C., during the war, their navy, which blockaded New York City, was deterred from entering the harbor. The island forts never had to fire a shot.

By 1820, New York claimed 123,706 inhabitants, surpassing Philadelphia as the most populous city. The number soared to 813,669 by 1860; a quarter of the newcomers were Irish immigrants. A similar boom occurred throughout the rest of the nation, bringing with it an increase in crime and poverty and stirring fears that America's church, family, and social order were in jeopardy. The government, which was run by a hand-ful of wealthy men, turned to newly developed institutions, like the asylum and the prison, to keep the underclass in check. To maximize segregation, municipalities nationwide routinely placed institutions well outside the city limits; for its part, New York City bought up islands, which were nearby, yet isolated. Between 1828 and 1892, the government turned first to Blackwell's Island, then to Randall's, Ward's, Hart, North Brother, Rikers, and Ellis Islands for warehousing the sick, criminal, indigent, and immigrant. Hoffman and Swinburne Islands were built from scratch as quarantines to pacify citizens opposed to a quarantine on Staten Island.

These islands "were waste places that could be spared very readily," John Van Dyke wrote in his 1909 book, *The New New York*. However, Van Dyke added, public opinion was changing, and New Yorkers were ques-tioning whether the city had "given up to its crippled and aged, its thugs and thieves, its paupers and prisoners, the most livable and lovable por-tions of the town." This sentiment, combined with the escalating cost of operating these isolated institutions and revelations about widespread bru-tality and corruption there, led to a change in policy beginning in the 1930s.

While institutions still occupy some islands, many have been reclaimed for the public good, hosting everything from parks and wildlife sanctuar-ies to a new community and a historical museum. Indeed, the islands are now so desirable that the government and developers are clamoring to gen-erate big bucks by building upscale hotels and conference centers on Roosevelt, Ellis, and Governors Islands. And in the last two decades migratory birds have adopted long-abandoned islands like North Brother, enlightening New York on the virtue of preserving open space in this ultra-urban environment. That these islands play host to rare and significant birds is "a real challenge to our notion of ourselves," says Omie E. Medford of the Waterfront and Open Space Division of the New York City Planning Commission. "We are challenging ourselves to reinvent the city and the harbor, and these islands show there is room for serious environmental features, that nature doesn't have to be elsewhere."

Toward that end, the city, the state, not-for-profits, and private developers have recently sought to reconnect New Yorkers to their 578 miles of waterfront, from creating a major new park along the Hudson River to plans for a park along the Brooklyn waterfront, and even plans for walking and bike paths along the Bronx River. Entrepreneurs have also revived ferry service as an efficient and refreshing mode of city travel. As New York gets reacquainted with its splendid shoreline, we hope this book encourages people to look beyond the water's edge to the city's intriguing island empire.

Notes on the Archipelago

When we told people we were writing a book about New York City's islands, they invariably asked, "How many islands are there?"

Well, it depends. Some are islands when the tide is low. Jamaica Bay has many of these "now-it's-an-island, now-it's-not" types, like JoCo Marsh and Pumpkin Patch Marsh. Some were islands long ago. Landfill has fused many of them to the "mainland," changing the city's contours. Berrian's Island is now connected to Astoria, Queens, and is the site of a Consolidated Edison plant, while Crooke's Island has been transformed into Crooke's Point, a peninsula in Great Kills, Staten Island. Some, like Goose Island in the Bronx, are mere bumps in the water with few tales to tell.

We almost had another island to add, one fabricated from toxic materials dredged from the harbor. Proposed in 1994, it was to be constructed off Coney Island, and later, Staten Island. But the government bowed to pressure from environmentalists and anglers, and instead Toxic Island has been relegated to an out-of-state dump.

For our book, we've profiled forty-two islands and former islands; some offer an engaging anecdote, whereas others have a rich, detailed history to share. There's the tragic plane crash on High Island, the burning of Coney Island's Dreamland, and the failed scheme of Solomon Riley, who wished to build an amusement park for blacks on Hart Island.

The book is organized geographically. For example, the chapter on Hoffman Island can be found in the *Lower New York Bay* section, while

Roosevelt Island is in the *East River* section. Most sections are punctuated by a chapter called *Forgotten Islands,* a roundup of smaller islands and former islands in the region.

Blocked off within most island chapters are stories related to the island's history that warrant their own moment in the spotlight. These *Historical Detours* feature compelling characters like Nellie Bly and Typhoid Mary, and dramatic vignettes like the burning of the excursion steamer *General Slocum.* We've included a brief profile of Robert Moses up front (see *Island Emperor*), since he influenced the fate of so many islands.

Because of their isolation, islands often exist in worlds of their own, breeding myths and misinformation. Rather than perpetuate fable as fact, we've included various versions when historical accounts are irreconcilable.

Exploring the Islands

While we hope none of our readers has cause to spend time on Rikers Island, many of these islands boast attractions worthy of a day's outing.

We have, in the *Exploring the Island* and *Where to Eat* sections, described these experiences—from riding the Cyclone at Coney Island to climbing the Statue of Liberty—in a narrative style filled with historical tidbits that should make the excursions enjoyable even to the armchair traveler.

We have included phone numbers and addresses so you can call ahead to check on prices and hours, since they change so frequently. (If it's free, we let you know.) The *Island Hopping* section will tell you how to get there, with accessibility icons to tell you at a glance how you can get there.

   by boat   *by subway*

   by bus   *by tram*

   by car   *by foot*

Island Emperor

Robert Moses, who once held twelve city and state posts simultaneously, wielded more authority and did more to shape New York City than any other figure in the twentieth century. Even the islands of New York didn't elude Moses' grasp. His endless drive to add parkland to the city—and bring ever more territory under his control—prompted him to acquire remote spots like Fort Lafayette and Hoffman, Swinburne, and Mill Rock Islands. He also used landfill to connect Hunter and Twin Islands to the mainland Bronx, and joined Randall's and Ward's Islands and Sunken Meadow in the East River.

Randall's Island, with ball fields and the buttresses of the Triborough Bridge dominating the landscape, perfectly symbolizes the master builder's two most significant achievements: the creation of parks and the construction of bridges. During his reign, Moses created more than two million acres of parkland and built twelve bridges.

Robert Caro, in his Pulitzer Prize–winning biography of Moses, *The Power Broker*, depicts Randall's Island as the capital of Moses' empire. Isolated from the city by the moat of the East River, and hidden from public view beneath the Triborough Bridge, Moses wielded untold power from Triborough Bridge and Tunnel Authority headquarters from the 1930s until the 1960s; as appointed head of this revenue-generating public authority, he was not accountable to the public.

Caro wrote that to enter Moses' kingdom, everyone—even top city officials—symbolically paid tribute at the Triborough's tollbooth. Once on the island, visitors were subject to the Authority's rules, not city law. Moses also maintained a splendid dining room with a full-time staff. Businessmen and officials were often kept waiting in an anteroom decorated with pictures of Moses with mayors, governors, and presidents. Once in the dining room, visitors enjoyed a fine repast while submitting to the emperor's monologues . . . and his will.

Born in Connecticut in 1888, Moses moved to New York with his family when he was nine. He studied at Yale, Oxford, and Columbia Universities. He was a genius—sharp in intellect and long in vision—who never lost his superhuman capacity for work.

He entered the city's political arena after attaining power in the 1920s as one of Governor Al Smith's top associates. In 1934, Moses became the city's first parks commissioner as well as head of the new Triborough Bridge and Tunnel Authority. He also later held a seat on the planning commission and the all-purpose title of city construction coordinator. In addition to these official roles, Moses controlled both the housing authority and often the mayor's office from behind the scenes.

While he started out as an idealist reformer, politics and an unslakable thirst for power transformed him into a ruthless, autocratic despot. As

Moses poured out ideas fifteen hours a day, decade after decade, he shifted sharply right on the political spectrum. His brutal philosophy included maxims like "Nothing I have ever done has been tinged with legality" and "If the end doesn't justify the means, what does?"

His accomplishments were touted as gifts to the masses, yet Moses cared little for the people themselves. Thus the highways he built ushering in New York's automobile age often came at the expense of mass transit, leaving idyllic places like Hunter or Randall's Island inaccessible to poor and working-class folks.

Moses died in 1981, leaving an island legacy that is mixed. He razed historic buildings on Hunter and Twin Islands and helped accelerate the decline of Coney Island's amusement area. His grandiose park plans for Hoffman and Swinburne Islands went unfulfilled, yet his benign neglect allowed them to develop into sanctuaries for migrating birds. He created the Jamaica Bay Wildlife Refuge at Broad Channel, but fortunately he failed in his effort to obliterate the community there.

Part I

Upper New York Bay

GOVERNORS ISLAND • LIBERTY ISLAND • ELLIS ISLAND • FORGOTTEN ISLANDS OF UPPER NEW YORK BAY

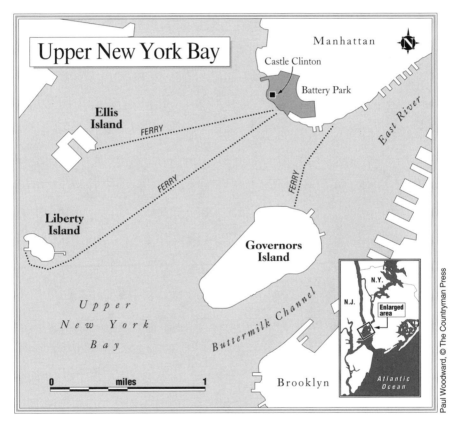

Hugged by New Jersey and Staten Island to the west and the Battery and Brooklyn to the east, the five-mile-long and four-mile-wide Upper New York Bay is the confluence of the Hudson and East Rivers.

1. Governors Island

"In 1800, New York magnanimously gave the Island to the Federal government to provide for the Nation's defense. It is only just that Governors Island now be returned to the people of New York, and that its historic efforts are protected."

—SENATOR DANIEL PATRICK MOYNIHAN
MAY 2000

Governors Island

FROM THE EARLIEST DAYS of colonial New York, the unique location of Governors Island captivated military and political leaders. Resting between Lower Manhattan and Brooklyn—where the East and Hudson Rivers converge and spill into Upper New York Bay—the island's strategic importance inspired its development as one of the city's great garrisons, a post that contributed to every war in American history.

While many of New York City's other islands—such as Roosevelt, Liberty, and Hart—changed with the times, Governors Island remained a bulwark of consistency for two centuries. But the island's days as the oldest continuous military post in the United States ended with the Coast Guard's departure in 1997. For the first time in centuries, this prime piece of real estate sits unused, facing an uncertain future.

When settlers sent by the Dutch West India Company reached New York Harbor in 1624, Governors Island was lush with groves of oak, hickory, and chestnut trees, and known to the Manahatas Indians as Pagganck, or "land of nut trees." The island's locale was so appealing that the Dutch built a fort there—even before settling Manhattan. The following year, more Dutch pioneers arrived, bringing some 103 head of cattle to what they called Nooten Eylandt, or Nutten Island. Little pasturage was found, however, and the bovines soon joined the colonists on Manhattan Island, where newly erected Fort Amsterdam succeeded the Nooten Eylandt fort.

Governors Island's 160 acres were then left to the Native Americans until 1637. In that year, the Falstaffian Wouter Van Twiller, who was governor and director general of New Netherland, acquired it from the Manahatas in exchange for two ax heads, a string of beads, and a few nails. The plump and prosperous leader envisioned lounging in an executive mansion there, a fantasy that never materialized. Strong tides made sailing to the island difficult, and Van Twiller was damned by his own corpulence—he was too big for the narrow rowboats of the day. A year later, Van Twiller was stripped of his title and properties after being accused of illegal land dealings and extorting money from his employer, the Dutch West India Company.

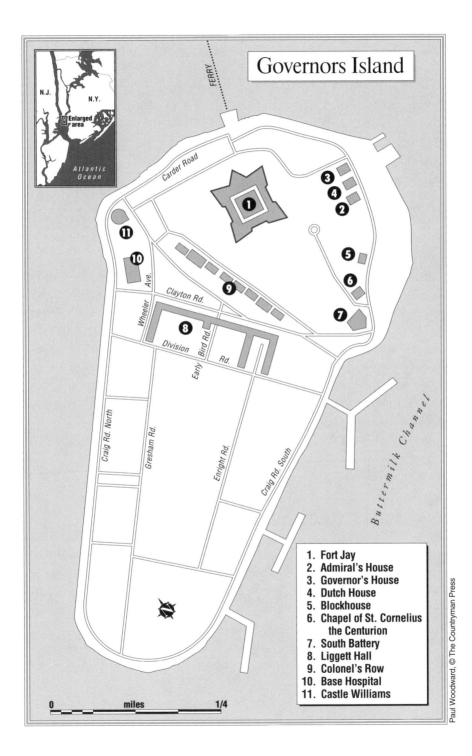

Governors Island

FERRY

Carder Road

N.J.

N.Y.

Enlarged area

Atlantic Ocean

Wheeler Ave.

Clayton Rd.

Division

Early Bird Rd.

Rd.

Craig Rd. North

Gresham Rd.

Enright Rd.

Craig Rd. South

Buttermilk Channel

1. Fort Jay
2. Admiral's House
3. Governor's House
4. Dutch House
5. Blockhouse
6. Chapel of St. Cornelius the Centurion
7. South Battery
8. Liggett Hall
9. Colonel's Row
10. Base Hospital
11. Castle Williams

0   miles   1/4

Paul Woodward, © The Countryman Press

The British gained control of New Amsterdam and Nooten Eylandt in 1664, renaming them New York and Nutten Island. To protect idyllic Nutten Island from falling into private hands, a decree in 1698 proclaimed it "the Denizen of His Majestie's Governors," thereby granting the island its name.

This rural retreat inspired manorial visions in yet another colonial executive, England's Lord Cornbury, Sir Edward Hyde. Cornbury was a peculiar fellow and a lackluster leader, revelous and unscrupulous. He was also rumored to be partial to women's clothing, which some say he donned publicly, as tribute to his cousin Queen Anne. A formal portrait of the outlandish governor, which today hangs in the New-York Historical Society, features Cornbury in a cinched blue gown and ladies' gloves, with a bow in his hair—although some historians question whether the drag queen who posed for the painting is indeed Cornbury.

In 1703, Cornbury capitalized on fears of a French invasion by instituting a tax to fund fortification of Governors Island. It included levies on people who wore pearl rings, men who donned periwigs, and bachelors twenty-five years of age or older. No fort was built, however, and Cornbury used the money to finance his estate, which, according to legend, was built on high ground overlooking Buttermilk Channel, between the south shore of the island and Brooklyn. He called it "the smiling garden of the sovereigns of the province." When Queen Anne learned of her cousin's controversial financial dealings, she yanked him from office.

Whether Queen Anne's later use of the island is tied to this family feud is speculation, but she nonetheless thought Governors Island the proper place to quarantine thousands of plague-infested Palatine refugees. These German Protestants had been routed from their homes in the lower Palatinate of the Rhine for religious reasons by France's Louis XIV in 1689. The exiles eventually wandered to England, where they petitioned Queen Anne to send them to the colonies, and in 1710 they were granted land near what is today Newburgh, New York. But when hundreds fell ill aboard ship, the queen quarantined the passengers on Governors Island. Many died and were buried there, but one teenage survivor later played a critical role in American history: John Peter Zenger became publisher of the *New York Weekly Journal* and, in 1735, established the legal precedent for freedom of the press when he was acquitted of seditious libel charges brought by the British government.

When the threat of war with France resurfaced in the mid-eighteenth century, British governors called for the fortification of Governors Island. Again, nothing was built, but in 1755, during the French and Indian War,

Historical Detour: Sub-Par Sub

In September of 1776, with the British commanding New York from Governors Island and Brooklyn Heights, the Continental army summoned an untested, top-secret weapon for a guerrilla attack on the warship of British admiral Richard Howe. Invented by American David Bushnell, the *Turtle* was the first submarine used for military purposes and was designed to destroy hostile ships by detonating explosives under their hulls.

Sitting in the primitive *Turtle* was like being inside a barrel—in the dark. Only six feet wide and seven and a half feet long, the wooden ship accommodated one man, who powered it with a hand-cranked propeller. A brave and adventurous army sergeant, Ezra Lee, left on his mission from the New York shore the night of September 6, and was soon thrown off-course by the tide. Lee cranked the strange vessel for more than two hours until he arrived—going about three miles an hour—underneath Howe's HMS *Eagle* sitting in New York Harbor.

When the sub's detonating device malfunctioned, Lee floated to the top to investigate. Much to his chagrin, he discovered that the fleet hadn't been destroyed and day was dawning, putting him in danger of being discovered. He quickly descended again and headed back to New York, but a broken compass required him to pop up occasionally to check his course.

His zigzag route brought him within several yards of Governors Island, where he attracted hundreds of redcoats to the parapet. When a small group of these armed curiosity-seekers began rowing out to the *Turtle*, Lee gave the defective magazine one desperate last try. The enemy retreated and the bomb drifted in the other direction, exploding far from Governors Island in the East River. Lee cranked away at the *Turtle* and made it safely back to New York.

the Fifty-first Regiment of the British Colonial Militia became the first troops stationed there. They were later joined by a British army regiment made up entirely of colonists known as The Loyal Americans, or The Royal American Regiment, Sixtieth Foot.

At the start of the American War for Independence, however, the Sixtieth Foot was transferred to British colonies in the West Indies to avert possible allegiance with their colonial brethren. The remaining redcoats, ill equipped to contend with anti-British sentiment, vacated the island and New York on June 7, 1775 . . . with plans to return in force.

In the spring of 1776, General George Washington sent General Israel Putnam and more than a thousand men to erect the first garrison of purely American troops on Governors Island. They were later aided by other regiments, including the famous Seventh Continental Infantry that fought at Bunker Hill. Determined to test the city's defenses, British warships sailed from Staten Island to the Hudson River on July 12 and were met by a barrage of artillery from Governors Island. Although the fray lasted about an hour and one ship was damaged, the navy proceeded unimpeded north to Westchester.

On August 27, the British army—confident they could overwhelm any American defenses and capture New York—successfully attacked Washington's troops in central Brooklyn, driving them back to Brooklyn Heights. The British could have easily captured Washington and his men—effectively ending the Revolution—if their navy had attacked Governors Island and sailed into the East River to cut off a colonial escape. Modern historians contend that Governors Island was spared this confrontation when strong tides and bad weather prevented an invasion.

In the wee hours of August 30, a beaten Washington and his battered troops withdrew to Manhattan under the protection of nighttime fog. The next day, the British navy, surprised by the maneuver and unsure whether any Continental forces remained, fired on Governors Island from a great distance. The island never felt the attack, and that night the island's Continental troops destroyed the cannons, packed up artillery and provisions, and joined Washington in retreat. The British completed their capture of New York on September 15, 1776, occupying the city and Governors Island until 1783.

During peacetime, the singular purpose of Governors Island was briefly forgotten; it was used as a racetrack, another quarantine station, and, in 1791, an elegant summer resort. But Britain and France were warring, and America's maritime commerce with both countries placed the young nation in the middle—bringing the United States to the brink of war with Britain and France. New York, again feeling vulnerable to attack, begged for protection. Congress eventually appropriated funds for new fortifications on Governors Island, but Governor George Clinton felt the sum was inade-

Shaped like a horseshoe and built on the northwest corner of Governor's Island, Castle Williams held an ideal vantage point from which to protect New York Harbor.

quate. He enlisted the help of students and faculty from Columbia College as well as local organizations. Between 1794 and 1798, they erected Fort Jay, named for John Jay, who had helped negotiate peace with Great Britain and had served as the first secretary of foreign affairs.

In 1800, seeking to shore up the nation's defenses, the federal government assumed control of Governors, Bedloe's, and Ellis Islands. During the next decade, while the British attacked American ships and impressed American seamen, fortifications were rapidly erected. Fort Jay was replaced by a more durable structure in 1803; it was later renamed Fort Columbus because of the unpopularity of Jay's treaty with Britain. The original name was restored in 1904. Castle Williams was completed on the island's northwest corner in 1811. Designer Colonel Jonathan Williams of the U.S. Army Corps of Engineers conceived the red sandstone roundhouse to work together with its sister fort, Castle Clinton, at the Battery. Of all the city's defenses, Castle Williams was the most impressive and influential. Based on a French design, it was the first casemated fort in North America—its multi-tiered parapets provided greater firepower than earlier forts. In 1812, defenses were strengthened when the South Battery was built to guard Buttermilk Channel. During the War of 1812, the British made no attempt to enter New York Harbor, and the islands' fortresses never fired a shot.

By the middle of the century, the harbor islands were nearly obsolete as forts, since the increased range of ships' cannons required confronting attackers out at sea. Governors Island, however, took on myriad military responsibilities. The local army headquarters in New York was transferred there in 1821, and from 1833 to 1920 the island housed one of the army's most important arsenals. The island was even briefly headquarters for the entire U.S. Army under General Winfield Scott in the 1840s.

With the outbreak of the Civil War in 1861, both the Union and Confederate armies thickened their ranks by instituting the first drafts. Understandably, a provision allowing Union men to buy their way out of the war for $300 did not sit well with less fortunate men. More than a thousand men were killed or injured when draft dodgers rioted in New York in 1863. When troops from Governors Island rushed to Manhattan to guard the Sub-Treasury on Wall Street, rioters intent on pillaging the unguarded military post rowed to the island. They quickly reversed course after a group of civilian employees lined the shore brandishing clubs, guns, axes, and knives, while others pretended to make ready at the garrison's cannons.

Far from the bloody battlefields of the Civil War, Governors Island processed and assigned thousands of volunteers and draftees and served as an assembly point for out-of-state militia organizations en route to the South. Castle Williams became a prison for Confederate soldiers; "Johnny Rebs" convicted of espionage and awaiting execution were usually jailed separately in the basement of a building near Fort Columbus.

The crowded brig and barracks on Governors Island bred postwar epidemics, forcing the government in 1870 to destroy contaminated buildings, including a strip of wooden houses nicknamed Rotten Row. In 1878, the War Department relocated army administrative operations to Governors Island and began modernizing the facilities.

By 1900, erosion had reduced the original 160 acres purchased by Wouter Van Twiller to a mere 70 acres. To reclaim the original dimensions, the U.S. Army Corps of Engineers built a bulkhead surrounding some 103 acres of submerged land adjacent to the south and southwest portion of the island and filled it with rock and dirt dredged from channels and excavated during the construction of New York's Fourth Avenue subway.

Even before the project was completed in 1912, the expanded island had become a showcase for daring innovators in the emerging field of air travel. On September 29, 1909, Wilbur Wright took off from the new ground on the first flight from Governors Island, circling the Statue of Liberty before returning. Later that year, he flew from the island to Grant's Tomb in

Upper Manhattan and back. In 1910, fellow pioneer Glenn Curtiss landed on Governors Island, completing a solo flight from Albany and winning a $10,000 purse offered by *New York World* publisher Joseph Pulitzer.

With the arrival of World War I, Governors Island reverted to its military role. On April 6, 1917, eighteen minutes after the United States declared war on Germany and the Central Powers, a battalion of the Twenty-second Infantry stationed on Governors Island jumped into the waiting boats of the Revenue Cutter Service (forerunner to the Coast Guard) and sailed across the Hudson to Hoboken, New Jersey. There the doughboys carried out the country's first hostile act of World War I—capturing German steamships berthed in Hoboken and impounding their crews at Ellis Island—all without firing a shot.

For the rest of the war, the island functioned as a military prison, hospital, supply base, and embarkation point for troops, a job requiring new warehouses, barracks, roads, and docks—all told, seventy buildings were erected. To access these scattered structures, the Governors Island Railroad was built. The smallest railroad in the world, it was outfitted with eight miles of track and steam locomotives that operated day and night. The railroad fell into disuse after the war, and in 1921 was sold as scrap metal.

After the war, the Army Air Service encouraged cities to build airports, and by the 1920s sophisticated airfields were needed to accommodate larger, rapidly evolving aircraft. Arguments were made for and against putting the first municipal airport at Governors Island, with certain military kingpins determined to preserve what they called a necessary military presence. One pugnacious New York congressman named Fiorello H. La Guardia called the island a "playground for generals who like to play golf and give garden parties," and accused the military of building new barracks on the island to forestall attempts to build an airport there. In the middle of this controversy, Floyd Bennett Field opened in Brooklyn in 1928 as the city's first municipal airport.

La Guardia's New York City dreamport, however, would not die easily. After being sworn in as mayor in 1934, the Little Flower launched a full-scale effort to build an airfield on Governors Island. He planned to seduce airlines away from Newark Airport and institute express passenger service at Governors Island as a supplement to Floyd Bennett Field. In defiance of critics who said Governors Island was too small, La Guardia proposed using landfill to increase the island by twenty-nine acres. President Franklin Roosevelt even considered a $100,000 survey to study connecting Governors Island to Lower Manhattan, and a local organization called

Community Councils advocated constructing a 615-acre airport island just south of Governors.

Well-known aviators like Amelia Earhart supported La Guardia's idea, but many airport operators and other experts insisted that Governors Island, which passengers could reach only by boat, was a poor site. Not only was it near a busy harbor and densely built financial center, but the island, critics argued, was plagued by fog and prevailing winds that would force descending planes to fly dangerously close to skyscrapers. In addition, they felt that with technology constantly producing bigger planes, the island would soon prove too small for a landing field.

La Guardia was unable to effectively counter those arguments, so the flamboyant leader focused instead on countering the army's claim that military readiness was needed close to New York City. (Terrorists had bombed Wall Street in 1920.) To illustrate his point, La Guardia masterminded a fantastic publicity stunt in April 1935. Leading a delegation of the House of Representatives' Military Affairs Committee, La Guardia made an unscheduled stop at the Sub-Treasury, where he asked Deputy Police Commissioner Harold Fowler to turn in a riot call. "I'll show you whether we need soldiers on Governors Island," La Guardia said.

Sirens blared and bells rang in alarm. Thirty seconds later, patrol wagons, radio cars, and 450 city policemen—unaware that this was merely a test—rushed to the scene, only to find La Guardia triumphantly announcing that his point had been proved.

La Guardia's stunt wasn't totally in vain. The House unanimously approved a bill in 1936 to turn Governors Island into an airport, but the bill died in Senate committee. La Guardia then turned his attention to North Beach Airport in Queens (now La Guardia Airport), and the army remained on Governors Island.

During World War II, Governors Island served much as it had during World War I. New York's induction stations were concentrated there; new warehouses, barracks, and extra hospital wards were erected; and some of the island's historic cannons and cannonballs were thrown on the scrap heap, contributing 2,321,000 pounds of metal to the war effort. Another postwar building program produced new apartments and a strange octagonal tower of white masonry built at the island's northeast tip to provide ventilation for the new Brooklyn Battery Tunnel. The army called Governors Island home until 1966, when the base was one of ninety-five closed around the country.

With the island declared surplus, developers envisioned building luxury high-rises with sweeping views of Lower Manhattan. But the U.S. Coast

Guard stepped in, maintaining the island's military legacy. On June 30, 1966, the solemn music of "Retreat" played as the army bade farewell to the island it had occupied for 172 years. Minutes later, a saluting battery thundered a Coast Guard welcome as the admiral's flag was raised high above Fort Jay, establishing Governors Island as the largest Coast Guard base in the world.

For three decades, Governors Island was home to a multi-mission base charged with search and rescue, protection of life at sea, environmental protection, port security, and even military readiness, with troops dispatched through the years to Haiti, Cuba, and the Persian Gulf. However, in 1997, the Coast Guard relocated operations, dispersing four thousand members and their families to bases along the East Coast. The closing of the base saves the Coast Guard about $30 million a year—$10 million in housing, fire, and police expenditures, and $20 million in ferry costs.

The Coast Guard's departure opens up one of the most exciting real-estate opportunities New York has had in years. Despite its military history and proximity to Manhattan, Governors Island is surprisingly idyllic. Architecturally, it resembles an Ivy League campus, with brick and stone edifices, manicured lawns, and elegant Victorian homes overlooking the stately trees of Nolan Park. Several redevelopment plans are being discussed. Indeed, the island's future may take one of many paths, depending upon how a tangle of political, planning, and financial realities sort themselves out.

In 1995, President Bill Clinton, sharing a helicopter ride over the city with Senator Daniel Patrick Moynihan, asked about the island's history. Clinton then offered to sell the island back to New York State for $1 if the city and state could agree on a plan that would benefit the public. Despite Clinton's offer, Congress would have to pass special legislation to allow the transaction before 2002. Most congressional Republicans, however, prefer auctioning the island to the highest bidder. Compounding matters, in 1997, Congress factored a $500 million sale price (since reduced to $300 million) into its Balanced Budget Act, meaning that it would have to make cuts elsewhere to give New York the island.

New York's initial development proposal got bogged down when Mayor Rudolph Giuliani insisted that only a casino would make access to the island affordable. Historians, preservationists, and much of the public found this outrageous. Additionally, casinos are not currently legal in New York. Even after Giuliani backed down, he and Governor George Pataki, bitter political rivals, feuded over how much control the city and state would each have over the project.

In 2000, the mayor and governor finally agreed upon a plan, one that is both all-encompassing and vague enough to allow for numerous changes. Their proposal relies upon finding $300 million in private investment as well as a significant amount of government funding; a state-run development corporation would administer and govern the island.

Governors Island, which has been off-limits to visitors for more than two centuries, would be reborn as a public oasis. The plan calls for a fifty-acre park, a branch of an existing museum, small new museums, a sculpture garden, artists' studios, a motel, a museum of military history, an amphitheater, an educational center with a maritime museum, an aquarium highlighting the Hudson River's marine life, and a sports complex to be leased to New York University and other schools. There would also be commercial development—a hotel, spa, and conference center, as well as residential apartments and retail stores—to generate enough revenue to cover the maintenance of the park and historic buildings and to offset development costs. The conference center would snap up the spectacular former officers' houses in beautiful Nolan Park. A private concessionaire would provide ferry service.

How much of this plan ever becomes reality is still anyone's guess. However, in one of his final acts in office, President Clinton named the island's two fortresses—Fort Jay and Castle Williams—national monuments. The move created a twenty-acre national park, thus preventing this swath of land from ever being sold. The park is expected to open to the public by 2003.

While the forts' fate seems to be resolved, Clinton's decision does not solve the rest of the island's future. If Congress doesn't allow for transfer of the island to the state, private developers like Donald Trump will no doubt start lining up, checkbooks in hand, for the chance to turn the island into one of the city's most affluent and desirable neighborhoods.

Once valued for its strategic importance, Governors Island served well as the citadel protecting a busy harbor and illustrious city. With its military service now spent, the island has come almost full circle. When Wouter Van Twiller looked south across the half mile of open water to the shores of Governors Island, he beheld property fit for an executive mansion and retreat from the city. More than three centuries later, opportunistic eyes are again fixed on Governors Island as it waits out its fate.

Exploring the Island

Governors Island is not generally open to the public. However, the federal government's General Services Administration—which along with the Coast Guard is administering and maintaining the island—is allowing a local tour group to continue offering public tours. **Big Onion Walking Tours,** (212) 439-1090, offers monthly tours of the island's historic section from April through November. This area—a national historic landmark district and a city landmark district—includes sixty-two buildings on ninety acres.

Your tour begins with a walk up a small hill, past what's left of the nut trees that once proliferated on the island, and straight ahead to **Fort Jay.** An elaborate sculpture on the fort's archway depicts the original seal of the War Department with its mortar-cannon-eagle-flag insignia. It was carved by an army prisoner and former stonecutter who won his freedom during the course of the work. According to legend, the fort commander's young daughter was walking through the main gate when a chunk of red sandstone broke loose. The stonecutter jumped down from his ladder and placed himself between the girl and the falling debris, saving her life. For his heroism, he was pardoned.

East of Fort Jay are two of the island's more stately residences: the **Admiral's House** and the **Governor's House.** The twenty-seven-room Admiral's House (circa 1840) was originally home to the army's commanding general, including World War I general John J. Pershing. The building is flanked by two cannons cast in the late sixteenth century and was captured in Cuba during the Spanish-American War of 1898. In 1988, a historic diplomatic meeting was held there between President Ronald Reagan and Soviet leader Mikhail S. Gorbachev.

The Georgian-style Governor's House is the oldest building on the island. Purportedly constructed in 1708 as the residence of Lord Cornbury, there is some doubt as to whether it indeed dates back that far. The house, however, was substantially altered in 1749. During the American Revolution, so the story goes, the house had an underground tunnel allegedly large enough for the governor's coach and four horses. The tunnel was connected to a private dock so the British leader could escape the island if hostile forces attacked. There is no evidence that this tunnel ever existed. In between the two estates is the **Dutch House,** which was built in 1845, it was used as a commissary storehouse until 1920, and, later, as officers' quarters. The brick building is an authentic replica of homes built by early Dutch settlers.

Historical Detour: Great Escapes

Prisons often incite breakouts, and the stockade at Governors Island was no exception. Its island location often enhanced the drama; three escapes are particularly memorable.

Days before the Civil War ended in 1865, Captain William Robert Webb, a Confederate prisoner held in Castle Williams, decided he could wait no longer for freedom. Webb, the first Confederate soldier to escape the island, swam to the Battery, where he emerged wet and disheveled in his Confederate grays. For days, Webb explained his story to anyone who would listen, but nobody believed him. He was left to wander the city and eventually made his way home to Tennessee, where he was later elected a senator.

In 1918, Grover Cleveland Bergdoll, a German American, proclaimed he would never fight against the fatherland and went into hiding. Two years later, the twenty-one-year-old was caught at his mother's mansion near Philadelphia and jailed in Castle Williams as a World War I deserter. Within several months, he escaped by convincing federal authorities he needed to retrieve some money he had stashed on a Maryland farm while a fugitive.

En route to Maryland, Bergdoll persuaded his keepers—two armed military police sergeants—to stop for lunch at his Pennsylvania home, conveniently located along the train route to Maryland. The chaperons were soon puffing on cigars and downing German beer at the family estate while Bergdoll entertained them with readings from Shakespeare. Pleasantly fuddled, the guards thought nothing of Bergdoll going to answer a telephone call. When Bergdoll didn't return to the party, the sergeants realized they'd been duped and took their shameful selves back to Governors Island, where they avoided court-martial only because they hadn't benefited financially.

Bergdoll made it to Germany, where he staved off kidnapping attempts by the United States while his mother tried to effect his repatriation. In 1939, Bergdoll showed up in New York without warning, was court-martialed on Governors Island, and sentenced to seven and a half years in Leavenworth Penitentiary. He was released for good behavior in 1944.

Melvin Blanton, twenty-three, had thrice wriggled out of

other disciplinary barracks across the country before being sentenced to Governors Island for desertion and jailbreaking. But the Ohioan didn't stay there long either. On July 20, 1934, Blanton was working a manual labor detail on the island's south side when a friend, armed with a revolver, came ashore and ordered the only guard—a private on his first hitch—to hand over his weapon. The duo then made their anticlimactic getaway, rowing a mile and a half to Red Hook, Brooklyn. The *Daily News* called the escape "the most spectacular prison delivery in the history of eastern penal institutions," embarrassing the island's army personnel charged with safeguarding the Port of New York.

Blanton and a companion went on a crime spree in Ohio and Indiana, holding up filling stations with a gun stolen from a guard at an Indiana fort. In August, they were in a friend's car in Indianapolis when the driver was pulled over for running a traffic light. None of the three men gave his real name, but Blanton, who was recognized because of his much-publicized escape, was promptly rearrested.

Farther along the street is the **Blockhouse,** built as a fortification in 1840. It later served as a hospital, headquarters, and officers' quarters. Lieutenant Ulysses S. Grant lived there from April to July 1852. In a letter to his wife, he wrote: "We can go to the city at almost all hours of the day in small boats belonging to the government which ply regularly for the convenience of us all." But Grant preferred Governors Island: "We get the benefit of the sea breeze here, while in the City we would get but little of it."

The granite church south of the Blockhouse is the **Chapel of St. Cornelius the Centurion.** Of English Gothic design, it was completed in 1906 to replace the original wooden church built nearby in 1847. Lining the chapel's nave are many battle and regimental flags, including the Civil War guidon General Philip Henry Sheridan carried to victory at the Battle of Five Forks in 1865 and the bullet-riddled flag that flew atop the building where Philippine insurrection leader Emilio Aguinaldo made his final stand against the United States in 1898. The church is also notable for its stained glass, artwork, and a credence table carved of stone from the Château de Rouen, where Joan of Arc was imprisoned in 1431.

Across from the church is the **South Battery,** erected in 1812 to defend Buttermilk Channel between the island and Brooklyn. Largely hidden by some of the island's younger infrastructure, it was used as an officers' club by the Coast Guard. In July 1993, it hosted the United Nations–sponsored peace talks between exiled Haitian president Jean-Bertrand Aristide and Lieutenant General Raoul Cédras, which helped restore democracy to Haiti.

Turning north, back toward the ferry, it's hard to miss immense **Liggett Hall** on your left. Completed in 1930 as barracks for the entire First Army regiment, it's the largest building on the island, cutting clear across its middle. The hall's classical cupola above the sally port is so conspicuous that it shows up as a landmark on nautical charts.

Before walking through the hall's sally port, retreat to Hay Road on the perimeter of Nolan Park and take a gander at the row of butterscotch-colored, high-ceilinged Victorian houses where senior officers and their families once lived.

On the way to Castle Williams, check out the former **base hospital** to your left. Ruth Smothers gave birth here to two boys who later tickled the country's funny bone: Tommy Smothers was born on February 2, 1937, and Dick on November 20, 1938, while their father, Major Thomas Bolyn Smothers, was stationed on the island.

Straight ahead awaits **Castle Williams,** a mammoth stone citadel on the island's northern tip known as the cheese box because of its circular shape. It was a stockade from the Civil War through World War II; Walt Disney and Rocky Graziano served time there for being absent without leave. Ivy climbs its eight-foot-thick red sandstone walls fitted with three tiers of windows from which one hundred guns once poked their menacing muzzles.

Island Hopping

The ferry to Governors Island departs from the Battery Maritime Building at 39 South Street in Manhattan. To reach South Street:

🚗 **By car:** From the West Side of Manhattan, take the West Side Highway south to West Street, then south to Battery Park and South Street. From the East Side, take the FDR Drive south to South Street. Street parking is close to impossible, but there are several parking lots by Battery Park.

🚇 **By subway:** From the West Side, take the 1 or 9 to South Ferry. From the East Side, Brooklyn, or the Bronx, take the 4 or 5 to Bowling Green. From Queens or Brooklyn, take the N or R to Whitehall Street.

By bus: From Midtown, take the M6 or M1 to Battery Park. From the East Side, take the M15.

By boat: From Staten Island, take the ferry to the Manhattan terminal, which is down the street from the Battery Maritime Building.

Island Bonus

Check out the notorious Lord Cornbury painting, which hangs in the **Great Hall of the New-York Historical Society,** 2 West Seventy-seventh Street, Manhattan, (212) 873-3400.

2. Liberty Island

"At the threshold of this vast continent, full of new life—where all the ships of the universe arrive—the statue will rise from the bosom of the waves. She will represent 'Liberty Enlightening the World.'"

—FRANCO-AMERICAN UNION, LAUNCHING THE CAMPAIGN TO BUILD THE STATUE OF LIBERTY, 1875

Liberty Island

WHEN THE *ISÈRE* ENTERED New York Harbor on June 19, 1885, more than one hundred ships poured out to greet her as guns from Fort Wood on Bedloe's Island and Fort Columbus on Governors Island roared an enthusiastic welcome. It had taken seventeen days to load the 214 boxes—each weighing between 150 and 6,000 pounds—onto the *Isère*, and nearly a month for the ship to travel from France. But New York would have to wait to see the Statue of Liberty emerge from the crates.

Liberty's agonizing journey from conception to completion had taken two decades, yet America was still struggling to finish the pedestal on which she would stand. So, for more than a year, Lady Liberty—a gift from France extolling American ideals—lay in pieces on Bedloe's Island.

According to her sculptor, Auguste Bartholdi, the statue was born out of a dinner conversation in 1865 at the home of Edouard de Laboulaye, France's preeminent political thinker. The topic was whether camaraderie could truly exist between nations. Laboulaye said France and America had shared struggles for independence, thus creating an indestructible bond. This notion, Bartholdi later wrote, "remained fixed in my memory."

Yet other factors also helped shape Liberty. Bartholdi traveled to Egypt in 1867 and 1869, hoping for a commission on a gargantuan lighthouse for the new Suez Canal being built by Bartholdi's friend Count Ferdinand de Lesseps. Bartholdi designed a robed woman carrying a torch, "Progress: Egypt Carrying the Light to Asia," but his concept was rejected. An American newspaper later accused Bartholdi of repackaging this failure into the Statue of Liberty to turn a profit. The sculptor vehemently denied this, claiming, "I never executed anything for the Egyptian ruler except a little sketch which remained in his palace," but the subsequent discovery of several "Progress" studies betrays this lie. Nevertheless Bartholdi's $20,000 and fifteen-year commitment to Liberty imply that his was more a labor of love than a moneymaking scheme.

After France's bitter defeat in the Franco-Prussian War (1870–71), Bartholdi's work turned more political. His concept for a Liberty monument was seen by the democracy-minded Laboulaye as excellent anti-monarch propaganda. Laboulaye, however, realized the statue was too potent a symbol to be countenanced in a politically unstable France. The scholar had written extensively on America, using the distant land to convey his views on democracy and individual freedom. So he wrote Bartholdi letters of introduction and sent him to America to propose building the monument there as a symbol of the affinity between the two countries.

Bartholdi first arrived in New York in June 1871, "in the pearly radiance of a beautiful morning," he later wrote. Awed by the harbor—"the gateway to America"—and "the magnificent spectacle of those immense cities" (Brooklyn and Manhattan), Bartholdi immediately envisioned his statue there. His eye fell upon a twelve-acre site, Bedloe's Island, which he soon learned belonged to "all the states."

The Mohegan Indians called the isle Minnissais, or Lesser Island. Early colonists named it Great Oyster Island, but Bedloe's Island was the name that survived. On December 23, 1667, Richard Nicolls, New York's first British governor, granted the island to Captain Robert Needham, but the next day Needham sold it to Isaak Bedloo. Bedloo, an alderman and wealthy merchant, had been one of 252 Dutch settlers who signed a pledge of loyalty to England in 1664. Rewarded with a string of influential and lucrative political jobs, Bedloo anglicized his name to Bedlow. In the eighteenth century, it was corrupted to Bedloe. (The family battled for more than a century to correct the error, but in 1940 the U.S. Board of Geographic Names rejected the evidence. The island remained Bedloe's until 1956, when it was renamed Liberty Island, belatedly fulfilling Bartholdi's request.)

In 1738, fearful of a smallpox outbreak, New York took over the island, where it established the city's first formal quarantine station. Incoming ships anchored there to wait for a doctor to row out from Manhattan and inspect the passengers and crew. Archibald Kennedy, commander of the British naval station and later the eleventh Earl of Cassilis, bought the island in 1746 and built a summer home. But when the smallpox threat returned in 1758, Kennedy sold the land back to New York City.

On the eve of the Revolution, British troops seized Bedloe's Island, establishing a refuge for Tory sympathizers and setting the stage for an unusual incident. On the night of April 2, 1776, colonists snuck out to Bedloe's to capture the Tories, but found none there. The British either had been tipped off or had heard the boats approaching and removed all their men. With no one to take prisoner, the four hundred rebels instead swiped

STUART MILLER

Star-shaped Fort Wood serves as the foundation for the 151-foot-tall Statue of Liberty and her 89-foot-tall pedestal.

tools, coats, and poultry, and torched the island's buildings. *Asia,* a British warship in the harbor, meanwhile fired two cannon shots at the island, but there were no casualties.

After the war, New York tried renting out the island, but stipulated that it would revert to a quarantine as needed. Not surprisingly, the city found few takers. The French navy leased it as a quarantine from 1793 to 1796, at which point the city turned Bedloe's five buildings over to the state for a quarantine hospital. Four years later, the island was ceded to the United States for the harbor fortification project. A star-shaped battery with thirty guns was completed on Bedloe's Island in 1811; in 1814, it was named Fort Wood after Lieutenant Colonel Eleazer Wood, who died that year in the Battle of Fort Erie. The island served alternately as quarantine and garrison for the next half century, and Fort Wood functioned as an ordnance depot and recruiting station during the Civil War.

After arriving in New York, Bartholdi traveled for five months, meeting both ordinary citizens and power players like industrialist Peter Cooper, President Ulysses Grant, and *New York Tribune* publisher Horace Greeley. While Bartholdi found this nation of conformists reluctant to embrace his unusual proposal, he felt America's love for the grandiose would ultimately ensure Liberty's success.

On returning home, he minimized his model's sensual contours and, under Laboulaye's guidance, replaced the broken chain in Liberty's left hand with a tablet reading, "July 4, 1776." To raise the $60,000 needed to build Liberty, Laboulaye established the Franco-American Union, which launched its campaign in 1875. That same year, the Third Republic restored democracy to France, with Laboulaye co-writing France's new constitution. Liberty was to be presented during America's centennial celebration, but the project was more costly and progressed more slowly than anticipated. Its final cost was four times the estimate, and the subscription wasn't completed until 1880.

Bartholdi believed his career was on the line, and worked doggedly to ensure Liberty's success. If the project failed, he wrote, "I would look like a ridiculous day dreamer and an inefficient man." Under his supervision, craftsmen from the renowned Gaget, Gauthier and Company toiled seven days a week, ten hours a day before spectators. The public viewing promoted the cause and raised cash; three hundred thousand gazers paid to see Liberty take shape. In October 1881—in a publicity stunt tied to the centennial of the last major battle of the American Revolution at York-town—Levi Morton, the U.S. minister to France, drove the first rivet into Liberty's left foot. The following year, Bartholdi invited key members of the press to lunch . . . in the Lady's knee.

When Liberty's old-school engineer, Eugène Viollet Le Duc, died in 1879, Bartholdi turned to inventive bridge builder Gustave Eiffel (whose Parisian tower was still a decade away). Like his contemporaries— Bartholdi, de Lesseps, and American architect Richard Morris Hunt, who designed Liberty's pedestal—Eiffel was the quintessential impresario of that era: self-confident and ambitious, with a steadfast faith in technological progress as wrought by intrepid individuals. (Several cutting-edge advances, such as reinforced concrete, electric light, and Bessemer steel, were used in the statue and pedestal.) Eiffel's own innovation—an iron-and-steel skeleton with a secondary tier of braces attached separately to each of Liberty's copper plates—replaced Le Duc's primitive plan to support Liberty by filling her to the hips with sand. Eiffel's idea later influenced the development of skyscrapers.

Laboulaye died in 1883, having lived to see the Third Republic firmly established and the completion of the statue assured. De Lesseps took over the Franco-American Union, but even when Liberty was completed the next year, it remained unclear whether she would ever make New York Harbor her home.

In America, preparations had become mired in divisive controversy. For starters, the United States had a limited cultural history, with a scanty tradition of public monuments, so people were less apt to grasp the significance of such a memorial. But the larger problem was money: Liberty was ostensibly a gift, so Americans were resentful about having to pay for the statue's foundation and pedestal, which eventually cost more than $250,000 (as much as Liberty herself). Raising the money proved a monumental task for the American Committee, which was stacked with prominent citizens and headed by William Evarts, a senator and respected lawyer who had successfully defended President Andrew Johnson against impeachment.

Between 1876 and 1881, little was accomplished. Public sentiment ran from indifference to cynicism; much of the press coverage was sensationalistic, irreverent, and even disdainful. Even when Bartholdi arrived at Philadelphia's Centennial Exhibition with Liberty's right arm and torch, he was met with skepticism. "Had the French sculptor honestly intended to complete the Statue of Liberty," opined the *New York Times*'s editorial page, "he would have begun at its foundation, modeling first the boot, then the stocking, then the full leg in the stocking."

Rumors that the French couldn't finish the sculpture without American funding persisted into the 1880s, severely hampering the pedestal drive (although the arm was a popular attraction at Madison Square for several years). That was only the beginning of the committee's tribulations; everyone found a reason not to contribute. The country considered it a New York issue. The poor and middle class expected the wealthy to pay, but the upper class disdained the icon's populist concept. Religious conservatives opposed adulating a secular sculpture that, with its torch held high, suggested "mankind receives true light, not from Christ and Christianity, but from heathens and her gods," according to the *American Catholic Quarterly* in 1880.

The site chosen for the statue also hampered the fund-raising. Some felt Liberty should be put at Coney Island as a tourist attraction, but most of

New York's ruling class and press preferred the tip of the Battery, where Liberty could be easily seen and visited. In fact, many wealthy Manhattanites refused to donate money for a statue on some out-of-the-way island. However, President Rutherford B. Hayes appointed Civil War hero General William Sherman to choose between Bedloe's and Governors; heeding Bartholdi's advice, Sherman selected Bedloe's, because on Governors, Liberty would have had her back to Europe or the Battery.

The debate raged on long after the decision, but some foes were eventually persuaded that Bedloe's would be the ideal spot. In 1884, the *Times*, a late convert to the Bedloe's camp, asserted that the statue would indeed be better "where it is not so very easy to reach . . . for, having made the trip, perhaps the visitors are likely to value the wonderful view the more." In this pre-skyscraper era, the paper also said siting "so colossal a mass" at the Battery would "make all the great buildings in the neighborhood look ridiculous."

Despite meager resources and public apathy, the American Committee hired Richard Morris Hunt in 1881 to design the pedestal. One of the nation's leading architects, Hunt had designed the main section of the Metropolitan Museum of Art as well as Newport mansions for society families. Hunt, who shared Bartholdi's love of ancient Egyptian colossi, produced plans for a 114-foot pedestal that threatened to overwhelm both the statue and its paltry budget. He scaled down the pedestal by twenty-five feet, but added more complex stonework that boosted the cost by $20,000.

With the committee scrounging for dollars, newspapers in cities like Cleveland, Baltimore, and San Francisco snidely suggested that New York didn't deserve the statue and claimed they would quickly raise the money and provide a proper home. Such commentary from Philadelphia and Boston in 1882 prompted the *Times* to demean them as "small but ambitious cities . . . jealous of our Metropolitan fame." While the vituperative war of words may have sold newspapers, it did nothing to aid the cause.

With donations trickling in, General Charles Stone, appointed engineer in chief in April 1883, wasn't able to begin work on the pedestal's foundation until October. The foundation was finished in May 1884, but the pedestal's six-ton cornerstone wasn't laid until August. In late autumn, work had to be halted because nearly all of the $182,491 raised had been spent.

Hunt solicited the Belmonts, the Vanderbilts, and the Astors for help, but was rejected. New York State's legislature appropriated $50,000, but Governor Grover Cleveland vetoed the bill as unconstitutional, stating that

New Yorkers shouldn't pay for a national monument. A congressional bill to provide the final $100,000 failed, in part because it was attached to an unrelated, unpopular bill. The press urged the French to pay for the pedestal, and publicized Liberty's flaws. The *New York Herald* found her design unappealing, while the *New York Evening Telegram* said the copper was too thin and Liberty balanced in an unnatural position.

In March 1885, only three months before the *Isère* arrived in New York, the project seemed doomed. Evarts and the American Committee issued a public statement noting that barring an immediate change in fortune, Liberty would be returned to France or given to another city.

Enter Joseph Pulitzer. This Hungarian Jewish immigrant had soared to prominence as a journalistic reformer and spokesman for the masses. Recognizing the promotional value of a good story and the merit of Bartholdi's majestic symbol, Pulitzer had launched a public campaign to fund Liberty's pedestal upon buying the *New York World* in 1883. "The dash of one millionaire merchant's pen ought to settle the matter," he implored. But Pulitzer's paper had a circulation of only fifteen thousand and was among the least popular of the city's sixteen dailies. He raised a meager $135 in the first four days and ended the drive within a month.

Two years and a hundred thousand readers later, Pulitzer responded to Evarts's plea with a second campaign. This drive was a different story. He encouraged the masses to take custodianship of the statue. "Let us not wait for the millionaires," he proclaimed. "Let us hear from the people." Pulitzer's consistent coverage excoriated the rich and prodded the poor; his shrewdest tactic was bestowing fame on the common folk by printing the letter and name of every one of the countless contributors.

"I am a poor man or I would send more than the enclosed 10 cents for the Liberty Fund . . . You go right on, Mr. World, and make it real hot for all the nobs and snobs," wrote E. James.

"We are twin boys—Yed and Joe . . . Enclosed you will find 50 cents, 25 cents each . . . If we live to be men it will be our pride to say: 'We helped place her here.'"

By May, there was enough money to resume work on the pedestal, and on August 11, Pulitzer triumphantly announced that 121,000 people had donated a total of $102,000; of that, $80,000 had been collected in sums of less than a dollar. The pedestal was finished April 22, 1886, and on July 12, with Eiffel's framework in place, the crates on Bedloe's Island were finally unpacked. "The dream of my life is accomplished," Bartholdi said when the statue was at last erected.

Historical Detour: A Delicate Situation

In April 1954, a man pined to perch on one finger atop the Statue of Liberty as a gesture of international goodwill. Nearly five decades later, his tomfoolery reads like a Dr. Seuss story, yet Viennese circus performer Franz Furtner almost pulled off this absurd and amazing stunt.

The Circumnavigator's Club, an organization for people who had traveled around the world, sponsored Furtner's balancing act as "a little something to bring about goodwill and world harmony." Furtner said it would "symbolize the freedom and happiness" he had found in America.

The petition to stage the spectacle was rejected by the statue superintendent, but National Park Service superiors in Washington approved it, erroneously believing the club was a charitable rather than a social organization, and that Furtner was an Iron Curtain refugee. When the government discovered that this Ringling Brothers acrobat had never been behind the Iron Curtain and, in fact, had served in the German army, they angrily revoked permission.

Furtner nonetheless made the papers. The *New York Times* reported that Furtner in fact accomplished his monumental feat during a practice session at the statue, but there were few onlookers that rainy day and no photos taken to validate the stunt.

From the beginning, the statue was a target for art critics, who considered Bartholdi an ordinary talent and Liberty lacking innovation or imagination. (The image of a woman bringing forth freedom could be traced from ancient Rome to Delacroix; before Liberty, America's symbol was a patriotic woman called Columbia.) As recently as 1976, art historian Marvin Trachtenberg referred to Liberty as "presentable but no great sculptural beauty," while Richard Seth Hayden and Thierry Despont, who headed the statue's renovation in the 1980s, wrote that when working on a smaller scale, Bartholdi was an "average sculptor."

However, as Eiffel noted, conventional standards don't always matter: "There is in the colossal an attraction, a particular charm to which the theories of ordinary art are hardly applicable." The Statue of Liberty is today more national icon than revered artwork. While no Michelangelo, Bartholdi should be hailed for realizing his lofty dream using a blend of neoclassical sculpture, high-tech engineering, astute entrepreneurialism, and perseverance. From the moment he recognized the symbolic significance and aesthetic appeal of Bedloe's Island until his tireless efforts brought Liberty to fruition, Bartholdi displayed a keen understanding of the entire artistic process.

When the Statue of Liberty was dedicated on October 28, 1886, "a hundred Fourths of July broke loose . . . to exalt her name," the *Times* proclaimed. The day was wet and foggy, but the celebration's fervor vanquished the elements. Starting at Fifth Avenue and Fifty-seventh Street, the parade's grand marshal, General Stone, led twenty thousand marchers south past one million spectators; at Wall Street, the only area not closed for the holiday, spools of ticker tape spilled from hundreds of office windows, filling the air and the streets with white curlicues. The ticker-tape parade was born.

The celebration moved to Bedloe's Island, where about thirty-five hundred men—mainly the wealthy who had previously snubbed Liberty—beheld the statue's dedication. With the exception of Bartholdi's wife, Jeanne-Emilie, and de Lesseps's daughter, Tototte, women were barred from the festivities. The Battery and Governors Island were packed with spectators, and the harbor brimmed with boats—including one filled with women protesting their exclusion, led by Lille Devereux Blake, president of the New York State Suffragette Association.

Bartholdi waited anxiously inside Liberty's crown to pull a cord that would swish away the French flag covering Liberty's face. Evarts, a long-winded fellow who had given eight days' worth of closing arguments in the notorious adultery trial of celebrated preacher Henry Ward Beecher, launched into his presentation. When Evarts paused for breath, a young man charged with signaling Bartholdi mistakenly gave the sculptor the go-ahead and Bartholdi unveiled his statue. Evarts's oration was drowned out by what the *Times* described as "one thundering paean of acclamations that swept down the Bay on the wings of the northeast gale and smote the hills of Staten Island with a huge shock of sound." (Translation: fifteen minutes of exploding gunfire, blasting whistles, blaring bands, and wild cheering.) The litany of speeches continued until nightfall, when the guests—panicked about being stranded on the island overnight—turned into a stampeding mob in a race to the boats. At least one elegant Vanderbilt was bloodied in the crush.

While Liberty was designed to enlighten the world, financial and technical difficulties often left her in shadows, and even darkness, for the next thirty years. Though Bartholdi wanted a gilded copper torch illuminated by outside lights (as is the case today), the government made an eleventh-hour decision to cut open the torch and install lighting inside. Under the aegis of the Lighthouse Board, the statue's pedestal lights and the torch—to be visible for one hundred miles—were turned on one week after her premiere.

The weak pedestal lights, however, often left Liberty's head and shoulders in semidarkness, while the torch light's faint glow looked like a faded star unconnected to the statue. And the lights lacked more than wattage—within a week, a money outage darkened the statue completely. Although funding was restored, this embarrassing situation was repeated periodically throughout the next three decades. What's more, when the lights did work, they were often depressingly dim.

Bartholdi, who died in 1904, made one final visit to the United States in 1893. Already distressed that his statue hadn't brought him the prestige, artistic opportunity, or financial gain he had hoped for, he found Liberty's condition disheartening. "I was somewhat disappointed at the effect," he said. "The lights do not show up well at all."

In its early years, the Statue of Liberty was not a major tourist attraction, although twenty-five cents bought admission to the island and a rented bathing suit. The army maintained a presence on Bedloe's Island, with soldiers doubling as monument guards, and in 1902 the Lighthouse Board ceded the entire island to the War Department. Four years later a *Times* reporter, whose ferry to Bedloe's included only forty other visitors, found the island's pier and buildings neglected and dilapidated.

Even the indomitable Lady was in poor shape. Her copper skin was green, and there was concern that the salt air had weakened her joints. Plans to paint the statue were met by cries of dismay from artists, who said the patina, or green layer, provided a mellow hue and enhanced the statue's contours. Scientists explained that the patina naturally occurs when copper is exposed to air, and actually protected the metal from erosion. So when Liberty was spruced up in 1907, her exterior was not painted, a strategy adhered to ever since.

The statue's funding and lighting woes were finally resolved in 1916, when the *World* again intervened, raising $30,000. Gutzon Borglum, who later chiseled Mount Rushmore, redid the statue's torch, using translucent amber cathedral glass to allow more light to shine through. Floodlights, the latest technology, replaced the ineffective lightbulbs at the statue's pedestal—although Liberty's face was still haunted by some shadows until more powerful floodlights were installed in 1931.

During a celebration dinner, French ambassador Jules Jusserand toasted the statue, which, unlike most monuments, did not honor a single man or nation: "It was raised to an idea . . . the idea of Liberty." While that had been true at the statue's conception, the French connection was slipping from the public's memory by 1916. Liberty was stepping into a new role, a more assertively nationalistic one. She had developed into America's foremost symbol, a patron saint who represented the country's foundations more clearly than did flag-bearing Columbia, and more majestically than Uncle Sam.

During the First World War, as ships set out under this guardian's gaze, Liberty lent her name and image to four bond drives that raised $15 billion—half the cost of the war. Campaign posters touted her as a woman warrior or draped her in the American flag, urging patriotic citizens to "remember your first thrill of American Liberty." In 1924, she was designated a national monument, and in the 1930s—when the army passed the torch to the National Park Service—she began receiving her due as a tourist attraction.

By her golden anniversary in 1936, Liberty's image had been reinvented in the public mind. She had become the "Mother of Exiles." Although few immigrants were arriving—the United States had yanked away its welcome mat in the 1920s—Liberty had beckoned and guided millions of Europeans to this country during the prior half century. These firmly rooted new Americans celebrated Liberty as their guardian angel.

Liberty's association with the "huddled masses" was reinforced in 1965 by the opening of the Museum of Immigrants at the statue's base and President Lyndon Johnson's signing of a new immigration bill there. The law reopened the gateway to America by undoing the bigoted quota restrictions of 1924. Increasingly, other disenfranchised groups have appropriated Liberty's all-embracing symbolism: Vietnam War protesters, Puerto Rican nationalists, Native Americans, Iranians opposed to the Ayatollah, and even Al Sharpton and his disciples have staged freedom protests there.

Although Liberty's reputation remained vital, by the 1980s her body had begun to show its age. A 1981 report by French researchers detailing the monument's deterioration sparked an unprecedented campaign to renovate both the statue and the immigration depot at Ellis Island in time for their centennials in 1986 and 1992, respectively.

While the Statue of Liberty indeed looked resplendent at her rededication, achieving that end involved nearly as much energy and strife as had her construction. With President Ronald Reagan's blessing, virtually the entire restoration was done without the federal government, testing the Republican theory that the private sector can accomplish what the public sector cannot. This proved both the project's greatest strength and its gravest weakness. Without bureaucratic restrictions, a phenomenal amount of money was raised and a staggering amount of labor performed in a short time. However, the lack of government oversight bred bruising behind-the-scenes battles and allowed fund-raisers to mislead the public about the money being donated.

The Franco-American Committee, the Statue of Liberty–Ellis Island Foundation, and several other not-for-profit American fund-raising organizations all vied for the right to oversee the restoration. The Franco-American Committee was done in by its inability to raise money. Meanwhile, the Statue of Liberty–Ellis Island Foundation, headed by Chrysler chairman Lee Iacocca, came up with the cash and demanded more say; it was anointed sole fund-raiser by the government in 1985.

The foundation was accused of egregious commercialism when it licensed dozens of companies to sell Liberty air fresheners, ashtrays, and other dust collectors. Still worse were denunciations that the foundation's fund-raising methods tarnished Liberty's image. In 1985, the *Times* reported that the foundation had solicited multi-million-dollar pledges from major corporations in exchange for official-sponsor status. These "donations," however, often came from consumers who paid to participate in promotions and events thinking they were contributing directly to the statue's refurbishment, when they were actually covering the companies' pledge. Richard Rovsek, the marketing maven and Republican insider who conceived the fund-raising campaign, was fired from his $50,000-a-month foundation job after it was revealed that when he signed up sponsors, he also accepted payment on the side to create their Liberty ads.

Critics questioned the foundation's fund-raising means, complaining that its grassroots efforts had been trampled by deals made with big business. But many felt the end—$400 million in funds—was perfect justification. (Repairing Liberty and her island cost $87 million; the remaining money was used to restore Ellis Island and Castle Clinton and to create an endowment.)

The seamy details surrounding the restoration of the Statue of Liberty were largely hidden from the public, as was Liberty herself. Her makeover required more than a nip and a tuck, and for more than two years, she was screened by scaffolding. Workers discovered birds' nests, graffiti, busted rivets, and, although most photos hadn't shown them, unbecoming cracks on her nose and chin. (In typical celebrity fashion, Liberty's photographs had been touched up for years.)

On July 4, 1984, Lady Liberty relinquished her torch. The 1916 version had been improperly sealed, and rainwater had corroded the torch and the arm's framework. Twelve French craftsmen, using Bartholdi's original gilded copper design, built a new torch in a Liberty Island workshop, combining the ancient repoussé technique of hammering copper into sculptural form with the latest in computer modeling. American union workers—many ignorant of the statue's French origins—picketed the island, unhappy about foreigners working on an American job. The artisans' expertise, however, eventually won the respect of most Americans.

The restoration team's most surprising discoveries involved discrepancies between Bartholdi's plan and the completed statue. Liberty's right arm, connected at an improper point, was so weak that it swayed in the wind. Because her head tilted slightly to the right, one of her diadem's spikes poked into her right arm. Research traced the irregularities to the original assembly in Paris. After lengthy debate, the team opted to fortify her shoulder and shorten the spike, rather than tinker with history and restructure the statue.

Liberty's refurbishment required imagination as well as research. Removing the seven coats of paint inside Liberty with traditional materials like solvent would have carried the risk of a deadly explosion, so liquid nitrogen—supercooled to minus 325 degrees Fahrenheit—was used. Underneath the paint were two layers of tar. Since most conventional cleansers threatened to scrub through Liberty's copper skin as well, everything from ground walnut shells to corncobs was tried. Finally, workers discovered baking soda; forty tons of it did the trick.

When July 4, 1986, arrived, with a weekend-long celebration that filled New York Harbor with tall ships and fireworks, the Statue of Liberty looked grand. And today, long after the last echoes of ceremonial pomp have faded, the Statue of Liberty still silently exalts the freedoms upon which she and this country were founded.

Exploring the Island

Bartholdi designed the **Statue of Liberty,** (212) 363-3206, to be seen from the water, and the boat ride allows you to bask in the majesty of his creation. So stand out on deck, because the best view (and photo opportunity) comes as the boat passes around the island to the dock. Liberty's persona changes along with your perspective—on the approach she stands erect, with an indefatigable mien, but as her right side comes fully into view, she appears to stride purposefully forward to enlighten the world about democracy.

Unless you are perversely attracted to long lines, visit during the week in spring or autumn. A beautiful April day means only eight thousand visitors and minimal waiting, whereas summer attracts sixteen to twenty thousand people per day, making the trek to the crown an arduous three-hour journey. Even reaching the pedestal will take two hours by foot or ninety minutes by elevator. Another strike against summer visits is that Liberty's interior is about thirty degrees hotter than the outside temperature. On 80-degree days, it's 110 degrees as you trudge slowly upward. That's why the faces on those unending lines resemble Emma Lazarus's "huddled masses." Rangers say that people often don't heed their temperature warnings and occasionally pass out during the journey.

The Statue of Liberty is a timeless symbol of America's most cherished virtue, but it is also, from the ground up, a remarkable combination of art, architecture, and engineering. To best experience this wonder, climb to the pedestal's balcony or Liberty's crown; an elevator, which is handicapped-accessible, will take you as far as the balcony. (The torch, never open to more than twelve people at once, has been closed since 1916, after several explosions in New Jersey weakened the arm's structure.)

Visitors' lines form outside the wall of star-shaped **Fort Wood;** built for the War of 1812, it now houses the base of the statue. To produce the statue's foundation, the fortress's center was filled with 23,500 tons of concrete—then the largest single mass poured at one time. The stepped-terrace structure you see rising above the fort's walls was added by the National Park Service in 1965 and is home to the **statue's museum.** This belatedly fulfills the vision of the pedestal architect, Richard Hunt, who had to scrap his tiered base for budgetary reasons.

Inching along the line, you eventually reach a set of immense bronze doors leading to the lobby. Added during Liberty's mid-1980s restoration, the door's icons commemorate the toil of everyone who participated in the project, from plumbers to architects. One panel depicts wrenches and pliers, another features compasses and slide rules; one even shows the scaffolding that caged Liberty during her rehabilitation.

Once inside the lobby, you'll get an up-close view of the amber-glass torch designed by American sculptor Gutzon Borglum. It was held aloft by Liberty from 1916 until 1984.

Historical Detour: Emma Lazarus

In the autumn of 1883, Emma Lazarus, whose poetry was praised by contemporaries Ralph Waldo Emerson and Ivan Turgenev, was asked to compose a piece for the Statue of Liberty's pedestal fund-raiser. Lazarus tersely replied that she could not write to order. Soon afterward, however, Lazarus visited Ward's Island, where two thousand Jewish refugees from Russia's pogroms were crammed into filthy temporary quarters with no heat, water, or food. Lazarus had no personal connection to the immigrant experience—her Portuguese ancestors were among the first twenty-six Jews in New York in 1649 and her father, Moses, was a wealthy sugar refiner—yet she was appalled by the conditions she encountered. She complained directly to Mayor Franklin Edson—and was inspired to pen "The New Colossus":

> *Not like the brazen giant of Greek fame,*
> *With conquering limbs astride from land to land;*
> *Here at our sea-washed, sunset gates shall stand*
> *A mighty woman with a torch, whose flame*
> *Is the imprisoned lightening, and her name*
> *Mother of Exiles. From her beacon hand*
> *Glows world-wide welcome; her mild eyes command*
> *The air-bridged harbor that twin cities frame.*
> *"Keep ancient lands your storied pomp!" cries she*
> *With silent lips. "Give me your tired, your poor,*
> *Your huddled masses yearning to breathe free,*
> *The wretched refuse of your teeming shore.*
> *Send these, the homeless, tempest-tost to me.*
> *I lift my lamp beside the golden door!"*

That December, a portfolio with her poem and works by Walt Whitman and Mark Twain brought $1,500 at auction, but "The New Colossus" slipped into obscurity. When Liberty's dedication-day parade commenced in 1886 one hundred feet from Lazarus's East Fifty-seventh Street home, she was in Europe. A year later, she died at age thirty-eight from Hodgkin's disease. Her obituaries mentioned many of her poems, but not the one that in 1903 was

quietly posted in Lazarus's memory on a plaque on Liberty's
pedestal. It wasn't until the 1930s, after America had put strin-
gent curbs on immigration, that Lazarus's poem became heralded
as the statue's poignant theme.

Then the urban mountain climb through the pedestal begins. The stair-
wells are narrow and can get claustrophobic since the lines often back up.
However, the two-step-and-wait pace means the hike doesn't get tiring. The
pedestal's interior—concrete walls, metal beams, an exposed elevator
shaft—is cold and industrial. But rewards await at the **balcony level,**
where you can step outside and marvel at the spectacular view: the city's
sweeping skyline stretching from the Empire State Building to the World
Trade Center to the Brooklyn Bridge.

Back indoors, the odyssey continues skyward, through the Lady herself,
where you experience the wondrous sensation of stepping inside the soul of
a sculpture. Looking at the folds of softly illuminated copper, you can
appreciate the enormous task that faced the nineteenth-century artisans.
Although metal casting had long since replaced repoussé in most sculpt-
ing, Auguste Bartholdi felt this ancient technique—which allowed Liberty's copper skin to be hammered to a mere three-thirty-seconds of an inch
thick—was the only way to tackle a job this size: Thin sheets used less copper, saving money and reducing weight for shipping.

What you see are three hundred thin copper sheets spliced and lapped
over one another, then riveted together and fitted to Gustave Eiffel's innovative framework. Each section is supported independently, so the skin
"floats," allowing the copper skin to expand and contract with outside temperature changes. Some 1,799 stainless-steel bars were installed in the
1980s, replacing rusted iron reinforcements. This was a particularly
tedious task for the steelworkers, since only four old bars could be safely
removed at a time.

The pace of the line picks up within the statue, but along the tightly
wound spiral staircase it still takes a while to reach the Lady's knee. (If
you're tall, duck.) From there, it's fairly quick to the midriff and, finally, the
crown. But climber beware. Unlike the pedestal balcony, which has enough
room for you to take a leisurely stroll while absorbing the panoramic vistas,
the crown proves somewhat anticlimactic. "This is it?!" is perhaps the most
common response. The windows are narrow and the view is limited since

Liberty, designed primarily to greet ships, not accommodate tourists, faces south, away from Manhattan. A greater problem is that pensive contemplation is impossible in this cramped headdress—the unending trail of the curious takes a look and keeps on marching.

Although it may be tempting to cram Liberty and Ellis Islands into one ferry trip, each monument is worthy of a separate visit. After journeying to the pedestal or the crown, save enough energy and time (about forty-five minutes) for exploring the informative and entertaining **Statue of Liberty Museum** on the second floor. You are greeted by a full-scale copper replica of Liberty's face, which provides both an otherwise unattainable perspective of the statue's mammoth proportions and a perfect photo op. (Go ahead, touch the nose. Everyone does.) Many historians believe the stoic visage of Lady Liberty was inspired by Bartholdi's widowed mother, Charlotte.

The museum's first two rooms offer a fairly comprehensive account of the statue's conception and construction, using models, drawings, written narrative, and video. There are reproductions of Bartholdi's 1869 watercolor and terra-cotta studies for "Progress: Egypt Carrying the Light to Asia," which later evolved into the Statue of Liberty, and a series of models depicting Liberty in her various incarnations: In one, Liberty's crown has no diadem; in another, she isn't bearing a flame; in a third, there's no tablet in her left hand. A continuously running video demonstrates the repoussé process, while old photographs, writings, and models depict the entire construction process.

But producing Liberty took more than sculptors and engineers. Raising the requisite funds required an unprecedented marketing and merchandising blitz that was a harbinger of twentieth- and twenty-first-century campaigns. As a licensed logo in France, Liberty's likeness showed up on cognac bottles and Camembert cheese labels, which are displayed alongside criticism of this commercialization. Also on view are satiric attacks on America's uninspired attempts to pay for the pedestal—an 1884 cover of *Life* (not related to the popular twentieth-century periodical) depicts a wilted, wrinkled Lady Liberty, as she was expected to look by the time the funds were raised.

The statue's story doesn't end with her unveiling. In the next room is a compelling textual and audio presentation recounting the reactions of immigrants who, after arduous voyages to America, beheld the Statue of Liberty for the first time. This is a moving reminder that Liberty is more than a statue; she is a symbol of hope, freedom, and opportunity.

"She was a beautiful sight after a miserable crossing that September," wrote Eleanor Kenderdine Lenhart, whose letter about her journey from England in 1921 at age seven is on display. "She held such promise for us all with her arm flung high, the torch lighting the way—opening a new world to those who would accept the challenge."

The wall opposite is covered with posters featuring Liberty hawking everything from war bonds to sheet music for such nationalistic songs as "Liberty Statue Is Looking Right at You," illustrating the patriotism with which she became associated in World War I.

Since then, the statue has developed into an American icon—revered and parodied in popular culture and appropriated for political statements and commercial interests. A display case features hundreds of Liberty post-cards—from black-and-white classical shots to Liberty with her robe blowing upward à la Marilyn Monroe to a 1918 aerial view of eighteen thousand soldiers at Camp Dodge in Iowa assembled in the shape of the statue. The walls are also lined with Liberty novelties—statuettes, clocks, lamp bases made of copper and jade, and even a Tiffany lamp with a Liberty motif. Photos and posters range from wacky to tacky: the Marx Brothers dressed as Liberty, the Lady wearing a pair of red-white-and-blue jeans in a Levi's advertisement. Although a long way from Bartholdi's lofty vision, these images are testaments to the powerful hold his statue has had on the world.

The Lady's Figures

Although the Statue of Liberty's history is extraordinarily well documented, some basic data is surprisingly uncertain. Bartholdi wrote that 179,000 pounds of copper were used for the statue, but the National Park Service lists Liberty at 200,000 pounds. A book about the Liberty restoration places her total weight—including framework—at 560,000 pounds, but the park service weighs her in at 450,000 pounds. Liberty's nose is either four feet, six inches long (according to the park service) or three feet, eight inches (per the restoration book). There are, however, a few facts that appear to be as solid as Bartholdi's monument:

LIBERTY'S VITAL STATISTICS

Height: 151 feet
Waist: 35 feet around
Right arm: 42 feet long
Index finger: 8 feet long

Pedestal: 89 feet high

Steps: 354—192 steps to the pedestal, 162 from pedestal to crown

Visitors: In 1938, about 300,000; in 2000, about 3.2 million

Gum: 8 pounds swept and scraped out per day in summer

LIBERTY'S SYMBOLS

Shackles: The broken shackles at Liberty's feet signify escape from tyranny.

Torch: The flame represents the light of truth and justice illuminating the world.

Crown: The seven rays of Liberty's diadem suggest the seven seas and seven continents.

Tablet: Held in her left arm, it is inscribed JULY 4 MDCCLXXVI (1776), the date America's Declaration of Independence was signed.

Where to Eat

Liberty Island is an enchanting picnic spot—cool breezes, magnificent views, no cars. Even when the statue's line snakes on forever, the rest of the island has a mellow, uncrowded feel. But bring lunch, since the cafeteria is unimpressive: The menu is limited, food greasy, and prices inflated. Highlights include Liberty lollipops and plastic torches filled with chocolate candies. Picnic on the patio if you want chairs and tables, but for a meal with a view, venture off and find a spot on the grass facing Manhattan—a practice that National Park Service rangers don't encourage but don't condemn.

Island Hopping

The statue can be reached from both New Jersey and Manhattan. New Jersey ferry service runs from Liberty State Park in Jersey City, exit 14B on the New Jersey Turnpike, (201) 435-9499. Manhattan ferry service runs from Battery Park; tickets are sold in Castle Clinton, (212) 269-5755. To reach Castle Clinton:

🚗 **By car:** From the West Side of Manhattan, take the West Side Highway south to West Street, then south to Battery Park and South Street. From the East Side, take the FDR Drive south to South Street. Street parking is close to impossible, but there are several parking lots by Battery Park.

By subway: From the West Side, take the 1 or 9 to South Ferry. From the East Side, Brooklyn, or the Bronx, take the 4 or 5 to Bowling Green. From Queens or Brooklyn, take the N or R to Whitehall Street.

By bus: From Midtown, take the M6 or M1 to Battery Park. From the East Side, take the M15.

By boat: From Staten Island, take the ferry to the Manhattan terminal. Follow the signs through Battery Park to Castle Clinton.

3. Ellis Island

"At Ellis Island, I was born again."
—EMANUEL GOLDENBERG, WHO ARRIVED FROM ROMANIA IN 1903 AT AGE
TEN AND WENT ON TO MOVIE STARDOM AS EDWARD G. ROBINSON

Ellis Island

ON THE FIRST DAY OF 1892, Annie Moore, a fifteen-year-old Irish lass, entered the United States at the new immigrant depot on Ellis Island. The first one through the gate, Moore—one of 148 arrivals on the steamship *Nevada*—was presented with a ten-dollar gold piece in a ceremony commemorating the occasion.

And then the jostling began.

For the next sixty-two years, Ellis Island was the sieve in America's immigration process; its Great Hall, crammed with people of many nationalities determined to become Americans, was the consummate melting pot. For the hundreds of thousands of aliens deported from Ellis Island, it symbolized the shattering of a tightly held dream. But for the twelve million foreigners who entered America there—from Knute Rockne to Frank Capra to Felix Frankfurter—Ellis Island was the first step in a new world. Today, nearly 40 percent of all Americans trace their roots through Ellis Island.

The women waiting in the Great Hall "had expressions of fear on their faces," recalled Raffaele Cotugno, whose account is just one of many preserved in the Ellis Island library. Cotugno, who journeyed from Italy in 1909 at age ten, remembered that children "had streaks on their cheeks where tears had dried on unwashed faces. Buttons were missing on well-worn garments. Belongings were carried in pillow cases, blankets and shawls."

Cotugno's first meal is what lingered longest in his memory, particularly his amazement at the wondrously soft white bread he mistook for cake. "I crammed my pockets full of slices in fear of never getting any again."

Estelle Belford traveled with her mother from Romania in 1905 at age five. She remembered being startled by a big, strange man who came to greet them. "I didn't know him. He picked me up and I started to cry." Then Belford's father put his arms around her mother and the reunited couple wept with joy.

Manny Steen, who arrived from Ireland in 1925 at age nineteen, remembered Ellis Island as an unsettling place. "The building was grimy and hot as a pistol . . . All they had was a couple of rotating fans that did nothing but raise the dust. But the worst memory was the physical," he continued. "The doctors testing for social diseases were seated at a long table with a basin full of potassium chloride. You had to reveal yourself right there in front of everyone. This was very demeaning."

But most inconveniences were a small price to pay for a new life, recounted Arthur Tracy, who came to this country from Russia in 1906 as Abraham Tracovutsky. (Tracy, who became an international star as a radio crooner in the 1930s, died in 1997 in New York at the age of ninety-eight.) His father, Morris Tracovutsky, unable to stay in the family's hometown of Kamenetz after pogroms and the drowning of one son, took his wife and seven children—including six-year-old Abraham—to America. "We left everything as it stood in the house. We took only what we could carry," Tracy said. They bribed guards in every Russian city en route to Hamburg, then journeyed to Liverpool; six long weeks later, they arrived at Ellis Island, where an inspector clucked disapprovingly at the long, unpro-nounceable family name, and snipped six letters from Tracovutsky. "He performed a little circumcision," quipped Tracy.

With their futures at stake, this vast, impersonal pit stop rife with uncertainty terrified many immigrants. But 80 percent passed smoothly through Ellis Island within five hours. The rest were detained for health or legal reasons; and whereas only 2 percent were sent back to their homelands, that seemingly small number added up to about 240,000 broken dreams.

The Ellis Island ordeal was endured only by those who couldn't afford a first- or second-class steamship ticket. Moneyed newcomers received cursory inspections on board ship and were sent to Ellis only if they were seriously ill or lacked the proper papers. Even on Ellis Island, they were kept separate from the masses. The derogatory slur *immigrants* was reserved for the teeming hordes of poor packed into dangerously unsanitary conditions in steerage, the lower decks near the ship's steering mechanism.

Although America had always been a nation of foreigners, most aliens who came through Ellis Island were from markedly different cultures than previous generations of newcomers. During the 1780s, about 5,000 people emigrated to America annually; by the 1820s, some 150,000 were arriving each year. More than 90 percent of these arrivals were from northern or western European countries—England, Ireland, Germany, France, Holland, Belgium, and Switzerland. By contrast, immigrants between 1880 and 1924 were largely from southern and eastern European nations—Italy, Russia, Austria, and Hungary.

Government oversight of the immigration process increased gradually in the years leading up to the opening of Ellis Island in 1892. Until the mid-nineteenth century, ships simply docked at the city's many piers and unloaded passengers. New York State established a board of emigration in 1847, but it focused almost exclusively on quarantining those with contagious diseases. Then, in 1855, the state opened a formal processing station at Castle Garden in Lower Manhattan. During the next thirty-five years, nearly eight million aliens entered America there. Ostensibly a place to check paperwork and provide job, home, and transportation counsel, Castle Garden developed a venal reputation because of corrupt employees and the predatory swindlers and con men who lurked nearby.

The federal government established procedural rules in the 1880s—including a head tax of fifty cents per arrival—but the state continued running the show until 1890. Finally, the federal government stepped in, announcing it would operate the depot from one of its harbor islands. The takeover, and the subsequent isolation of immigrants, would help end exploitation and restrict the flow. Many Americans of northern and western European heritage disdained the new immigrants, whom they viewed as poor, uneducated, peasant Jews and Catholics who dressed and spoke strangely, and whom they suspected of political radicalism. The *New York Times* endorsed the takeover, writing, "We want no more immigrants who are fitted for no higher work than digging ditches and paving streets."

William Windom, secretary of the Treasury, had three islands from which to choose. His first selection, Bedloe's Island—where the Statue of Liberty had been placed four years earlier—was met by public outrage. U.S. Senator William Evarts and Joseph Pulitzer's *New York World* denounced the idea, as did Auguste Bartholdi, who called it a "monstrous plan" and "downright desecration." The military shot down Windom's request for Governors Island. That left Ellis Island, just north of Bedloe's and right off Jersey City, even though Windom deemed it too small and "not a desirable place."

The island Windom scorned was an unimpressive three-acre speck of land. The Native Americans called it Kioshk, or Gull Island, for the birds that loved the water's seafood. It was Oyster Island to Dutch settlers who picnicked there. The English called it Oyster, but also Gibbet Island after several pirates were hanged there in the 1760s. (Executions were held there sporadically through 1860.) Little else is known about the island before 1785, the year Manhattan merchant Samuel Ellis put it up for sale. Although he also offered "a few barrels of excellent fat shad . . . and a few thousand red herring of his own curing," Ellis found no takers.

Ellis, who also owned a farm in Bergen County, New Jersey, died in 1794, bequeathing the island to his unborn grandchild—if it was a boy named Samuel. When his heir died in childhood, a family dispute ensued. Ownership remained unsettled until 1808, when the federal government, which had built a fort on the private property, paid the family $10,000 for the island. The fort was replaced by a one-tiered battery built for the War of 1812; two years later, it was named for Colonel James Gibson, who died in the Battle of Fort Erie. Although the fort was dismantled in 1861, a naval magazine operated there until 1890, when, despite Windom's many objections, Congress voted to double the island in size and replace the munitions with immigration facilities.

After Ellis Island opened, immigration levels plunged from 445,987 in 1892 to 178,748 in 1898. The drop was caused by a cholera scare in 1892, a nationwide economic depression the following year, and a slew of new immigration regulations. The 1885 Contract Labor Law, which prohibited companies from importing cheap labor, was expanded to prevent advertising for workers overseas; steamships were required to pay for the detention and return of any passengers; and the federal government began inspecting immigrants aboard ship for a variety of ailments, ranging from idiocy to insanity to contagious diseases. This last change caused friction with New York State, which still inspected all ships entering New York Harbor, quarantining anyone with a contagious disease at Hoffman and Swinburne Islands.

Improvements continued at the Ellis Island facilities, built of Georgia pine with slate roofing, until June 14, 1897, when a devastating fire wiped out seven years of work. While a new station was being constructed, immigrants were admitted through the Barge Office at the Battery in Manhattan. Ellis Island reopened in 1900 with a stylish new French Renaissance building designed by a small firm called Boring & Tilton. The exterior was red brick with ironwork and limestone trim, highlighted by intricate stonework and four towers capped with cupolas and spires. The interior was dominated by the large Registry Room on the second floor. The Great Hall, as it was also known, was two hundred feet long, one hundred feet wide, and fifty-six feet high, with twelve narrow alleys divided by large iron railings to direct inspection lines. In 1911, wooden benches replaced the railings.

While the building's stately design was visually stirring, it was equipped to administer no more than half a million incomers a year. The chaos and overcrowding of the next fifteen years—when more than nine million people arrived—proved this a disastrous miscalculation. The government soon used landfill to expand the island for a new hospital and other buildings. By the 1920s, Ellis Island had grown to its present size of twenty-seven and a half acres.

Between 1900 and 1914, three-quarters of all immigrants who reached America came through Ellis Island. In 1907, the busiest year, 1,004,756 people filed through the Great Hall. While the crowds averaged 5,000 a day, the peak that year was 11,747 in a single day. The staff, which ranged in size from 500 to 850, routinely worked twelve-hour days in a vain attempt to keep up. (Immigrants not examined when they arrived had to stay another night on the ship.) The influx continued until World War I reduced arrivals; by 1918, only 28,867 were admitted. After the war, business boomed again, climbing to 315,587 in 1924.

Upon reaching New York Harbor, the immigrants—already dehumanized from having been herded like livestock in steerage—were piled onto barges and then deposited on Ellis Island, where they were funneled into lines for a medical exam and legal inspection.

The medical exam was called a "snapshot diagnosis." After trudging upstairs to the Registry Room, immigrants were glanced at by an exhausted doctor (charged with examining as many as two thousand people a day) who judged whether they suffered anything from lameness to typhus. The line then shuffled to a second set of doctors, who looked for trachoma, a contagious eye disease causing blindness. Those who failed these exams received a chalk mark on their coat indicating the problem and were pulled out of line. Those suspected of feeblemindedness were given a battery of basic puzzles and tests, although many were so culturally biased that the results were absurd. One demonstrated that 80 percent of all eastern Europeans were "morons."

"It is no more difficult a task to detect poorly built, defective or broken - down human beings than to recognize a cheap or defective automobile," wrote Dr. Victor Safford of this assembly-line approach. However, they often made highly speculative diagnoses. Some doctors believed that dull strands of hair hanging on the left side of a foreign woman's head meant she was pregnant. While scientific advances and increases in Ellis Island's medical staff led to more rigorous examinations, these changes also resulted in more medical exclusions. Less than 2 percent of exclusions were for medical reasons prior to 1898; by 1913, the figure had climbed to 57 percent.

After the medical exam, each person waited to see an inspector, who peered at information provided by the ship's manifest and asked questions

Newcomers endured a battery of examinations at Ellis Island, including an eye inspection for trachoma. (Circa 1920.)

ELLIS ISLAND IMMIGRATION MUSEUM

about age, economic status, relatives in the country, and job skills. With the help of translators who spoke an average of six languages each, the inspectors determined if a person was "clearly and beyond a doubt entitled to land" in America. Immigrants also had to prove they had the then considerable sum of $25, a rule implemented by Commissioner William Williams in 1909 and informally enforced even after it was deemed unfair and repealed. In 1917, the lines slowed down and the number of detainees increased because of the Basic Immigration Act passed by Congress, which required a literacy test and a more detailed exam.

Those who passed went to the railroad and telegraph rooms and then departed Ellis Island. (One-third of the twelve million new residents settled in New York.) Those who failed to meet these standards were stuck in a screened-in area awaiting a hearing before a three-member board of special inquiry.

In the early years, Ellis Island was as riddled with corruption as Castle Garden had been. To rectify the situation, President Theodore Roosevelt appointed Williams commissioner in 1902. A wealthy New Englander who

Historical Detour: The War Between the States

Ellis Island, New Jersey. Historically, it makes no sense. Emotionally, it seems plain wrong. But legally, it is largely true. While the island is actually owned by the federal government, in 1997, the U.S. Supreme Court issued a shocking decision that carved jurisdiction over the land into two chunks. About five acres, including the famous museum, sit in New York, while the remaining twenty-two and a half acres reside in New Jersey. This put to rest a battle dating back three centuries.

What are now Liberty and Ellis Islands were formally annexed to New York in 1691, although both islands are geographically closer to New Jersey. The Garden State soon claimed that this was an unjustifiable case of Empire State Building. Although ownership was given to the federal government around 1800, the states continued their turf war. In 1834, they signed a compact designed to settle the dispute. It said that New York would "retain its present jurisdiction of and over" the islands while New Jersey kept "exclusive right" to the waters around them. The issue continued to simmer, with court cases occasionally popping up.

Ultimately, New Jersey's main goal was not historical but financial—it wanted tax revenue from concessions and employee salaries, particularly if Ellis Island's south side, home to thirty rapidly decaying buildings, were ever redeveloped. In 1986, the two sides patched up their differences by agreeing to split the revenue and, appropriately, spend it on low-income and homeless housing. The plan, however, was scrapped by the New York State legislature, which was not inclined to give away money to New Jersey or to the poor.

Finally, in 1993, having lost a Liberty Island battle, New Jersey asked the Supreme Court to decide Ellis Island's fate. New Jersey claimed that the areas created by landfill after the 1890s were in New Jersey's waters as decreed by the 1834 compact. New York emphasized its historical connection to the island, perhaps not arguing strenuously enough that the language technically gave it jurisdiction over anything called Ellis Island.

The war between the states grew ugly, with the *New York Times* lambasting New Jersey's efforts as "unfriendly, unbecoming, un-American, untoward, unhelpful, unprincipled, unseemly, unwarranted, and underhanded."

But in the end, New Jersey won. The question now is, What is its prize? The south side is eerily quiet and off-limits to visitors. Long, tight corridors connect the old insane wards, the vaultlike machine used for disinfecting quarantine mattresses, and the commissioner's quarters, where a valance or two still hangs. It is an important part of Ellis Island's history, yet most of the public doesn't know it exists and thinks the work on Ellis Island has been completed. In 2000, Hillary Rodham Clinton presented a Save America's Treasures grant of $500,000 to the National Park Service to help stabilize the ruins of what the First Lady called one of the eleven most endangered sites on the Treasures list of 550. New Jersey Governor Christine Todd Whitman kicked in an additional $1 million.

A state commission has made recommendations for developing the south side, while a Save Ellis Island committee has been formed to raise money. The ideas seem fitting and potentially popular—a center on immigrants' contributions and ethnic studies, a public health learning center, a center for historic preservation, a regional history center, and a conference center that would generate revenue and help the project eventually become self-sufficient.

"We want to be respectful of Ellis Island's heritage and history," says Save Ellis Island executive director Judy McAlpin. "We want to keep the immigrant experience front and center." (The commission pointedly avoids taking a stand on the "temporary" bridge linking New Jersey to the island, which was erected during the Main Building's restoration. Many New Jerseyans want to make it permanent, allowing residents to walk or even drive to the island, while many historians and others argue that visitors should arrive by boat as the immigrants did.)

Yet the final say belongs to the National Park Service, which will offer a plan of its own in late 2001. And raising the money to stabilize and restore the buildings—likely in excess of $200 million—will clearly be a national project, not a statewide one. In the meantime, millions of visitors each year converge on the Ellis Island Immigrant Museum. That's Ellis Island, New York.

had graduated first from Yale and then from Harvard Law School, Williams was a brilliant administrator and hands-on leader. Although scandals flared up throughout the Ellis Island years, Williams, who served two non-consecutive terms as commissioner, curbed the most egregious excesses. His first report in 1902 decried the depot's "vicious practices" and the way arrivals were "hustled about and addressed in rough language" that left them "bewildered and frightened." To keep out swindlers, Williams forced visitors to apply for passes.

But the gravest problems were woven into the daily fabric of Ellis Island life. Inspectors coerced testimony, covered up their own mistakes, and detained immigrants at whim, often trying to extort bribes. The operations contracted out to private businesses were no better. The dining-room floor was often covered with grease, bones, and other debris, while immigrants ate from unwashed bowls without utensils. During one period, the only meal served—day in and day out—was prunes and rye bread. The rates at the island's money exchange were arbitrary and unfair, and sometimes phony paper currency was issued.

Williams replaced corrupt officials and booted out profiteering contractors. These politically connected men took their case to the Oval Office, but Roosevelt sided with the new commissioner. Williams, however, sometimes seemed at odds with himself. While he planted nasturtiums, ferns, and pansies to brighten the dreary facility and posted signs reading ALL IMMI-GRANTS ARE TO BE TREATED WITH KINDNESS AND CONSIDERATION, he nonetheless sided with the public regarding the new immigrants.

"Rigid means should be adopted to keep away those who are undesirable," he wrote in an initial report targeted at Russian, Syrian, and Italian peasants. When 6,839 immigrants were deported from Ellis Island in 1903, Williams was accused of operating a star chamber. Roosevelt reminded Williams to be more judicious, writing that to send an immigrant back "is often to inflict a punishment upon him only less severe than death itself."

With the sharp decline in immigration at the start of World War I, a compassionate new commissioner, Frederic Howe, transformed Ellis Island into a welcoming place, offering everything from classes to folk dancing for those confined there. In an effort to give more freedom to immigrants who had been locked indoors for six weeks, he let them out for recreation. "They rolled upon the grass," he wrote in *Survey* magazine in 1916. "Hundreds of them wept at the contact with the earth again."

Howe's reforms, however, made enemies in the bureaucracy. When Howe tried improving food on the island, Congressman William Bennet, who had once been the attorney for the food contractors, called Howe a "half-baked radical with free-love ideas" and demanded an investigation of Howe's leadership.

When the United States entered the war, Ellis Island was mostly used to hold captured German sailors and suspected spies. After the war, anti-Communist and anarchist hysteria fueled the desire for increased expulsions of "new immigrants," and Howe found himself more jailer than immigration commissioner. Attacked in Congress as a suspected Communist after refusing to deport people without hearings, Howe resigned in September 1919. As the Red Scare peaked that winter, hundreds of immigrants caught in nationwide raids were sent to Ellis Island and deported back to Europe.

The literacy tests and anti-anarchist laws passed in that era were followed by a 1921 quota rule that had boats racing to New York every month to unload passengers before their nation's quota was filled—a tragedy for those who had given up everything only to arrive too late. Even so, there were too many outsiders for public taste. In 1924, stricter quotas allowed entry to only 2 percent of the total number of people from any one country who had established U.S. residency by 1890. The front door to America was swinging shut.

In addition to the new quota, fewer and fewer immigrants stopped at the island because they were being inspected at their point of embarkation. The huge crowds dwindled to five hundred a day, and the only arrivals were those who were sick or detained for a board of special inquiry hearing.

The final blow to Ellis Island was dealt by a ruling rendered during the Great Depression. Aliens who might take jobs from Americans or become public charges were banned, leaving Ellis Island operating almost entirely as a detention and deportation center. The tide had turned: Once a symbol of hope throughout the world, the island had come to represent America's disdain for outsiders. As immigration sank to its lowest totals in a century, deportations continued to rise (as did the number of Europeans voluntarily returning home in the face of anti-immigrant sentiments and massive unemployment). In 1932, more than twice as many aliens left through Ellis Island as had arrived.

With the focus of Ellis Island on detention, armed guards and barred windows were installed to control criminal aliens waiting to be kicked out of America. Diminishing government support made the services of volunteer organizations and social workers—who had been helping immigrants for more than a century—even more vital. The General Committee of Immigrant Aid at Ellis Island included groups like the Belgian Bureau, the

National Council of Jewish Women, Daughters of the American Revolution, and the Italian Welfare League. They provided sewing materials, classes, concerts, games, and, most important, friendly faces and familiar tongues to ease the immigrants through these difficult times.

But the days were extremely regimented—detainees were forced to while away the hours on hard benches and were led only occasionally into the courtyard for fresh air, where they walked silently in single file. Paul Laric, a Yugoslavian immigrant, was held with his family there for three weeks in 1940 because his brother's paperwork was not in order. "We spent the entire time in the Great Hall," he later told the island's librarians. "There was a feeling of desperation. The Statue of Liberty was showing us her back as if she was sending us a message."

During World War II, the island was an internment camp for people from enemy countries, be they captured sailors, immigrants, or even naturalized U.S. citizens. Surrounded by barbed wire, Ellis Island held as many as fifteen hundred prisoners; although there were more Germans than Italians or Japanese, the Japanese received the harshest treatment. European prisoners played big-stakes poker and drank Scotch at night, then skipped breakfast in the morning and bought food on the black market later. The Japanese were segregated from the Europeans and had a strict schedule, including earlier wake-ups. They were served meals completely alien to their diet, like pig's knuckles with sauerkraut. (The Coast Guard was also stationed there from 1939 to 1946.)

When the Internal Security Act was passed in 1950, the island again hosted hundreds of immigrant detainees. A response to the new Red Scare, the act demanded that suspected Communists and anyone with past links to fascism be held. Soviet Union propaganda gleefully proclaimed America's Ellis Island a concentration camp, but by material measures life there was more agreeable than ever. Whole families of detainees were given rooms of their own, with fresh linen and cleaning services. Movies, concerts, Ping-Pong, billiards, occasional ball games, and a Salvation Army–run library with twenty thousand books and foreign-language periodicals filled the time.

The officials were "very kindly people" who went to extraordinary lengths, within the system, to make the stay there "as little like a nightmare" as they could, George Voskovec, a Czechoslovakian refugee, told *The New Yorker* in 1951. Although he landed at La Guardia Field with a valid entry permit, Voskovec was suspected of Communist affiliations, driven to the ferry, and shipped to Ellis Island.

Despite the creature comforts, the experience was psychologically unsettling. Many individuals, accustomed to totalitarian regimes, feared stepping out of line and were preoccupied with self-preservation. There was also little camaraderie because the population was so transient. Voskovec felt "walled in by silence" during his ten-month stay.

Since the war, there had been occasional talk of abandoning Ellis Island, especially with much of it in disuse. In 1951, the *New York Journal–American* made a push for establishing a juvenile drug rehabilitation center there. It ended up on North Brother Island instead. Finally, in 1954, the Immigration and Naturalization Service shifted the island's limited operations to 20 West Broadway in Lower Manhattan. On November 12, the last detainee, a Norwegian seaman named Arne Peterssen, left Ellis Island, and the Great Hall fell silent. Although the island was never forgotten, the thirty-five buildings were left to deteriorate as its fate was debated during the next three decades. Laundry carts, filing cabinets—even an American flag—lay discarded, disturbed only by an occasional vandal.

In 1956, the government put this surplus property up for sale, touting it in newspaper ads as ideal for manufacturing or storage. There were many development proposals in the next decade—a resort hotel, a marina with sail-in movies, a liberal arts college, a school for the mentally retarded, senior citizen housing, and a futuristic city designed by Frank Lloyd Wright just before his death. Some bids were too low; others never got past the talking stage. Concerned citizens, meanwhile, pressured the government to preserve this crumbling shrine to the American Dream.

A monument or museum concept for Ellis Island, in fact, had been tossed around since the compound had first closed. Then, in 1965, President Lyndon Johnson conferred national monument status on the island, allocating $6 million for refurbishing the site. Renowned architect Philip Johnson, who designed the scheme, proposed demolishing some buildings and stripping others down so they could be preserved as "stabilized ruins." He also planned a garish 130-foot circular tower as a tribute to the Ellis Island immigrants. Johnson's concept was forsaken when the money was shifted to Vietnam War spending.

In 1974, Dr. Peter Sammartino, whose parents had come to Ellis Island from Italy, formed the Restore Ellis Island Committee. The head of Fairleigh Dickinson University, Sammartino lobbied Congress, which provided some preservation funds. In 1976, limited tours of the run-down buildings began. Finally, in the 1980s, the rehabilitation of Ellis Island was included in the Statue of Liberty restoration project. Unlike Johnson's abstract concepts,

Historical Detour: The Prince of Ellis Island

Most detainees didn't call New York's immigration center "The Palace at the Isle of Ellis." And most didn't parlay their illegal alien status into vaudeville engagements and a friendship with Frank Sinatra. But most people were not Harry Gerguson.

In fact, by his telling, Harry Gerguson wasn't Harry Gerguson ... he was Prince Michael Romanoff.

Gerguson was first detained at Ellis Island in 1922 as a stowaway from Europe. Gerguson swore he was a New Yorker, but recalled little about the city, his neighborhood, or his school days. His excuse? After ten years of solitary confinement in a German jail for killing a German nobleman, he'd lost his memory. He soon escaped Ellis Island by stowing away on the *Ellis Island* ferry, although he perpetuated a tale that he had been one of the island's few successful "swimaways," dragging his signature walking stick with him through the water.

This small, dapper man with a thin mustache and British accent (he alternately claimed to have attended Oxford, Cambridge, Yale, Princeton, and Harvard) resurfaced soon after in Manhattan as Prince Michael Alexander Obolensky, a descendant of Russia's royal Romanoff family. He later simplified his persona to Prince Michael Romanoff.

As Romanoff, Gerguson spent the next year persuading the press and high society from New York to Wichita that he was a down-on-his-luck nobleman, willing to groom horses for cash. But he mostly lived off the generosity of others and also earned money lecturing on conditions in Russia. He was subsequently exposed as a con man and returned to Ellis Island to face deportation. Immigration officials were forced to free him, however, because they couldn't prove he was not an American.

Romanoff crisscrossed the United States, living off his forged identity and periodically landing in jail for writing bad checks. In 1932, he fled to France, where he again ran into trouble with the law. He stowed away on a boat back to America, but was detained at Ellis Island, where he charmed officials and even helped run the island library before engineering his next escape. Four staff members were suspended for allowing

Romanoff to slip away, although he telephoned Ellis Island brass from his hideout to say his guard should not be blamed. Romanoff was caught two weeks later at one of his regular haunts—an East Side speakeasy—and was shipped back to France to serve the jail sentence he'd left behind. He snuck back into the United States later that year, but ended up again on Ellis Island after the manager of Dunhill's tobacco shop on Fifth Avenue reluctantly turned in one of his favorite customers.

Romanoff was released in January 1933, on the condition that he would relinquish the Romanoff persona. Instead, he capitalized on his notoriety with a brief stint on the vaudeville circuit as the prince. He later went to Hollywood, where an entertaining con was something to be admired. In 1940, after three years of party-hopping, he opened Romanoff's, a restaurant in Beverly Hills, with the financial backing of pals like John Barrymore, Humphrey Bogart, and Charlie Chaplin.

For the next twenty-two years, Romanoff was restaurateur to the stars and big spenders (he also opened eateries in Palm Springs and San Francisco). His celebrity enabled him to finally attain U.S. citizenship in 1958, when President Dwight D. Eisenhower signed a bill written specifically for the occasion. Until Romanoff died in 1971, he had bit parts in many movies, especially anything starring his closest friend, Frank Sinatra.

According to Ellis Island officials, Gerguson was born in Russia in 1890, arriving in New York at age six. When his parents died a few years later, Gerguson became a troubled truant, passing through six orphanages and earning the label "incorrigible." He ran away from his uncle, was arrested for petty larceny, and as a teen was sent with other orphans to live on a farm in Hillsboro, Illinois. This peripatetic soul later returned to New York to peddle newspapers on East Broadway. But the life of a regular joe held little appeal for Gerguson, so he began trying on new, glamorous identities, eventually settling on the Romanoff persona.

Gerguson built a life around tales so fantastical as to make the most polished fiction writers envious. His most honest comment was, "No one has ever discovered the truth about me, not even myself."

the primary goal this time was to restore the Main Building as a museum re-creating the immigrant experience.

Unlike Liberty Island, where supplies delivered by barge had to be scheduled around the tides, Ellis was close enough to New Jersey to permit the erection of a temporary bridge, which saved millions of dollars. (Although no longer used, the bridge has not been dismantled.) The Ellis Island restoration was generally more mundane than the Liberty project. Tasks included repairing the water-damaged Main Building and removing a piece of anachronistic architecture tacked on by the Coast Guard in the 1940s—an exposed staircase ascending from the Registry Room to its bal-cony. The most dramatic undertaking required that helicopters set four new fifteen-hundred-pound spires atop the Main Building's towers.

The Ellis Island project did, however, stir up plenty of controversy. In 1982, the National Park Service endorsed a plan for a conference center and Sheraton Hotel on the island's southern end. Lee Iacocca, who headed both the government's advisory committee and fund-raising for the Statue of Liberty–Ellis Island Foundation, belittled the concept as too commercial and a tax break for the rich, since finances depended heavily on tax shelter investments. Iacocca delayed the project and leaned toward an "ethnic Williamsburg" featuring exhibits, shops, and cultural events highlighting immigrant contributions to America. Both plans involved razing most buildings other than the Main Building.

Even after developers erased the hotel from the plan, Iacocca refused to budge. Then in 1986, Secretary of the Interior Donald Hodel fired him from the government's committee. Iacocca—who said his firing "borders on un-American"—averred that the conference center was the reason he was ousted. But others found his positions on the fund-raising and government committees (not to mention the Chrysler Corporation) a conflict of interest. Later that year, Iacocca was bumped up to chairman emeritus of the foun-dation fund-raising campaign.

At that point, the National Park Service wrested creative control from the foundation, which still held the purse strings. The two-headed monster was a disaster for the project's contractors, the *Daily News* wrote in 1990. The architects and engineers reported to the government, but the founda-tion handled the contractors, several of whom went bankrupt or needed bonding companies to complete the job. Although officials denied charges of bad management and undue interference, claiming that restoration work posed special challenges, they approved twenty-five hundred change-orders for tasks as minor as shifting soap dispensers by inches. "No matter what people say, this is not the palace at Versailles," said contractor David Demick of Danaco. "This is a utility building. Restoration should not have been a big deal."

Despite the finger-pointing, the $162 million renovation was an overwhelming success. The Main Building looks as regal and dignified as it had to immigrants in 1900, but the Ellis Island Immigrant Museum inside is more welcoming still. Plans to raze the rest of the island's abandoned buildings for development faded, and the foundation even restored two of them for maintenance and administration, providing extra space in the Main Building for the museum and library.

In the 1980s, record numbers of immigrants began pouring into the United States, stirring up in many Americans those old xenophobic attitudes about dubious foreigners—who now come largely from Asia and Latin America. While citizens worry about the ruination of America, many people journey to the Immigrant Museum to celebrate their own family's arrival. Perhaps at Ellis Island they will appreciate the irony of spewing the same prejudices their immigrant ancestors endured.

Exploring the Island

The **Ellis Island Immigrant Museum,** (212) 363-3206, is a magnificent treasure, blending a meticulous collection of artifacts, text, photos, and oral histories with the **Main Building** itself to bring the immigrant experience to life. The museum is so packed with stirring, often poignant information that you might feel almost as overwhelmed as one of the twelve million newcomers who trudged through here.

The museum doesn't get as jammed as the Ellis of old (or Lady Liberty today), but in summer an early start is advisable in order to reach the smaller rooms on the second floor before they get crowded. Don't rush through everything; you'll need an entire day, with a break for lunch (we recommend a picnic), to absorb it all.

There are several ways to enhance the experience—a film, a live performance, tours, an audio guide. The half-hour film, *Island of Hope, Island of Tears,* is screened in two theaters; one show includes a brief overview by a ranger, the other does not. The footage takes viewers from European villages through the arduous trip to Ellis Island. Although not a must-see, the film, especially when interpreted by a ranger, provides a fine visual and factual introduction to the island's history. In the twenty-five-minute play *Ellis Island Stories,* costumed actors bring to life oral histories that can also be heard throughout the museum on special phones. The hour-long guided tours are lively, although poor acoustics in the cavernous Registry Room make hearing the ranger a challenge for those standing in the back. The audiocassette tour is the most thorough and can take up to two hours to complete. Like the ranger tour, it re-creates the tension and drama of the Registry Room in a way that the room's small plaques cannot. Many of the voices from the exhibit phones are also on the tape.

The tour begins with the **Baggage Room,** just inside the main entrance, with a display of original luggage—from wicker handbaskets to heavy trunks—toted by some of Ellis Island's twelve million immigrants. The striking photos of these immigrants, who brought only what they could carry, accentuates this sculpture of human determination, which symbolizes the fortitude and courage required to leave everything behind for an unknown new world. Baggage handlers could often pinpoint an immigrant's country of origin by the style of the luggage or the way ropes had been tied around the bulging caches.

Take the stairs on the right up to the **Registry Room,** retracing the steps immigrants took en route to their medical and legal inspections. The room today is bright and spacious, so it requires a vivid imagination to visualize crowds of bewildered, exhausted immigrants filling up every inch of it. The elegant vaulted ceiling was installed in 1918 after a 1916 explosion detonated by German saboteurs on Black Tom Wharf in New Jersey damaged the Main Building's interior. The new ceiling was designed by Rafael Guastavino, whose family had emigrated from Spain. Workers installing it dangled from safety belts without scaffolding; they did such a solid job that during the 1980s renovation only seventeen of the 28,282 tiles had to be replaced.

The former processing rooms—now the **Peak Immigration Years** and **Through America's Gate** exhibits—complete the tour of the immigrant's entrance to America through Ellis Island. In the medical exam room, the buttonhook used to lift eyelids in search of trachoma will make your eyes twitch. In the board of special inquiry waiting room, graffiti left by restless immigrants is preserved on the walls. Special tests and puzzles designed to determine feeblemindedness are exhibited as well. The museum also showcases the contributions of charity workers and civil servants, including a most famous alumnus, Fiorello La Guardia, who before entering politics earned $1,200 a year as an Ellis Island interpreter. He spoke Italian, German, and Croatian and often put in eighty-hour weeks.

Now climb to the balcony overlooking the Great Hall to see the dorm accommodations where detainees slept three hundred to a room, in cots stacked one above the other and suspended from the ceiling.

This is a good time to break for a picnic lunch outside and a stroll around the **Immigrant Wall of Honor** behind the museum. The 652-foot, double-sided, semicircular wall is adorned with nearly five hundred thousand names, commemorating immigration from its earliest days—from Myles Standish on the *Mayflower* to Paul Revere's father, Paul Rivoire, to the ancestors of Stan Musial and Mario Cuomo and thousands of less famous citizens.

The tour resumes inside with the **Peopling of America** exhibit, located behind the Baggage Room. In eye-catching and easy-to-understand charts, the display illustrates changes in America's population. One exhibit depicts the early geography of Native American tribes, while another maps out the forced migration of the Atlantic slave trade. There is more than cold statistical data here: A video features recent arrivals talking about immigrating today, and the **Word Tree** demonstrates how America's English has been enhanced by its many ethnic influences. For example, *phooey* derives from German, *gung ho* from Chinese, *raccoon* from Powhatan, and *patio* from Spanish.

The final stop is the third floor, where three compelling rooms await. **Ellis Island Chronicles** tells the island's tale from the government perspective. Models and photographs depict the building and landfill additions, while mini-biographies introduce commissioners like William Williams, who is quoted as saying, "Aliens have no inherent right to land here." The wheel of the *Ellis Island,* the steel-hulled ferry that traveled a total of nearly a million miles between the island and the Battery transporting immigrants from 1904 to 1954, is on display. (The abandoned ferry sank in her slip in 1968; the hull can be seen at low tide, but attempts to raise her fragile remains have been unsuccessful.)

Treasures from Home preserves those belongings immigrants could not bear to leave behind: mirrors and teddy bears; a long-stemmed pipe from Norway; a violin from Ukraine; a cake plate from Italy; and a sewing machine from England.

The final room, **Silent Voices,** recalls the post-1954 years, when the island sat abandoned. Black-and-white photos serve as backdrop to displays of dusty, run-down benches, signs, and other relics—all fitting reminders of what went into transforming this once forgotten building into a tribute to America's immigrants.

Island Hopping

Ellis Island can be reached from both New Jersey and Manhattan. New Jersey ferry service runs from Liberty State Park in Jersey City, exit 14B on the New Jersey Turnpike, (201) 435-9499. Manhattan ferry service runs from Battery Park; tickets are sold in Castle Clinton, (212) 269-5755. To reach Castle Clinton:

By car: From the West Side of Manhattan, take the West Side Highway south to West Street, then south to Battery Park and South Street. From the East Side, take the FDR Drive south to South Street. Street parking is close to impossible, but there are several parking lots by Battery Park.

By subway: From the West Side, take the 1 or 9 to South Ferry. From the East Side, Brooklyn, or the Bronx, take the 4 or 5 to Bowling Green. From Queens or Brooklyn, take the N or R to Whitehall Street.

By bus: From Midtown, take the M6 or M1 to Battery Park. From the East Side, take the M15.

By boat: From Staten Island, take the ferry to the Manhattan terminal. Follow the signs through Battery Park to Castle Clinton.

4. Forgotten Islands of Upper New York Bay

Castle Clinton

Castle Clinton

WELDED TO THE MAINLAND by landfill and dwarfed by skyscrapers, Castle Clinton has been reduced to a bit player, the launching point for the tourist ferry to Ellis and Liberty Islands. But before Ellis Island became America's front door, this fort was the immigrants' gateway to the United States. And long before the majestic Statue of Liberty stood in New York Harbor, the tiny isle of Castle Clinton was the pride of New York City.

The man-made island, constructed from stone in 1807 as a fortress site, was positioned about two hundred feet from the Battery at Manhattan's southwestern tip. The Southwest Battery, completed in 1811, had both the Hudson and East Rivers in its sights. It had twenty-eight cannons and walls eight feet thick, and was connected to Manhattan by a wooden bridge.

The Battery never fired on the British, but during the War of 1812 it went head-to-head with Fort Columbus on Governors Island in annual morale-boosting competitions to blow up old ship hulks. In 1815, the fort was renamed Castle Clinton after Mayor De Witt Clinton, and remained headquarters for the Third Military District until 1821, when the central offices shifted to Governors Island and the island fort was given to the city.

In 1824, it was reborn as Castle Garden, and during the next three decades was the city's premier showcase, hosting celebrity galas and concerts, political rallies, and fireworks displays. The fortress was lavishly remodeled to accommodate its new personality. The gunrooms boasted marble busts and painted panoramas. A promenade was constructed along the building's crest, allowing guests a romantic stroll. In 1825, Castle Garden became one of the first public buildings lighted with gas. A massive fountain was installed in its interior in 1843, and the next year a roof was added, turning the former fort into the city's largest indoor concert hall.

Virtually every president from Andrew Jackson to Franklin Pierce was feted at Castle Garden, also home to outstanding assemblies. Daniel Webster delivered some of his greatest orations; Henry Clay, "the Great Compromiser," held conventions intended to defuse growing tensions between the North and South; and Hungarian freedom fighter Louis Kossuth made his celebrated 1851 speech here.

Castle Garden was also home to high culture. It introduced Americans to grand opera performed by supreme Italian vocalists Giulia Grisi and Giuseppe Mario, and hosted the first American performance of Beethoven's Ninth Symphony. Indeed, two events were hailed during their time as the social affairs of the century: a grand reception honoring Revolutionary War hero Marquis de Lafayette on his visit from France, and the American debut of Europe's most popular singer, Jenny Lind, "the Swedish Nightingale."

Castle Garden had been open only a few months when the city's cannons roared one hundred times to welcome Lafayette to America on September 14, 1824. The city was impressed by the Marquis's appearance and awed by the fort's transformation. Reviewing the bash for the *New York American,* James Fenimore Cooper wrote that with its blazing lights and extravagant decor, "the Castle presented a more magnificent spectacle than this country has before witnessed."

The fort was decked out in red, white, and blue, and hung with flags depicting the armorial insignias of the thirteen original states. Each of the gala's five thousand guests wore a medallion bearing the Frenchman's likeness. Beyond the pomp and circumstance the party was also a memorable one, with music and dancing continuing until 4 AM.

Jenny Lind's arrival on September 12, 1850, was more demure—the music of flutes, not the blast of cannons, welcomed the soprano. Lind sold out all six thousand seats for six evenings, but there was little chaos thanks to the masterly organization of her manager, the legendary P. T. Barnum.

Barnum auctioned off the tickets. While the average ticket cost about $6, John Genin, a hatter and friend of the showman, was persuaded to pay $225 (about $4,375 in 1999 dollars) for the first seat, A1, a cushioned, crimson velvet chair directly in front of Lind. Barnum assured Genin that the astronomical sum was a good buy, and would reap untold publicity for the hatter. Indeed, "Genin" hats became a fashion statement ballyhooed across the nation.

People traveled from Philadelphia and Boston for the debut, although many ladies, fearing a crush, stayed away opening night. Those without seats took to the water, encircling Castle Garden in their boats. On premiere night, two hundred vessels surrounded the concert hall, filled with fans listening to Lind's voice floating beyond the fort's walls.

"Never did a mortal in this city, or perhaps in any other, receive such homage," proclaimed a front-page story in the *New York Herald.* "From the ceiling to the stage it was one dense mass of human beings."

Lind, whom the *Herald* anointed "the greatest prodigy in song that ever appeared upon the theater of this world," donated her opening-night purse of $12,000 to various New York charities, and gave her tour earnings to Swedish schools. Her generosity and talent prompted the newspaper to proclaim her "goddess of the people."

Lind returned to Castle Garden in 1852 for a series of farewell concerts, but the hall's glory days were nearing an end. Three years later, the island was joined by fill to Manhattan and given over to the state, which turned the old palace into a depot for immigrants. When it closed in 1890, Castle Garden's legacy included the admission of 7.9 million newcomers to America. So embedded was the name Castle Garden in the immigrant psyche that for years after Ellis Island opened, many arrivals referred to the new depot as Castle Garden.

In 1896, the building was remodeled and converted into the New York Aquarium—the city's most popular public institution, drawing at its peak two and a half million visitors annually. But in 1941, Robert Moses, head of the Triborough Bridge Authority, closed the aquarium and threatened to demolish the building as revenge against upper-crust reformers and politicians who had defeated his proposal for a Brooklyn Battery Bridge.

The aquarium never reopened, but Moses' planned destruction of the historic building was thwarted when reformers successfully lobbied the federal government to preserve the site. After several decades without funding, the National Park Service restored Castle Clinton to its original state.

Exploring the Island

Most visitors merely pass through **Castle Clinton,** (212) 344-7220, stopping only at the Ellis and Liberty Island Ferry ticket gazebo. They miss a chance to learn about the fort itself through a dioramic exhibit or ranger-led tours. While they may not warrant a separate trip, the exhibit and tour are worth allotting time for on your way to Ellis or Liberty Island. The rangers time the twenty-minute tours so you'll make the next ferry and they provide details not found in the exhibit, such as the fact that the fort only had officers' quarters—infantrymen had to commute to the garrison or sleep next to their cannons during emergencies.

The exhibit is in a small room off to the right as you enter the fort and offers an entertaining look at the fort's evolution and how drastically the contours of New York have changed. (There is also a short film about the Hudson River.) It features three large models and murals depicting the

Castle Clinton area in 1812, 1886, and 1941. The 1812 rendering shows an open fort on a small island connected by a wooden bridge to Lower Manhattan, with the nearby shores of Brooklyn essentially undeveloped. By 1886, Castle Clinton was enclosed, surrounded by Labor Bureau buildings for receiving immigrants, and connected to Manhattan by landfill. An elevated train chugs through Manhattan, which is linked by a magnificent bridge to rapidly developing Brooklyn. The 1941 version shows the castle in its final days as New York's aquarium, now three stories covered by white stucco. Landfill has pushed the fort farther back from the shore, and skyscrapers dominate the skyline.

To complete the experience, step outside: The small fort that may have seemed stodgy and uninspiring upon your arrival now has a stubborn dignity; it is a stark reminder of the country's hard-won independence.

Island Hopping

By car: From the West Side of Manhattan, take the West Side Highway south to West Street, then south to Battery Park and South Street. From the East Side, take the FDR Drive south to South Street. Street parking is close to impossible.

By subway: From the West Side, take the 1 or 9 to South Ferry. From the East Side, Brooklyn, or the Bronx, take the 4 or 5 to Bowling Green. From Queens or Brooklyn, take the N or R to Whitehall Street.

By bus: From Midtown, take the M6 or M1 to Battery Park. From the East Side, take the M15.

By boat: From Staten Island, take the ferry to the Manhattan terminal. Follow the signs through Battery Park to Castle Clinton.

Part II

Lower New York Bay

HOFFMAN AND SWINBURNE ISLANDS •
FORGOTTEN ISLANDS OF LOWER NEW YORK BAY

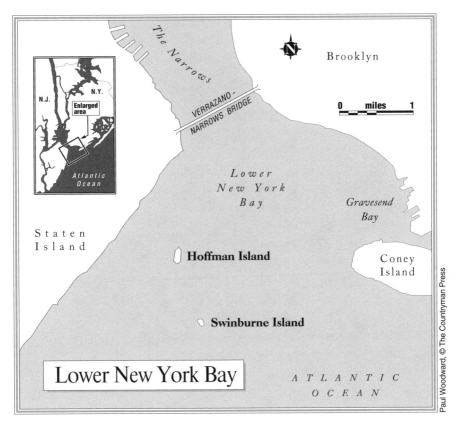

*Linked to the Upper Bay by The Narrows, a mile-wide tidal strait, the
Lower Bay borders the eastern shore of Staten Island and the western coast
of Brooklyn, and opens up into the Atlantic Ocean.*

5. Hoffman and Swinburne Islands

"Peopled only by the shades of those who were banished there by disease to die or recover, the isle has held a morbid fascination for occasional visitors curious to see this forsaken spot."

—STATEN ISLAND ADVANCE, JULY 17, 1934,
REFERRING TO SWINBURNE ISLAND

Hoffman and Swinburne Islands

STATEN ISLANDERS HAD had enough. In 1858, after more than fifty years as New York's dumping ground for people with contagious, deadly diseases—yellow fever, typhus, cholera, and smallpox—infuriated mobs burned the New York Quarantine Hospital to the ground. In the face of this unsurpassed expression of NIMBY-ism, the government was forced to create two artificial islands, Hoffman and Swinburne, to house the ill.

Establishing a quarantine had never been an easy endeavor; its location inevitably distressed nearby residents. The first official quarantine was established at Bedloe's Island in 1758, but after a deadly cholera epidemic spread to Manhattan, detainees were shuffled off to Governors Island, and then, in 1801, to Tompkinsville at the northeast corner of Staten Island. (The Seamen's Retreat in nearby Stapleton was used from 1831 to 1882 to separately quarantine seamen and their families.)

Staten Islanders protested vehemently. Their opposition to the Tompkinsville quarantine intensified in 1848, when 180 locals contracted yellow fever. The legislature ordered the quarantine—which detained anyone with a contagious disease, not just immigrants—moved again, this time to Sequine's Point, Prince's Bay, far away at the southern end of the island.

Soon after building began there in 1857, angry residents burned the new structures and piers. Martial law was declared and the militia patrolled the quarantine site, but another series of new buildings was also razed. Frustrated, the state tried reopening the old quarters at Tompkinsville, but north shore residents proved as furious and destructive as their southern neighbors. On September 1, 1858, lawless islanders armed with fiery fagots of straw broke through the quarantine gates and burned the main buildings. The militia was called in to save what remained, but as soon as rumors spread the next day that the quarantine would be rebuilt, the mob returned, dragging patients onto the lawns and setting the last buildings ablaze.

Desperately, the quarantine commissioners set their sights offshore and established a temporary detention center for yellow fever sufferers on two old ships—the *Florence Nightingale* and the *Illinois,* which they anchored in New York Harbor. Smallpox victims were sent to Blackwell's Island (now Roosevelt

Island), and typhus sufferers went to Ward's Island. The arrangement so effectively restored calm on Staten Island that the commissioners replaced the ships by constructing two small islands in a shallow area in Lower New York Bay called Orchard Shoals, about one mile southeast of South Beach and west of the main channel leading into and out of New York Harbor.

Beginning in the mid-1860s, piles of sand dredged from New York Harbor were heaped into two mounds until they formed the new Quarantine Islands—Hoffman and Dix Islands—each about two and a half acres in size. Administrative buildings and a boarding station to inspect incoming ships were built several miles north, at Rosebank, on Staten Island.

Hoffman Island was named for John T. Hoffman, mayor of New York City from 1866 to 1868 and governor of New York State from 1869 to 1872. Dix Island was named for John Dix, a New York senator from 1845 to 1849 and governor from 1873 to 1875, but the moniker was soon changed to Swinburne Island in honor of Civil War hero and surgeon Dr. John S. Swinburne, who as port health officer oversaw the development of the islands.

Swinburne Island, or the Lower Quarantine, was completed in 1870. Hoffman Island, or the Upper Quarantine, was finished in 1873. Immigration at the time was sporadic and manageable. In the beginning, Hoffman's three two-story brick buildings remained empty, while the hospital at Swinburne adequately cared for people infected with contagious disease. (Treatment for yellow fever included ingesting both iced champagne and spirits of turpentine.)

But in 1880, a great wave of immigration pounded the Port of New York. Twenty million foreigners immigrated to the United States between 1880 and 1920, the vast majority of them passing through New York.

Immigrants were typically crammed into steerage, with scant air, bad water, and decaying food. As a result, many were infected with or exposed to contagious diseases, putting a strain on the tiny islands, which were ill equipped for the deluge of human suffering. Those in the private quarters of first or second class were subject to inspection only if they came from a port where disease was prevalent.

Voyagers suffering from contagious diseases were hospitalized on Swinburne Island. Passengers exposed to, but showing no symptoms of, the deadly diseases were detained on Hoffman Island for observation during incubation periods, which generally lasted from a few days to two weeks. Immigrants were then sent to the receiving center at Castle Garden in Lower Manhattan and, after 1892, at Ellis Island; wealthier newcomers went straight to New York.

By 1884, the quarantine commissioners reported that unhealthy conditions—especially decaying wooden buildings that acted as disease conductors—at Hoffman Island were spreading infections to healthy detainees, who upon becoming ill were sent to Swinburne Island, which wasn't much better. In 1887, Hoffman was tagged "scarcely tenantable" and in need of at least $121,000 in repairs. Staten Islanders, meanwhile, successfully lobbied for a crematorium on Swinburne Island, to stop the burying of diseased corpses at Sequine's Point.

In 1892, as a massive cholera epidemic plagued the world, an average of fifteen ships a day arrived in New York. Between August 31 and October 8, quarantine officers discovered cholera on seven vessels: 914 cabin passengers, 3,405 steerage passengers, and 1,469 officers and crew members were held for observation on Hoffman and Swinburne Islands during those six frantic weeks.

A new three-story dorm was constructed hastily on Hoffman Island, increasing dormitory capacity from 850 to 2,100. Detainees were bathed, and their clothes and effects either disinfected with steam or boiled. The epidemic threatened national security and precipitated hostility among federal, state, and municipal officials, who accused each other of ineptitude. "The recent experience at the Port of New York sent a shudder throughout the whole country," wrote the *New Orleans Medical and Surgical Journal.* The federal government subsequently took over most quarantine stations, although New York State retained control of its facility until 1921.

When it became apparent that Hoffman Island couldn't accommodate the growing numbers of immigrants, the state—after buying Fire Island on Long Island, but deciding not to use it—enlarged Hoffman Island to 9.9 acres. The job was finally completed in 1896, but building didn't begin for several years due to lack of funds. The quarantine commissioners also implored the state legislature for money to improve existing conditions on both Swinburne and Hoffman Islands, but the requests were either denied or appeased with meager allocations.

Immigration peaked in the first decade of the new century. In 1901, 7,801 people were detained on Hoffman Island. While quarantine officials finally received some of the money they'd been requesting, most of the $64,000 allocated for Hoffman Island was slated for a luxury item—a building to segregate cabin-class travelers from steerage. Swinburne, which quarantine officials referred to as a "disgrace to the state," secured only $2,500 for minor repairs.

Despite hard times aggravated by overcrowding and insufficient funding, the islands were effective in keeping major epidemics from breaking
out in New York. The good work, however, was overshadowed in 1911 when
political maneuvering against the health officer of the Port of New York
resulted in a nasty trial rife with accusations of corruption and mismanagement. (See *Historical Detour: Tammany Goes Job Hunting.*)

New buildings were eventually erected and repairs made to the islands'
decaying infrastructures in 1916. Renovations continued through 1923,
but few people benefited from the enhancement, since the immigration
crunch was ending. Immigration was first interrupted during World War I,
and the islands' hospitals were used by the army and navy to care for thousands of soldiers with venereal diseases. Then, in 1921, harsh new laws
placed severe restrictions on immigration.

Only three people were detained on Hoffman Island after 1928, and
Swinburne Island closed that year. Some adventurous souls contented
themselves with nude sunbathing on Swinburne Island. In 1929, a *Daily
News* investigation discovered vandals pillaging the buildings, holding
"ghoulish orgies," using urns—like the one holding the remains of a five-
year-old Austrian girl named Anne Kowrah—for "target practice," and
carrying out other despicable frivolities. Fiorello La Guardia, a congressman at the time, arranged to have the remaining urns moved to Hoffman
Island. In 1934, a fire, believed to have been carelessly set by a canoeist,
destroyed many of Swinburne's buildings.

Hoffman Island's fate was not as forlorn as that of its sister island. From
1931 to 1937, Hoffman was used to quarantine imported parrots as a pre-
caution against psittacosis, or parrot fever. The feathered foreign commod-
ity was subsequently banned.

In 1934, Staten Island Borough President Joseph Palma flirted with the
idea of building a summer pavilion, dog track, and amusement park on
Hoffman Island. Three years later, then Mayor La Guardia proposed a
camp for disadvantaged children, but Parks Commissioner Robert Moses
criticized the plan, stating that the polluted water was unfit for swimming.
The city did briefly turn Hoffman Island into a picnic ground with a regular ferry run from Staten Island.

Since no one had been detained at Hoffman for years, the quarantine
was moved with little fanfare back to Staten Island in 1938. It was sited at
Rosebank, about a mile south of Tompkinsville, where eighty years earlier
an angry mob had burned the Quarantine Station to the ground.

The U.S. Public Health Service tried relinquishing the outcast islands, but neither state nor city wanted them. Then the government found a new use for Hoffman Island, and built a training school for merchant marines there. Operated under the U.S. Maritime Service, with training provided by the Coast Guard, the school opened in 1938 with one hundred students. By 1943, there were twelve hundred enrollees. Students applauded the program, but the National Maritime Union said it fostered anti-unionism and created a surplus of labor in a field already suffering widespread unemployment. Swinburne Island was revived during World War II as the electronic control center for underwater mines spread throughout the area to stop enemy submarines.

The Maritime Service eventually outgrew Hoffman Island, moving to Sheepshead Bay, Brooklyn, in 1947. Except for rats, both islands were then deserted. The neglected buildings and piers slowly rotted in the salty air until they were hollow and ragged with time.

Every now and then, an idea came up for the exiled islands. In 1950, Mayor William O'Dwyer rejected suggestions to build a homeless shelter and, later, a drug rehabilitation center there. Five years later, temporary housing for disadvantaged young people was proposed, but the islands failed inspection by city officials. The most grandiose plan was unveiled in 1956 by the most ambitious of planners, Robert Moses. The federal government was trying to sell the islands and Moses wanted to stop them from falling into the hands of private investors, whom he said would erect massive billboards on the islands and taint the majesty of the bay.

Moses persuaded financier and philanthropist Bernard M. Baruch to donate the $10,000 New York needed to purchase the islands. Moses planned to fill in the one-mile span between Hoffman and Swinburne Islands, creating a giant 250-acre island park with a boat basin, fishing piers, picnic areas, golf courses, and ferry service to and from South Beach and eventually extending to Brooklyn and Manhattan. By using ten million cubic yards of compacted waste to enclose the islands, Moses also claimed he'd extend the life of the Fresh Kills landfill by three years, allowing the city more time to develop a modern incinerator system.

Moses was inspired by an idea promulgated by Cornelius Hall, the Staten Island borough president during World War II. Hall had envisioned connecting the islands to Staten Island via a curved arm of land, thus forging an airport link with Miller Field in the neighborhood of New Dorp. Hall's Breakwater Island was also meant to protect South Beach from erosion.

But Moses' park project never moved beyond the planning stage. Once

more Hoffman and Swinburne were left vulnerable to the whims of mis-
chief-makers and the lust of boat-ready lovers seeking privacy amid the
ruins. In 1960, a fire destroyed three of Hoffman's sixteen buildings. In
1965, harbor police arrested three women and eight men shooting porno-
graphic movies on Hoffman Island. A year later, two Wagner College soph-
omores were ditched there during a prank orchestrated by fraternity
brothers, who headed off to the prom. The students were rescued after
winds swept their signal fire into a roaring blaze that caused rubbernecking
traffic jams on the Belt Parkway and Verrazano-Narrows Bridge.

The Baruch Park plan survived in modified form through 1967. The city,
facing a waste disposal problem, then suggested that Hoffman and Swinburne Islands be included in a massive landfill project linking them to Fort
Wadsworth Army Base on Staten Island. A concerned public objected to
the notion of garbage in the water, as it previously had to Consolidated Edison's proposal to build atomic reactor generating plants on the islands.

In the winter of 1968, the city took a small step toward its original goal
of creating a new city park. All the buildings on Hoffman Island were
razed, and grass was planted in their place. The city made permits available, concluding that the green space might appeal to day-trippers and
overnight campers who could travel there by boat. But virtually nobody
took advantage of the opportunity, and by the end of 1969, chatter about a
new city park ceased.

The islands, which once figured so prominently in U.S. history—and
were so enthusiastically corralled by the city—were deeded back to the
federal government in 1972 as part of the twenty-six-thousand-acre Gateway National Recreation Area, the country's first national park system
established for urban areas.

While Gateway maintains a popular and active network of recreational
areas, including the Jamaica Bay Wildlife Refuge in Broad Channel,
Queens, and beachfront in Sandy Hook, New Jersey, it has no plans for
Hoffman and Swinburne Islands. Gateway has, however, shot down proposals that would adversely impact the islands, such as Borough President
Guy Molinari's 1991 suggestion to move the city's sludge-composting operations there. Since then, the islands have become increasingly popular with
herons, egrets, and cormorants, as the city's Harbor Herons Project has
expanded from Prall's Island, Shooter's Island, and Isle of Meadow on the
northern and western sides of Staten Island. Hoffman Island is home to
about 130 black-crowned night herons as well as more than two dozen great
and snowy egrets.

Historical Detour: Tammany Goes Job Hunting

In 1895, when Dr. Alvah H. Doty was appointed health officer of
the Port of New York—in charge of the quarantine at Hoffman
and Swinburne Islands—he inherited a system close to collapse.
The island's facilities were inadequate to accommodate the thousands of immigrants requiring detention, and an emergency
three-story frame dormitory constructed in 1893 was still being
used, despite a quarantine commissioners' report calling it a "tin-
der box" and "death trap." Doty repeatedly pleaded with the state
legislature for funding to renovate and improve the facilities, but
he was largely ignored. Despite the difficulties, Doty prevented
infectious diseases from riddling the mainland and received
endorsements for reappointment from the medical community
and the *New York Times* throughout his tenure.

In 1910, the *Jewish Morning Journal,* on behalf of immigrants formerly quarantined at Hoffman and Swinburne, accused
Doty's administration of tolerating overcrowding, filthy conditions,
forced manual labor, and attacks on young women. The charges
were quietly investigated by Republican governor Charles E.
Hughes and quickly dismissed as baseless. It was not long, however, before changing political winds rekindled the controversy.

Later that year, Hughes was ousted by Democrat John Dix,
who broke a fifteen-year Republican stronghold on the governor-
ship. Tammany Hall, New York City's omnipotent Democratic
political machine, coveted Doty's state-appointed $12,000-a-year
position. Tammany persuaded State Senator Thomas F. Grady to
introduce a bill transferring the position of health officer from
state to city supervision. Tammany also pressured Dix (no relation
to Governor John Dix, for whom Dix Island—later Swinburne—
was named) to appoint Charles N. Bulger to reinvestigate conditions on Hoffman and Swinburne Islands.

This time, the allegations were scrutinized daily in the main-
stream press. The hearings lasted two and a half months during
1911 and included the testimony of some 250 witnesses, many of
them former quarantine employees and immigrants who were
paid a per diem witness fee by their attorneys to testify.

At first, Doty was so busy containing a cholera epidemic that he didn't attend the hearings. Nor did he retain counsel, since no charges had been brought against him and the hearing was ostensibly to familiarize the governor with the Quarantine Islands. But the hearings soon evolved into a witch hunt.

On June 27, an immigrant named Freida Alexandrowski detailed through an interpreter the incidents she'd witnessed on Hoffman Island: "I have seen quilts stuffed into the mouths of children by nurses to keep them from crying. I have also seen dying children carried out of the hospital into the open air on cold winter days in their cribs and left there for six hours. The food which the detention station authorities gave us to eat consisted of sour soup, stale, moldy bread which had been cooked in filthy vessels, bad eggs, and rancid butter."

While the practice of exposing to the cold children who suffered from pneumonia complicated by other diseases frightened many immigrants, it was an accepted medical treatment in its day, believed to increase patients' resistance.

Former Hoffman Island superintendent Frank Bartow testified about overcrowding and inadequate sanitary conditions on Hoffman Island. The next day, however, Dr. John W. Brannan of Bellevue and Allied Hospitals cited a letter written by Bartow a year earlier contradicting his testimony and referring to the quarantine as a model place under Doty.

On July 28, Arthur Denyse, a former employee, said he and other employees held orgies and parties in Doty's office after the health officer had left for the night. On one occasion, Denyse said, he emptied the cremated remains of former New York City street cleaning commissioner Colonel George Waring from an urn kept on Doty's mantel, and mixed gin rickeys in the vessel.

The *New York Times* discredited Denyse's story the next day, reporting that Waring's remains were buried in Stamford, Connecticut. It was also disclosed that Denyse had been fired from his quarantine job after fabricating a cholera scare that had fooled the press.

In August, Doty's friends convinced him to retain legal counsel. But Doty, kept away by a wave of cholera-infected immigrants and his own mental and physical exhaustion caused by the investigation, again failed to testify on his own behalf.

The hearing ended September 1. Awaiting Bulger's assessment, the American Hospital Association lauded Doty for his handling of the cholera crisis, and said, "It should be the shame of all citizens to remember the humiliating investigation to which the doctor has been subjected."

Bulger, however, was not to be deterred. On December 5, outlining a litany of misdeeds, violations, and ineptitude, Bulger recommended to Governor Dix that Doty be forced to resign. His final report accused Doty's administration of "gross incompetence and inexcusable negligence," adding that the health officer was "living the social, rather than the strenuous life," while the quarantined immigrants were suffering under inhumane conditions. He also said Doty's bookkeeping practices were "primitive, obsolete, unsystematic, and altogether unreliable." Bulger then recommended thorough reform and renovation of the Quarantine Islands—similar to what Doty had urged all along.

The *Times* and the Academy of Medicine rebuked the verdict, and an accounting firm countered that Doty's records had been maintained with "scrupulous honor and integrity," adding that the health officer had actually saved the state money.

Doty defended himself in a written statement: "For the past six months I have borne the brunt of this malignant attack upon me at a time when all my days and nights were devoted to a strenuous effort to keep cholera out of this country."

Despite these protests, it was reported three days later that Tammany Hall leader Charles F. Murphy would have final say in naming Doty's successor. On December 29, Governor Dix demanded Doty's resignation. Doty, whose term had officially expired almost a year before, refused to resign, but didn't contest the appointment of a successor.

More than two hundred men applied for the job as health officer of the Port of New York, and on February 14, 1912, Dix nominated Dr. Joseph J. O'Connell for the job. O'Connell moved into the health officer's quarters at Rosebank, Staten Island, on Christmas Eve 1912, the same day that Doty packed his family's belongings and departed.

For now, the islands live in quiet solitude, virtually unknown to those steering barges and tugs through the bay. Occasionally, a weekend angler will look past rod and reel, pondering the meager remains surviving on Swinburne Island. Or a party will dock its boat alongside the jagged periphery of Hoffman Island, and steal a peek into its jungle wilderness— perhaps unaware of its dark past, and the promise of resurrection never realized.

6. Forgotten Islands of Lower New York Bay

Fort Lafayette

Forgotten Islands of Lower New York Bay

Fort Lafayette

ARMED WITH SEVENTY-TWO cannons and standing on Hendrick's Reef—
a tiny ledge in The Narrows just four hundred yards from the Brooklyn
shore—Fort Lafayette was one of a series of citadels constructed to protect
New York during the War of 1812.

While the fort, completed in 1818, was built to keep intruders out, it
gained its greatest notoriety for keeping Americans locked up. During the
Civil War, this round brick garrison served as a jail for prisoners of war and
prisoners of state. (Originally called Fort Diamond, the name change hon-
ors Revolutionary War hero Marquis de Lafayette, who visited in 1824.)

Many of the prisoners came from Washington, D.C., a hotbed of espionage during the war, and Maryland, a crucial Union border state. In April
1861, with Union leaders worried about the capital being cut off from the
North, President Abraham Lincoln suspended the writ of habeas corpus,
allowing the government to detain people without warrants, charges, or trials. Suspected secessionists were rousted from their beds at night and trun-
dled off to Fort Lafayette and other prisons.

Perceptions of conditions at Fort Lafayette varied wildly, depending on
the source. Some captives felt it was among the worst of the bastilles, an
overcrowded dungeon where rights were tossed out the window; other prisoners felt they were treated fairly. Many Northerners thought the prison
lacked discipline, nicknaming it the Hotel de Burke, after commanding
officer Lieutenant Colonel Martin Burke, whose family was living in Maryland. In actuality, it was a perverse mix of harshness and laxity. Burke,
who'd earned three citations for gallantry in the Mexican War, cracked
down hardest on Union prisoners, but bent the rules for well-connected
Confederates.

Lawrence Sangston, a member of the Maryland Legislature, wrote in
1861 that he and his fellow prisoners could purchase good food, liquor, and
other provisions from Southerners living in the area. When the men weren't
eating, they passed the days reading, writing, and playing cards.

On the bleaker side, Sangston's sixty-six-by-twenty-two-foot quarters
held thirty-eight prisoners and five cannons, which took up half the space.

The group shared one writing table, three washstands, two water buckets, one tin cup, and two candles at night. There were tadpoles in the water and broken windows that weren't replaced when the weather turned cold. Nearby, a roomful of sailors and privateers who had violated the Union blockade were locked in chains and denied beds.

Among the prisoners were many prominent men, including George William Brown, Baltimore's mayor; Beale Richardson, editor of the *Baltimore Republican;* and General William Fitzhugh "Rooney" Lee, the son of Confederate army leader Robert E. Lee. (Ironically, in the 1840s, the elder Lee had been assigned to oversee repairs at Fort Lafayette.)

In May 1861, four Baltimore police commissioners were remanded to the one-acre island. Three months later, Kings County Sheriff Anthony Campbell arrived with a writ of habeas corpus ordering Burke to transfer the men to court custody. (Many judges, believing that Lincoln had overstepped his executive power, continued applying the writ.) Burke wouldn't let Campbell enter the fort, ignoring him for four days until the presiding judge dropped the issue. The commissioners were imprisoned until 1863.

One of the worst railroading cases involved General Charles Stone, commander of the Union troops routed at Ball's Bluff, a costly fiasco that followed the disastrous Battle of Bull Run. The press scapegoated Stone, and later, several soldiers secretly testified before Congress that Stone had met with Confederates prior to the battle. Stone testified at the same hearings without being informed of the accusations against him. On February 8, 1862, he was dragged from his home and locked up for forty-nine days at Fort Lafayette without exercise or outside communication. Stone, never formally charged, was acquitted in 1863, but not publicly exonerated. He lived in self-exile in Egypt for many years. His good name was finally restored when he returned to New York in the 1880s as engineer in chief overseeing the design of the Statue of Liberty's pedestal.

In 1863, a group of Confederate prisoners created a handwritten newsletter called the *Right Flanker.* (They later smuggled it out and published it as a book in London.) The *Flanker* detailed how a Confederate prisoner, whose daughter was friends with Burke's daughter in Maryland, convinced Burke to make life easier for Southern inmates. Burke removed prisoners to other forts to relieve overcrowding and asked Southern friends in New York to donate clothing to inmates who wouldn't accept anything from the Union government.

New Yorkers were outraged by the generous treatment afforded these traitors, and their fury was stoked by newspaper articles sensationalizing the rumors of Burke's laxity. One *New York Post* article claimed prisoners were using the fort's roof as a promenade to enjoy sunsets. After citizens and the press clamored for stricter treatment, the *Right Flanker* reported that Burke "tightened the screws," disallowing goods from the outside. Treatment of Northern prisoners also became more severe: Dr. Edson Olds of Ohio was put in solitary confinement for three weeks with no light and no toilet paper.

No one suffered a worse fate than Robert Cobb Kennedy, the final Confederate spy executed before the war ended. In November 1864, Confederate rebels unsuccessfully tried to burn down New York City's major hotels; only Kennedy was apprehended. He was sent to Fort Lafayette, and on March 25, 1865, he was hanged before a large crowd of troops, prisoners, and citizens. The public paid up to $50 for a pass to the island. The unusual gallows lacked a trapdoor; weights and levers violently jerked Kennedy off the ground at 1:16 PM. It took him twenty-nine minutes to die. Fifteen days later, General Lee surrendered and the war ended. The writ of habeas corpus was restored, but some prisoners were not released from Fort Lafayette for ten months.

On December 1, 1868, the fort made headlines again when a fire started by careless carpenters working on the structure's roof destroyed the garrison and threatened to obliterate a nearby neighborhood (today Bay Ridge in Brooklyn) surrounding Fort Hamilton. Everyone escaped the island unscathed, but fireboats couldn't quell the conflagration. They turned tail as rumors spread that fifty tons of gunpowder were stored in the fort. With a massive explosion apparently imminent, thousands of Brooklynites evacuated in a panic. The front page of the *New York Times* called the fire "an occurrence fraught with so much fear and trembling—so much dread apprehension of terrible calamity." The anticipated detonation never transpired, though live shells were found among the embers the next day.

In the decades after the fire, Fort Lafayette looked deserted but was actually a hub of activity, serving as the navy's loading station and munitions storage facility through World War II. When the fort was abandoned, Parks Commissioner Robert Moses persuaded top brass to lease it to his department, claiming that commercial interests would only create an eyesore like a nightclub, while he intended to transform this small island into a park. Although he prevailed over the American Legion, which wanted to establish quarters there, Moses never bothered developing Fort Lafayette—instead, he obliterated it.

In 1960, nearly 150 years after the brick fortress was built to keep intruders out of New York Harbor, what remained of Fort Lafayette was demolished to allow easier passage between Brooklyn and Staten Island. Hendrick's Reef became the foundation for the massive eastern tower that supports the Verrazano-Narrows Bridge.

Part III

Bronx Waters

CITY ISLAND • HUNTER AND TWIN ISLANDS • HART ISLAND •
FORGOTTEN ISLANDS OF THE BRONX

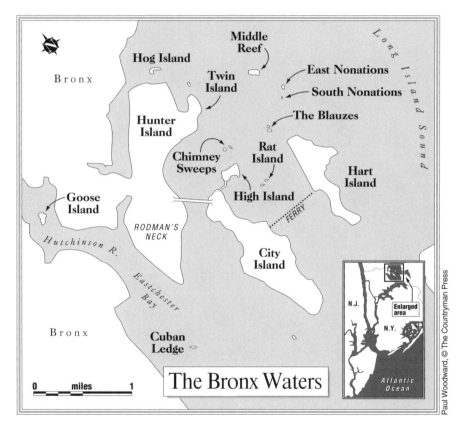

The spindly Hutchinson River widens into Eastchester Bay, which pours into Long Island Sound. New York's portion of the Sound is both the narrowest and the most congested, populated by nearly a dozen islands, some merely spots on a map.

7. City Island

"You'd hear the saws going and the intercoms calling different people through the yards. It was like a music around here. And you smelled the varnish and the paints and so forth. It was like a glamorous or romantic thing. Now, there are just as many boats, but the yards aren't like they used to be at all."

—TOM NYE, SAILMAKER AND FIFTH-GENERATION CITY ISLANDER

City Island

CROSS THE BRIDGE INTO City Island and enter a garden of nautical delights. Sailboats, cabin cruisers, motorboats, and rowboats bob in the water in rhythmic symphony. Jet-Skiers and water-skiers whiz around like seafaring motorcyclists. The air is cool, the bouquet briny, the waterfront peaceful. It's not as quaint as Nantucket, refined as Newport, or commercial as Mystic Seaport—places to which it is all too often compared. There's an urban edge to the island, which isn't surprising considering that most residents were either born here or moved to the island from other Bronx neighborhoods.

Its city sensibility is most noticeable in summer, when locals turn folding chairs into portable stoops and sit outside storefronts, and the rest of the Bronx descends on the island, blaring car radios and clogging the one-and-a-half-mile main drag. But it's also removed from the city—people move more slowly, say hello to strangers on the street, and swap four-digit telephone numbers. Everyone knows the island's exchange: 885.

And then there's the water—Long Island Sound to the east and Eastchester Bay to the west. From shipbuilding and sailmaking to recreational boating and open-air restaurants, the water is the island's livelihood and its soul. Many residents convey this aquatic connection by decorating their homes with sea paraphernalia—driftwood sculptures, whale weather vanes, seahorse birdbaths—while visitors live the islander's life vicariously by feasting on clams and lobsters or renting a boat for the day. The water has always been the lure to City Island.

In 1654, Englishman Thomas Pell became the first European to own what the native Siwanoy Indians called Minnewit, but no efforts were made to develop the island during the next century. Attempts to exploit the island's choice location—surrounded by the Sound's deep water and Eastchester Bay, convenient to both foreign and New England trade—began when Benjamin Palmer purchased Great Minnefords Island (the European name, also spelled Minniefords) in 1761. Palmer and a group of investors planned a busy seaport rivaling New York's, boasting that their "City Island" commerce center would save ships the hassle of passing

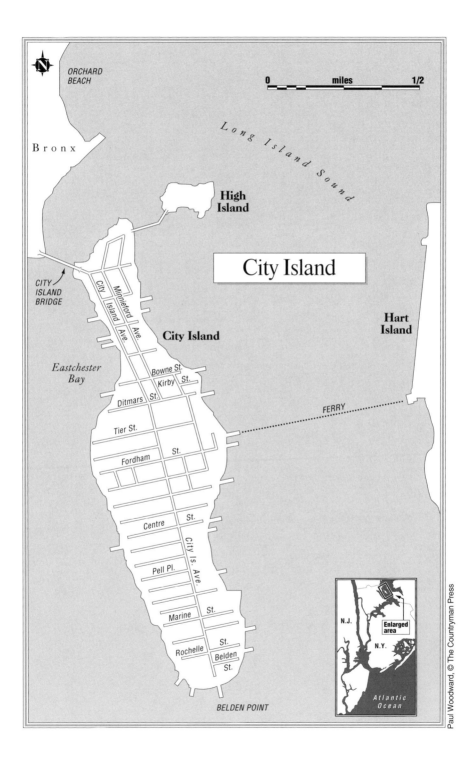

N

ORCHARD
BEACH

B r o n x

Long Island Sound

High
Island

City Island

CITY
ISLAND
BRIDGE

City Island Ave.

Minnieford Ave.

City Island

Hart
Island

Eastchester
Bay

Bowne St.

Kirby St.

Ditmars St.

FERRY

Tier St.

Fordham St.

Centre St.

City Is. Ave.

Pell Pl.

Marine St.

Rochelle St.

Belden St.

BELDEN POINT

N.J.

Enlarged
area

N.Y.

Atlantic
Ocean

Paul Woodward, © The Countryman Press

through the East River en route to New York. While it now seems laughable to imagine this modest 230-acre island competing with the great metropolis, New York was also young in 1761, developed only about as far as Houston Street.

The British Crown subsequently granted the Palmer party title to land extending out from the high-water mark, four hundred feet, around almost the entire island. (In the twentieth century, some islanders, marinas, and waterfront businesses exercised their Palmer Grant privileges by filling in land under the water, altering the island's natural contours.) The group laid out streets, lots for houses, shops, public buildings, and moorings for ships. The first ferries to the island were also established—one in 1763 from Rodman's Neck, and the other in 1766 from the north shore of Long Island.

The grand scheme had not progressed much past the planning stages when the American Revolution cast it adrift. On August 27, 1776, as British ground forces swarmed across Brooklyn, three Royal Navy vessels with one hundred armed men raided City Island. The British troops killed Palmer's livestock and "plundered many things, all of which they carried off and never paid for," Palmer later wrote. Two months later, Palmer sent a letter to British general William Howe, justifying the Revolution. This letter, Palmer would later claim, prompted Howe to seek revenge on the City Islander: In 1779, a Captain Brown of the British warship *Scorpion* captured Palmer, taking him and his family to New York against their will. Although he found a neighbor to farm his land, Palmer never again lived on City Island.

Talk of a commercial center was revived briefly after the war, but by then ports had been well established in Boston, Philadelphia, and New York. After unjustly losing his land in a war-related lawsuit, Palmer tried reclaiming his property and wrote to Governor John Jay and President George Washington as part of a lengthy but unsuccessful attempt to get reimbursed for damages incurred during the war. Future vice president Aaron Burr eventually raised enough money to support Palmer through his old age.

For the next eighty years, City Island remained isolated and sparsely populated. Most men made their living piloting ships through Hell Gate or fishing and clamming. The state legislature approved construction of a bridge between the island and the mainland in 1804, but the project was never funded. In 1819, forty-two acres at the island's southern end were sold to Pelham Town Supervisor George Washington Horton, the island's next entrepreneur, who laid out many streets. City Island was part of Pelham and hosted its town meetings, with Horton charging town fathers

$5 to hold their annual council at his house. (His home is now part of The Lobster Box, a restaurant that has operated under a number of names since the turn of the twentieth century.)

In 1847, there were still only seven houses on the island, but within two decades, City Island had grown into a small town. By 1868, eight hundred people lived in one hundred houses; the island also boasted three hotels, two shipyards, and two churches. City Island owed its newfound prosperity to the shipbuilding industry and a rough-shelled, highly sought mollusk: the oyster.

Orrin Fordham, an Englishman who moved to the island by way of Connecticut, was the first to cultivate oysters on artificial beds in American waters. In doing so, he made City Island the birthplace of the American oyster industry. "It had been a matter of common observation, that any object tossed into the water in summer, became covered with infant oysters," *The Drift*, one of the island's first newspapers, reported in 1895. Under favorable circumstances, this lasted until spring, when the oysters were large enough to be transplanted: "It was only a short step in logic to conclude, that if objects were thrown thickly into the water, on purpose to catch the floating spawn, a large quantity of oysters would be secured."

The business thrived through the 1890s. Oystermen who earned as much as $1,500 a week selling their catch in places like the Fulton Fish Market became some of the island's wealthiest residents. In the beginning, oystermen made their own sails for their skiffs and sloops, and boats were built by individual boatbuilders. In 1865, with the oyster business already well established, William Darling opened the first sailmaking loft on the island and produced sails for the oyster Fleet.

By this time, City Island was establishing itself as a center of commercial shipbuilding. Shipyards designed and produced oyster sloops, schooners, tenders, and, later, luxury and racing yachts. City Island was perfect for shipbuilding for the same reasons Benjamin Palmer thought the island would make a great seaport: extensive waterfront, a well-protected harbor, and deep water right off the yards. The industry eventually attracted "machine shops aplenty, where even a big Diesel engine can be repaired or overhauled, marine railways capable of hauling out all but the very largest yachts afloat, several good yacht clubs . . . awning makers and, in short, every facility and trade which is allied with yachts," wrote *Rudder* magazine in 1929.

The first commercial shipyard was built by David Carll on Pilot Street in 1862, although he had been building boats on the island since 1859. A native of Northport, Long Island, Carll was known for his three-masted schooners, small sloop yachts, and oyster sloops. Carll also helped build the island's first toll bridge in 1873, using timbers from the battleship USS *North Carolina*, which was dismantled in his yard. (The toll was abolished when City Island joined New York City in 1895.)

The Carll yard changed hands several times early on. It was bought in 1886 by Henry Piepgras, a master seaman, boatbuilder, and naval architect from Brooklyn. Piepgras introduced steel and iron ship construction to the island. "He was one of the pioneers in pouring lead keels, building hollow masts, and developing a strong waterproof glue made out of lime cheese and sour cream," says Tom Nye, a sailmaker and historian whose great-great-grandfather came to City Island in 1869 to work in the Carll yard (making Nye's two daughters sixth-generation islanders).

In 1900, Piepgras sold the yard to businessman Robert Jacob, who brought in expert builders and Ratsey & Lapthorn, a prestigious English sailmaking company. Jacob turned out yachts of all sizes and classes, including the largest yacht ever built on the island—the 187-foot *Caroline*, constructed in 1914. Frequently, when a boat was launched from the Jacob yard, the buyer treated workers to a bottle of champagne and a big party.

Another City Island pioneer was Augustus B. Wood, a Manhattan lawyer, boatbuilder, and yachtsman, who opened his shipyard on Pilot Street shortly after Carll. Wood developed a national reputation for building very durable, light boats, including oyster skiffs and the famed "Hell Gate" pilot boat. He moved his yard to the east side of the island in the 1870s, and, with his son, B. Frank Wood, built tenders and yachts, including *Feiseen*— in 1893, the world's fastest yacht. B. F. Wood also perfected the self-righting lifeboat, which was built for the government and exhibited at the 1893 World's Fair in Chicago. During this time, yacht yards also went from modeling and building boats themselves to hiring expert designers.

The industry's growth naturally affected development of the island. In 1886, William Belden created an amusement park, picnic grove, casino, and hotel at the island's south end, which soon became known as Belden Point. To attract tourists, Belden advertised in horsecars and elevated trains: COME TO CITY ISLAND, THE COOLEST SPOT WITHIN 100 MILES OF NEW YORK. Some visitors arrived by steamer; others took the railroad to Bartow Station, then transferred to the City Island horsecar.

At the turn of the twentieth century, millionaires like Vincent Astor, J. P. Morgan, August Belmont, William Randolph Hearst, the Vanderbilts,

The promenade overlooking Eastchester Bay and island marinas is a pleasant place to soak up City Island's ambience.

and Sir Thomas Lipton traveled to the island in their palatial yachts and dined at Thwaites Inn. (Belmont even began an underhanded effort to transform the island into a vacation spot and racetrack, sending agents posing as regular buyers to snatch up as much property as possible. When news of the scheme leaked out, residents raised their prices, ruining Belmont's plans. Soon after, Morgan financed another major development effort, City Island Homes. This project failed, too.) Boating clubs, restaurants, bathing pavilions, summer camps, and hotels dotted the landscape. At the foot of Ditmars Street, the well-known Macedonian Hotel (later known as the City Island Casino and Beach) attracted political and society figures, while less wealthy urbanites spent summers on the island in bungalow colonies.

This peaceful enclave became the city's latest diversion. "For more than a century, the intrusion of the urban resident or the man of commerce was resented," wrote Alice Payne in *Tales of the Clam Diggers*. "The native City Islander was content with his little world . . . and he hoped, as his ancestors had hoped before him that the invasion, now at flood tide, would never come."

Historical Detour: Linked to the Crime

On March 7, 1932, a retired school principal named Dr. John F. Condon wrote to the *Bronx Home News* offering to be an intermediary between Charles Lindbergh and the kidnappers of the aviator's infant son, forever linking City Island with the Crime of the Century.

The seventy-two-year-old Condon, described by some as eccentric and even senile, owned the Uncas Real Estate office at 313 City Island Avenue and had lived on the island before moving to the mainland Bronx. Some say Condon got involved in the case because he wanted to clear suspect Henry "Red" Johnsen, a yacht hand and boyfriend of the baby's nursemaid, Betty Gow. Others say the zealously patriotic and religious Condon was just angry because America's greatest hero—Lindbergh—had been wronged.

On March 8, the *Home News* published Condon's offer to intercede in the Lindbergh matter, and his promise to donate $1,000 toward the ransom money. While the kidnapping had occurred more than seventy miles away in Hopewell, New Jersey, the kidnappers immediately responded to the letter in this small, local paper, and sent a note the next day accepting Condon's offer. Condon even convinced Lindbergh to accept his proposal, too. To hide his identity as go-between, Condon adopted the name Jafsie, and delivered the ransom money to one of the alleged kidnappers in St. Raymond's Cemetery in the Bronx.

When the public learned Condon was involved in the case, he started getting hate mail. The case dragged on for two years, and authorities even accused Condon of being part of the kidnapping ring, although he was never arrested. Condon later picked suspect Bruno Richard Hauptmann, a Bronx carpenter, out of a lineup, and testified against Hauptmann during his trial. Hauptmann was convicted of the crime and electrocuted in Trenton on April 3, 1935.

There's a possibility that Condon may have simply recognized Hauptmann from City Island. Before his execution, Hauptmann explained that he kept his canoe at Dixon's boathouse on the island, where Condon rented canoes. Hauptmann had also visited City Island, where Condon had an office, about three to five times a week during the summers from 1932 to 1934. "And would I not have stayed away from City Island because I would have been afraid of being identified by Condon?" Hauptmann wrote to New Jersey governor Harold Hoffman in his plea for a pardon.

Condon spent much of the rest of his life lecturing about the case, particularly about how he believed that Hauptmann had acted alone in the kidnapping and murder. In 1936, he even wrote a book called *Jafsie Tells All*, and sold autographed copies for $2.50 from his City Island office. Skippy Lane, a longtime island resident, recalls Condon strutting about town in a black derby proclaiming, "You know who I am? I was the Lindbergh negotiator."

Condon died in 1945 at age eighty-four. In his obituary, the *New York Times* reported that "the Lindbergh case lifted Dr. Condon out of a placid existence and the role of village character into a complicated and troubled existence . . . with the fierce light of international publicity focused sharply upon him."

Despite islanders' wariness of city folk, City Island opted to leave the town of Pelham in 1895 and join New York City. It was a close call, though—with nine hundred votes cast, the city won by only two. The new government replaced the island's deteriorating wooden bridge with a steel structure and built a new school.

To improve transportation and accommodate visitors, a monorail—running from the City Island Bridge to Bartow Station—opened in 1910. Considered experimental, it was one of only two monorails in the country. When it worked, it reduced the fifteen-minute horsecar trip to five minutes. Unfortunately, it was plagued with problems from the first day, when it derailed, injuring several passengers. It broke down often, inciting residents who'd opposed it in the first place to shout, "Get a horse!" The ride was hot in summer, frigid in winter, and there was no ventilation for the hordes of customers crammed into its small compartments. The monorail didn't last long, closing in 1913. (The ruins of Bartow Station, designed by renowned architect Cass Gilbert, still remain on Pelham Parkway.)

During World War I, poor access limited the number of war contracts

City Island received, although many shipyards were busy building sub chasers, tugs, and other vessels instead of yachts. After the war, the Henry B. Nevins Shipyard, founded in 1907, built twenty Victory-class sailboats to revive interest in yachting. The boats were named in honor of yachts-men who had participated in the war. A number of great yachts were even built during the Depression. *Brilliant,* a City Island classic, was built in 1932 by the Nevins yard, and is "probably the best example of a wooden boat ever built," says Nye.

Just as the yards began building smaller boats to adapt to the changing economy and racing styles, World War II arrived. With access to City Island much improved, the shipyards won more contracting work. The yards constructed minesweepers, PT boats, tugs, and landing craft at a pace that necessitated hiring more employees, at least for a while. After the war, the round-the-clock hustle and bustle was gone, and so was the money. "Today, the island economy is struggling for survival," wrote the *New York Herald Tribune* in 1949. "Heavy taxes have discouraged owner-ship of pleasure boats and cast gloom over the whole nautical scene. Many wealthy families who once regarded yachts as a natural part of summer are doing without them: the yachts lie rusting at anchor or have been hauled up on shore and sit forlornly incased in weather-blackened clapboard with a 'For Sale' sign nailed to the stern."

Postwar America was also marked by a change in boatbuilding materi-als and new markets. Fiberglass made it more economical to churn out the small pleasure boats coveted by the growing middle class. Some shipyards moved overseas for cheap labor, or to inland facilities for lower property taxes. In response to the changes, some of the yards diversified, but most closed or sold out.

The end of the luxury-yacht era was punctuated by the death of Henry B. Nevins in 1950. One of the nation's most prominent shipbuilders, Nevins never wavered from his origins, working almost exclusively in wood despite technological advances. "And he always stuck to his price," says Nye. "You paid top dollar, but you got what you paid for. He was a fair man and everyone respected him." Four years after Nevins's death, his widow sold the yard to Carl Hovgard, one of the nation's leading yachtsmen, who bought it as a hobby more than a business. The yard closed in 1960.

The Minneford Yacht Yard, founded in 1926 by Henry Sayers, saw the changes coming and prospered by being adaptive. In addition to building twelve-meter racing yachts, Minneford offered an extensive marina, boat-ing services, and, eventually, condominium boat slips. Minneford also built four yachts that defended the America's Cup six times between 1964 and 1980, before becoming the last of the City Island yacht yards to shut down in 1983. (Another cup defender, the *Columbia,* was built on City Island in 1958, by the Nevins yard.)

City Island is still synonymous with boating, but now it's more recreational in scope. There are bait shops and marinas for fishermen, sailing and scuba schools, party boats, Jet Ski rentals, and dock-and-dine restaurants. For the past two decades, many islanders, especially members of the island's four yacht clubs—the City Island, Morris, Stuyvesant, and Harlem Yacht Clubs—have raced in the Eastchester Bay Yacht Racing Association's Wednesday-night regattas in spring and summer. But gone are the days when the four o'clock quitting-time whistle blew, spilling sailmakers and boatbuilders out onto the streets. UK Sailmakers, where Nye works, is one of a handful of sailmakers still on the island, and staff at UK have been cut dramatically in the last fifteen years. In addition to boat sails, they now make awnings for home-furnishing maven Martha Stewart. "It's changed quite a bit," Nye says. "The pie isn't that big anymore."

City Island can be a clannish place—anyone born there is a "clam digger," everyone else a "mussel sucker"—but there's also a healthy respect for the anonymity of city life. Years ago, when many islanders worked in the boating businesses, everybody knew everybody; now there's a sprinkling of strangers on most blocks, and many professionals have joined the stew. Once a neighborhood of private homes and bungalows, the island now has several waterfront condominiums, which have attracted New Yorkers—particularly those who work at Fordham University, the Bronx Courthouse, the Bronx Zoo, and the New York Botanical Garden—looking for a safe neighborhood within the metropolis. These days, timeworn sailors like Skippy Lane, a retired tanker captain whose family arrived on the island in 1880, are a novelty. He's usually in Rhodes, a restaurant-tavern popular among the locals, who generally leave the big seafood restaurants to the tourists.

City Islanders are socially, educationally, and economically a world away from the big city and its Bronx brethren. According to the 1990 census, the island was 96 percent white, mostly third-, fourth-, and fifth-generation islanders of Irish, Italian, and German ancestry. During the last decade, the island's population—just over four thousand—has grown and slowly diversified. In 1998–99, the island's elementary school, P.S. 175,

Historical Detour: Go West, Young Man

Riding the horse-drawn trolley his father owned on City Island was perfect training for Harry Carey, star of silent-film Westerns. After local mounted police taught Carey to ride, he often helped his father, Judge Henry DeWitt Carey, operate the horsecar between City Island and Bartow Station. Carey studied law at New York University, but missed his bar exam after developing pneumonia.

Born in 1878, Carey wanted to be an actor, not a lawyer, anyway. He performed at the island's Leviness Hall in productions of *Uncle Tom's Cabin* and *Montana*, a melodrama that he wrote, and kept a small film studio in the cellar of the family home on Carey's Point, opposite High Island. He made a few movies using local talent and sites. *Bride of the Sea* was filmed at Belden Point. He also went on location to High Island, taking palm trees and tropical vegetation for scenery, and was said to have kept some wolves there for his films.

Carey performed in New York, traveled with stage companies, and even took his hit *Montana* on the road from 1904 to 1908. Then he acted in three Westerns filmed on Staten Island. But it wasn't until he met D. W. Griffith at the East Fourteenth Street Biograph studio and lassoed a role in *The Unseen Enemy* with Lillian and Dorothy Gish and Lionel Barrymore that Carey's career took off.

In 1910, he moved to Hollywood, bought a ranch and fifteen hundred acres, starred in *The Sorrowful Shore*, and married leading lady Olive Golden. For the next twenty years, he starred in silent films, primarily horse operas. Although he made the transition to talkies, starring in Westerns like *The Last Outlaw* and *Law and Order*, he had tired of the cowboy stereotype. He broadened his career by taking character parts in other movies like *Mr. Smith Goes to Washington* and *The Prisoner of Shark Island*, and by appearing on Broadway, in *Heavenly Express* in 1940 and *But Not Goodbye* in 1944.

But Carey remained an old cowhand at heart: At his funeral in Brentwood, California, in 1947, Burl Ives sang "The

Cowboy's Lament" and John Wayne recited a poem. Then Carey
was put to rest wearing a black suit, shoestring tie, and cowboy
boots.

was 70 percent white. The Bronx, on the other hand, is largely Latino and
black; in 1990, less than one-quarter of its residents were white. City
Islanders are far more likely to have graduated from college than others in
the Bronx. In 1990, the borough's median household income was half of
the island's $40,727, a disparity that has likely widened in the years since.

Despite its relative stability, the island weathered some economic
storms through the years, primarily in the late 1950s and 1960s. In the
wake of the boating industry's demise, antiques shops and art galleries
blossomed along City Island Avenue in the 1970s. Ron Terner, a photog-
rapher and sculptor, was one of those who took advantage of the cheap
rents and empty storefronts. Frustrated with the Manhattan art world, this
Bronx native moved to the island in 1974, joining the budding bohemian
scene that revolved around a highly successful arts and crafts fair. Some
islanders were wary of these "hippies," says Terner, "but eventually, the
community begins to accept you." He opened Focal Point Gallery on City
Island Avenue and held out against the higher rents and materialism of the
1980s that sent most of the artistic community searching for greener pastures. Terner continued bartering photographic services for meals, while
his then wife, Niru, sold jewelry in addition to her watercolor paintings. In
recent years, the community of artists has slowly grown. Terner's gallery,
which showcases the artwork of City Islanders twice a year, no longer
sticks out on the avenue's palette. The mini-resurgence is evident in a
small crop of galleries, boutiques, and antiques shops. An umbrella group,
the City Island Arts Organization, briefly ran its own storefront gallery in
the mid-1990s; it is now reviving itself after suffering internal administrative problems.

The creative community wasn't the only arrival in the 1960s and 1970s.
In summer, droves of day-trippers from the Bronx, mainly blacks and
Puerto Ricans, descended on the island, heading to the southern tip where
fishing, a spectacular view of the Sound, and open-air restaurants awaited.
Traffic choked the island's two-lane main street so badly that frustrated
residents stayed home rather than spend more than an hour in traffic just
to cross their bridge. The residents cited the volume, not the ethnicity, of

the crowds as their objection, but tensions simmered throughout the sum-mer seasons. In fact, the community was accused of racism in 1970 when residents petitioned for the rezoning of the southern end to phase out the restaurants that attracted these outsiders. The issue was dropped. The eateries thrive today, and the traffic has abated somewhat since concession stands were added at nearby Orchard Beach. Still, it's rarely smooth sail-ing on summer weekends. Many islanders still consider outsiders an intru-sion, but more tolerant attitudes have eased racial tensions. In fact, the community itself has become more racially diverse in recent years, which most residents view as a positive sign.

The 1970s also saw land speculators aggressively pursuing the island's dormant shipyards, marinas, and related businesses. In an attempt to con-trol development and protect the island's seafaring identity, a special zone limiting new buildings to three stories was created in 1976. While modern development has been kept to a minimum on City Island (the six-story Pickwick Arms apartment house built in 1963 is the island "skyscraper"), several condominium complexes sprang up in the 1980s.

Today, City Island maintains three distinct identities: the crowded, open-air restaurant atmosphere of Belden Point; City Island Avenue, grittier and more urban than Newport or Mystic, but alive with restaurants, shops, and boat-repair yards; and the side streets, an eclectic mix of old Victorian homes, modest houses, weathered bungalows, and condominiums.

Island life remains affordable, but residents fret over continuing devel-opment. "Every last inch of vacant space is going," says Karen Rauhauser Nani, a "clam digger" and editor of *The Current,* the island's not-for-profit newspaper. More worrisome than the stores, offices, and restaurants, Nani says, are new condominiums and row houses, which have galvanized islanders to rally against a common enemy. The community is now trying to amend 1970s zoning rules to return the emphasis to single-family homes. Residents are apprehensive of change because they relish City Island's virtues—a low crime rate, a highly regarded public school, and strong community.

"The explosion of condos and row houses has actually inspired com-munity spirit," says Nani. "The resurgence of interest in limiting develop-ment has brought people closer together."

Also fostering community ties, she adds, has been "a greatly renewed interest in preserving our maritime heritage."

Ed Sadler, a retired Hell Gate pilot whose family moved to the island in the nineteenth century, says the island's boatbuilding and yachting heritage is what makes it special. "That's what I look back on, the fact that I was born and brought up in a nautical atmosphere," he says. "My children, even today, say, 'Dad, boy this was a great place to be brought up in.'"

Sadler, along with Skippy Lane, Tom Nye, and others, helped create the historical exhibits at the heart of the City Island Museum, which opened in 1995. In 1998, the island began sponsoring an annual Fleet Weekend, featuring historic ships, maritime awards, and races. And several not-for-profits have teamed up to bring an environmental study center to P.S. 175, even building a pond behind the school to enable students to study freshwater ecology firsthand.

While the island's shipbuilding heritage today survives mainly in recollection and culture, that doesn't diminish Nye's love of the island. "I walk home and count my blessings," he says. "I look down the end of the block and I see a view out there that a lot of people spend millions of dollars for. I don't take for granted what I have here."

Indeed, the water remains the lifeline of City Island. It moderates the island's climate, making it ten degrees cooler in summer and ten degrees warmer in winter than the mainland. And many residents own boats and belong to block associations that maintain private beaches.

Even for people who can't tell a schooner from a sloop, this slender strip is a salve for the soul. Jonna Gallo moved to City Island with her family when she was one year old; though while growing up, she didn't know much about its rich shipbuilding history, the island instilled in her "a real affinity for the water. I like the smell of the sea air," she says. "I like to walk down to the beach and just sit there."

Exploring the Island

In addition to its illustrious shipbuilding history, City Island is known for the Moby-sized portions served in its seafood restaurants. But besides eating, there are enough other things to do on the island for a day trip. Combined with some sailing lessons or a hike at nearby Hunter and Twin Islands, a visit can easily be stretched into a weekend getaway punctuated by a stay at City Island's charming bed & breakfast. The **City Island Chamber of Commerce** can be reached at (718) 885-9100; call for information about the island's Arts and Crafts Festival, held in June and September, and the Chowder Festival, also in September. For details about the annual Fleet Weekend held each June, call the not-for-profit group **IDEA** at (718) 885-3781.

Before feasting or heading out onto the great blue, get acquainted with this nautical community. A good place to start is the **City Island Museum,** 190 Fordham Street, (718) 885-1211. Operated by the City Island Historical Society, it's on the main floor of old P.S. 17, which was built in 1897 and closed in 1975. Once in the door, you're greeted by a tender built by the Robert Jacobs shipyard in the 1930s and a corridor featuring artwork—some depicting island scenes—by local artists.

The Walsh and Nautical Rooms are the small museum's most noteworthy attractions. The Walsh Room contains the historical library and features dozens of watercolors painted in the 1930s by former islander Professor Harold Vandervoort Walsh. They portray City, Hunter, and Twin Islands, Orchard Beach, and other local sites. The Nautical Room tells the story of the island's oystermen, shipbuilders, sailmakers, yacht brokers, and America's Cup defenders.

If you want to get truly waterlogged, browse through one of the city's most comprehensive collections of nautical books at the **City Island Library,** 320 City Island Avenue, (718) 885-1703. Organized in 1969, the Ship Collection contains nearly a thousand nonfiction and fiction titles on everything from building a ship in a bottle to accounts of old shipwrecks. Even the building itself has a nautical feel, with windows shaped like portholes.

If you're not in an oceangoing mood, dip into the shops, boutiques, and galleries on City Island Avenue. A shop nonpareil is **Mooncurser Antiques,** 229 City Island Avenue, (718) 885-0302. Even if you're not in the market for an old LP, it's worth visiting just to meet proprietor Roger Roberge, a young-at-heart, Latin-music-loving octogenarian with a long white beard and the credo, "Music makes you happy." Roberge also displays his private collection of old instruments—trumpets, bongos, tambourines, and fifty harmonicas—toy instruments, and two display cases of African American memorabilia and knickknacks. But the raison d'être of this neighborhood emporium is the seventy-five thousand albums for sale from every era and every genre. Pull up a ladder and pore through shelf upon shelf of vinyl. If you want to hear something, Roberge will gladly play it for you. If you just want to chat, that's okay too.

Among the galleries on the island are **Starving Artist Studio & Gallery,** 269 City Island Avenue, (718) 885-3779, featuring the nautical works of local artist Mark Whitcombe and the jewelry of owner Elliott Glick; **Fe Fi Faux,** 276 City Island Avenue, (718) 885-2024; and Ron Terner's **Focal Point Gallery,** 321 City Island Avenue, (718) 885-1403.

Other shops include **Silver Arrow Antiques,** 275 City Island Avenue, (718) 885-1598; **Lucid Dreams,** 278 City Island Avenue, (718) 885-1400; **Exotiqa International Arts,** 280 City Island Avenue, (718) 885-3090; **City Island Trading Company,** 282 City Island Avenue, (718) 885-1592; **Mood Light Candles,** 294 City Island Avenue, (718) 885-0125; **Early Ruth Antiques,** 319 City Island Avenue, (718) 885-0228; and **Corona's Hidden Treasure,** 329 City Island Avenue, (718) 885-1330, which sells nautical knicknacks. If you want to search through ancient marine equipment, try **Trader John,** 239 City Island Avenue, (718) 885-1658.

City Island's architecture is a hodgepodge, but within this miscellany you'll find two city-designated landmarks and a handful of other notable structures. Start at the southern end of the island and turn right onto Belden Street, a dead-end gravel road. The white house at 175 Belden Street with forest green trim and white picket fence overlooking Long Island Sound was built in 1880. It was designated a landmark in 1981 because of its cottage style, which is rarely found in urban areas.

Back on City Island Avenue, make a left onto Rochelle Street and go to the very end. On the left are four darling Norwegian-style country homes situated around a grassy common. They were built in the 1920s by boatbuilder Henry Sayers. Turn left again off the avenue to 95 Pell Place, a Sears, Roebuck & Company mail-order house called The Osborne. A bungalow with Oriental influences, this low-lying structure has a white stucco exterior, maroon trim, a full-width front porch, and a gabled roof supported by stucco-and-wood piers. It was built from a kit in 1930, when Sears was the largest home-building company in the world.

Grace Episcopal Church at 104 City Island Avenue is a typical New England style church built in 1861 with timbers hand hewn by employees of the David Carll yard. The church was founded by Adele Bolton, who regularly rowed over from Pelham (where her father, Robert, was rector of Christ Episcopal Church) to teach Sunday school and bring "grace" to the islanders. Her brother Cornelius became Grace Church's first rector; another brother, John, made the stained-glass window—a depiction of Palm Sunday—behind the altar. Hanging above the altar are two model-sized, square-rigged ships, one gold, the other silver. They were donated nearly a hundred years ago by sailmaker George Ratsey and Robert Jacob (who had purchased the Carll yard from Henry Piepgras in 1900). Facing in opposite directions, they symbolize birth and death and the belief that God is life's pilot.

The skinny five-story building at 284 City Island Avenue was the island skyscraper before Pickwick Terrace was built in 1963. Built in 1910 by sailmaker Tom Nye's great-grandfather, this black-and-tan building stands out among the avenue's unstylized structures with its gambrel roof and Palladian windows. Rhodes, a restaurant favored by locals, recently added an extension in the ground floor here.

Make a left onto Tier Street; at the end is a large Victorian surrounded by a concrete-and-stone wall overlooking Eastchester Bay. Built in 1894, this quirky three-story, brown-shingle house with conical roofs was featured in the 1962 film *Long Day's Journey into Night*, starring Katharine Hepburn. The house, which was designated a landmark in 2000, has a large Doric-style porch, inverted and protruding oriels, intersecting gables, and a whale weather vane.

Walk down Tier Street across City Island Avenue until you reach King Avenue, where you turn left. Located here since the 1880s has been Pelham Cemetery, a picturesque resting place set against Long Island Sound. The headstones read like a *Who's Who* of City Island history. The cemetery remains anchored to the community: Owner and islander John Ulmer is the fourth generation in his family to oversee it.

To experience City Island unabridged, a date with the water is required. Landlubbers can head to the southern tip where views of Long Island Sound and Stepping Stone Lighthouse await, or brave the seas like a true salt. The **New York Sailing Center and Yacht Club,** 560 Minnieford Avenue, (718) 885-0335, offers a full range of sailing, navigating, and racing classes as well as inexpensive, full-service facilities for boat owners.

Those already confident enough to captain a ship can rent rowboats and motorboats from **The Boat Livery,** 663 City Island Avenue, (718) 885-1843, or **Jack's Bait & Tackle,** 551 City Island Avenue, (718) 885-2042. If you want to drop a line for porgies, flounder, bluefish, or tuna, or want to see the sights, hop on a party boat. *Riptide III,* 701 Minnieford Avenue, (718) 885-0236, runs fishing trips daily from mid-March to mid-December. Its four-hour moonlight charters Wednesday and Sunday evenings take you under eight bridges on your way to the Statue of Liberty. *North Star,* 553 City Island Avenue, (718) 885-9182, and *The Apache,* 591 City Island Avenue, (718) 885-0843, also run daily fishing trips from March through November and offer group charters.

If bobbing on the water isn't adventuresome enough for you, **Captain Mike's Diving Services,** 530 City Island Avenue, (718) 885-1588, offers beginner and expert diving, night diving, underwater photography, and shipwreck diving courses.

Island Pearl

As unlikely as it sounds, there's a whisper of French countryside in the Bronx, where you can dine on *pâté de canard* and *selle d'agneau aux épinards* and indulge in the romance of Europe. Normandy-born restaurateur Pierre Saint-Denis, proprietor of the acclaimed Le Refuge restaurant in Manhattan, has breathed new life into one of City Island's nineteenth-century Victorian houses. **Le Refuge,** 620 City Island Avenue, (718) 885-2478, offers classic French cuisine and a charming bed & breakfast with eight rooms and a villa. The prix fixe dinners are served in a rustic dining room with beamed ceilings, a grandfather clock, and an ancient Zenith radio that plays classical music during meals. The menu changes according to Saint-Denis's culinary whims; while relatively expensive, the meals are beautifully presented and far and away the best on City Island. The assembly-line seafood houses don't offer a delightful blood-orange sorbet for cleansing the palate between vichyssoise and *canard au pamplemousse.* Saint-Denis's bountiful wine cellar boasts nearly two hundred selections.

Seven of the inn's rooms have shared baths; the other has a private bath and dressing room. Although there's no air-conditioning, the ceiling fans usually suffice. The rooms have a pastoral feel, from the decorative wallpaper to the mountains of frilly pillows on the bed. Stacks of French literature enhance the ambience. Front rooms look out onto sailboats docked in Eastchester Bay and offer a sunset view, but are also within earshot of the occasional car alarm and loud music—a reminder that you're still in New York. The separate villa with kitchen, living room, and three bedrooms is ideal for a small family.

Breakfast is a simple affair, with croissants and marmalade, fresh-squeezed orange juice, and the perfect cup of coffee. Le Refuge also hosts live chamber music Sunday afternoons in its homey parlor. There's a charge for visitors, while inn guests are admitted free.

Where to Eat

From pasta primavera to fried-shrimp-in-a-basket, City Island offers an eclectic banquet to satisfy every palate and pocket.

If you want to hobnob with City Islanders and enjoy inexpensive home-style cooking, try the **City Island Diner,** 304 City Island Avenue, (718) 885-0362. They serve hearty breakfasts, including seventeen omelets with nautical names like Man Overboard and Luxury Liner. Lunchtime sandwiches, salads, and Ports-of-Call burgers are similarly satisfying. Look for daily dinner specials and the diner's homemade soups and pies.

Another local hangout is pub-style **Rhodes,** 288 City Island Avenue, (718) 885-1538, decorated with old maps and island memorabilia.

The Black Whale, 279 City Island Avenue, (718) 885-3657, has experienced a rebirth. From the late 1960s until it closed in the early 1980s, this was the place to be for dessert and conversation on Friday nights. The building, according to local lore, was once part of a women's detention center on Hart Island and was brought over to City Island in the late nineteenth or early twentieth century, then plopped down backward with the front of the house facing the garden. In 1998, a resident, Bill Kenny, revived the restaurant, with its charming outdoor garden and mouthwatering desserts (including retro treats like hot fudge fondue and the rich but fluffy Black Angel, a hot fudge sundae over angel food cake). He also added a full and well-executed nouveau American lunch and dinner menu, making it the best choice for a moderately priced meal on the island. The Black Whale also screens movies on Tuesday nights, from *The Apartment* to *Pee-Wee's Great Adventure.* Popcorn is free.

Mona Lisa, 296 City Island Avenue, (718) 885-0947, is a sister restaurant to a well-respected Greenwich Village gourmet pizzeria; in addition to offerings like clams oreganata pie and chicken deluxe pizza, the restaurant also serves pasta and fish.

The island's newest restaurant is **The Tree House,** 273 City Island Avenue, (718) 885-0806. This small, modestly priced place serves solid northern Mediterranean fare that includes dishes from both Italy and the Middle East, including *shunka* wrappers (cheese rolled with bacon), *chevapas* (spiced, grilled sausages with feta cheese), and an array of pastas and kabobs.

Portofino, 555 City Island Avenue, (718) 885-1220, cooks up delicious northern Italian fare and offers outdoor seating overlooking Eastchester Bay. Try the chicken scarpariello with sausage and the baked clams oreganata.

For a cheap meal high in cholesterol and big on panorama try either **Johnny's Reef,** (718) 885-2086, or **Tony's on the Pier,** (718) 885-1424, both on Belden Point. Everything at these asphalt parks is served in cardboard carry-aways. Indoor and outdoor cafeteria seating is absolutely jammed in summer.

Big is the best way to describe City Island's numerous seafood establishments, which vary little from one to another. (In fact, five of the eateries are owned by the same restaurateur.) You get a big meal in a big restaurant with big crowds and big prices to boot. You get what you pay for; subtle sauces may not abound, but almost everyone leaves with a doggy bag. Stick with the mountainous seafood platters. In general, desserts and side dishes are uneventful.

The five hundred seats at **Sammy's Fish Box,** 41 City Island Avenue, (718) 885-0920, attract a special-occasion crowd, with a chorus of "Happy Birthday"s being sung at any given time. Request upstairs seating for a quieter meal. **The Lobster Box,** 34 City Island Avenue, (718) 885-1952, has tasteful decor and one of the nicest views of any island restaurant, with a large dining room overlooking Long Island Sound.

You'll find similar mouthwatering fare at the island's other seafood houses, including **The Seashore,** 591 City Island Avenue, (718) 885-0300; and the **Lobster House,** 691 Bridge Street, (718) 885-1459. Some restaurants offer dock-and-dine facilities, including **Anna's Harbor,** 565 City Island Avenue, (718) 885-1373, on Eastchester Bay; and **J.P.'s,** 703 Minneford Avenue, (718) 885-3364, on Long Island Sound.

Island Hopping

By car: Take the Throgs Neck, Whitestone, or Triborough Bridges to I-95 North (Bruckner Expressway) to the Orchard Beach/City Island Avenue exit. Follow Shore Parkway into City Island Avenue. The roundabouts on these roadways are confusing, so pay attention. Also remember that driving to the island in summer can be a lesson in patience, as traffic often backs up to the bridge. Once on the island, park on a side street and explore City Island by foot.

By bus: Take the 6 train to Pelham Bay Park, then transfer to the BX29 bus to City Island.

8. Hunter and Twin Islands

"It is ironic that there are probably fewer people that actually visit the back parts of Twin Island and Hunter Island, the less improved areas, now than there were in the 1920s. Now that they're accessible and the landmasses are all attached, it is fairly easy to wander up and down these trails, but not that many people do."

—THEODORE KAZIMIROFF JR., NATURALIST,
AUTHOR, AND LIFELONG BRONX RESIDENT

Hunter and Twin Islands

IN A CITY WHERE CHANGE is the only constant, the northeast corner of the Bronx is an extraordinary reminder of New York as the Native Americans saw it: pristine and picturesque. During the last two centuries, Hunter and Twin Islands have been home to a country squire's luxurious estate, settlement houses for the poor, and campgrounds for working-class immigrants, yet the islands—despite having been connected by landfill to the Bronx—look remarkably similar to the site Thomas Pell bought from the Siwanoy Indians in 1654.

Hunter Island is 166 acres of forest dense with pine, birch, oak, and flowering crab apple trees, as well as wild geraniums, violets, strawberries, and lilies. West of the island is a lagoon separating Hunter from the rest of Pelham Bay Park; to the east is nineteen-acre Twin Island—formerly two small cigar-shaped isles called East and West Twin—and Long Island Sound. Twin features schist rock striped with quartz that was carved out by glaciers thousands of years ago, and is the southern end of a sheet of bedrock that runs up to Maine.

Hunter was called Laap-Ha-Wach King, or "place of stringing beads," by the Siwanoy, who held religious rituals on the island's odd rock formations. In 1654, Pell—for whom Pelham Bay is named—bought the island and became the region's first English settler.

While Hunter Island changed hands several times, all was quiet there until John Hunter bought it for $40,000 around 1810. Hunter had followed his father into business near Wall Street, and he spent another $80,000 building, furnishing, and landscaping an extravagant Shangri-la for his family. Hunter, whose family had emigrated from Ireland, was married to Elizabeth Desbrosses, daughter of James Desbrosses, the warden of Trinity Church and patriarch of one of New York's oldest and wealthiest families. The winged three-story, Georgian-style mansion was made of brick and stone, and featured marble front steps, Doric columns, Palladian windows on the second floor, a wide veranda, and terraced gardens leading down to the water. Hunter also cleared many trees for farmland. The mansion's interior boasted extensive wine cellars, imported Turkish carpets, and silk draperies. The highlight was a collection of nearly four hundred paintings by artists like Leonardo da Vinci, Rembrandt, Rubens, and Van Dyke—assembled at a cost of $130,000.

Hunter, who also owned part of Hart Island and riparian rights to City Island, moved his family from State Street in Manhattan to their new home around 1813, but their peaceful days soon ended. Shortly after they arrived, Hunter's wife and their son Elias were thrown from a carriage on the island's new stone bridge. Elizabeth struck her head on a post and remained an invalid until her death in 1831.

Hunter, meanwhile, complemented his varied business interests with politics, serving as Westchester County supervisor and, later, a member of the state assembly. A friend of New York governors Silas Wright and De Witt Clinton, Hunter entertained lavishly. During the most celebrated of these festivities, in 1839, President Martin Van Buren was feted on calf brains *au suprême* in tomato sauce.

Hunter died in 1852, mandating in his will that his descendants live on the island or sell it. In 1866, Hunter's grandson, John III—a horse-racing magnate and future president of the New York–based Jockey Club—sold the property so he could live in Throgs Neck in the Bronx.

In an effort to provide parkland for the masses, the city bought Hunter and Twin Islands and nearby land in 1888, creating Pelham Bay Park. (Homes in the area, including the Hunter Mansion, were leased to charity groups for settlement houses, but were razed in the 1930s by the parks department.) Once the subway reached the region in 1894, German, Scandinavian, Czechoslovakian, and Russian immigrants discovered the islands, building rock shelters, and creating summer colonies where they sunbathed and swam. East and West Twin Islands, in particular, attracted boaters, and became known as Canoe Beach. When vandalism and over-crowding surged, the parks department temporarily banned camping and closed Hunter Island, but the beachgoers kept returning.

In the 1930s, Robert Moses created a magnificent new coastal getaway on Pelham Bay called Orchard Beach. It cost more than $8 million and took four years to complete the project, which joined Hunter Island to Rodman's Neck using two and a half million cubic yards of landfill. The finished beach accommodated two hundred thousand sunbathers, but Moses wanted room for more. In 1947, he linked the Twin Islands to Hunter Island, shifting the focus from the islands' rugged rocks and shady forests to a new sandy shoreline. With tremendous crowds packing Orchard Beach, Hunter and Twin Islands faded into the shadows.

The region's beauty was imperiled when the city turned part of Pelham Bay Park into a garbage dump in 1967. However, a group of local residents led by Dr. Theodore Kazimiroff—a dentist, Bronx historian, amateur archaeologist, and naturalist, who was well respected in scientific and academic circles—successfully halted the project. "Had that been allowed to continue," says his son Theodore Kazimiroff Jr., "Pelham Bay Park would have lost its character, its originality, and its heritage as the home of the former occupants of this country before any European settlers even came here, those people whom we call the Indians." To prevent further defilement of these environs, the group pressured the city into creating the Hunter Island Marine Zoology and Geology Sanctuary.

The elder Kazimiroff's passion for the region stemmed from a childhood friendship he had had with an Algonquin named Joe Two-Trees, says his son, who popularized this tale in a book titled *The Last Algonquin.* Joe Two-Trees is said to have lived in the Stone Age tradition of his ancestors in the park during the 1920s, where he spent many occasions telling stories to the young Boy Scout. While the younger Kazimiroff claims that *The Last Algonquin* is a true story, his father never mentioned the tale of Joe Two-Trees to friends, and no other Bronx resident ever met the Native American. However fanciful this tale, Kazimiroff's contributions to the region are real and enduring. In 1986, the city established a network of hiking paths on Hunter Island, naming it the Kazimiroff Nature Trail.

Exploring the Islands

They're just down the boardwalk from popular Orchard Beach, yet Hunter and Twin Islands seem isolated. Although connected to each other (and the Bronx) by landfill, the former islands maintain discrete identities. As one park ranger has described them, they are two ecosystems smashed up against each other. If you prefer a walk in the woods, head to Hunter; if scrambling along rocks is more your style, Twin is the place to be. The **Pelham Bay Environmental Center,** (718) 430-1832, on Twin Island, has maps available in summer, but don't rely on them too heavily—they don't illustrate every path.

Hunter Island is laced with an intricate network of trails. **The Kazimiroff Nature Trail** offers two paths; then there's John Hunter's old carriage road and various paved roads and trails. Although the mazelike environment can be frustrating, the island is chock-full of fascinating sights and sounds. Flowers, many originally planted for Hunter's garden,

flourish here: In spring and summer, orange daylilies, purple wild geraniums, goldenrod, pale blue periwinkles, and grape hyacinth color the
woods.

The parks department planted four acres of Norway spruce in 1918 to
reforest areas John Hunter had cleared for meadows. Atop the crest near
the center of the island where the mansion once stood, a grove of white
pine that Hunter planted as a buffer survives. (Brown stone blocks on
either side of the trail just northwest of the crest mark the estate's front
gate.) The island's woods comprise a diverse mixture of trees. Young members include dogwood, crab apple, honeysuckle, black locust, white
poplar, and black birch; the towering hickory, oak, and tulip trees on the
northern end are more than a century old.

From this forest pours forth a wild chorus of sounds. You might hear the
squawk of the pheasant or the song of the redwing blackbird. Other members of the choir include thrashers, goldfinches, and great horned owls.
Foxes, raccoons, opossums, and wild turkeys may occasionally be found
underfoot. Although these animals and birds steer clear of humans, the
mosquitoes don't. In summer, bring insect repellent or wear long sleeves
and pants.

To reach Twin Island, return to the boardwalk and make a left. Walk to
the end and clamber over the fence. Don't worry, it's permitted. Once
there, it's easy to give yourself over to the illusion that you're in Maine, not
the Bronx. In fact, this metamorphic rock is the southernmost part of the
New England mountain range created by glacial erosion. The glaciers polished these rocks, leaving swirling patterns of black, blue, tan, and white;
garnet and feldspar; and thick dikes of quartz. There are several massive
boulders, including a glacial erratic known as Sphinx Rock, just before the
informal trail bends west toward Hunter Island.

The view from this rocky path is glorious: High and Hart Islands to the
south, Westchester's David and Huckleberry Islands to the north, and sailboats navigating all around the Sound. The marshland and water attract
geese, herons, egrets, cormorants, bufflehead ducks, loons, and even
swans. Fishing off Twin Island offers bluefish, bass, and cod; but do not eat
more than a pound a month of anything caught in New York waters. (It's
not healthy.) To your left is a forest with several unmarked trails. You may
also see traces of long-gone summer colonies—mainly stairs and shelters
made from the island's rock and built by immigrants who canoed and
played chess and pinochle here.

Amid these hard, unforgiving surfaces are patches of lush green spartina, salt marshes, and tidal pools. Lady, blue, and green crabs wander here, while mussel, clam, and oyster shells—and even the occasional tropical fish—turn up. Although modern society does intrude in the form of graffiti and litter, people still sometimes find arrowheads left by Native Americans and artifacts from early European settlers.

The **parks department,** (718) 430-1832, offers occasional free tours of Hunter and Twin Islands.

Island Hopping

🚗 *By car:* Take the New England Thruway to the Orchard Beach exit or the Hutchinson River Parkway to the City Island/Orchard Beach exit. Follow the signs to Orchard Beach, and park in the far left corner of the parking lot. There is a fee from the week before Memorial Day to the week after Labor Day. From the parking lot, walk to the boardwalk, and turn left to Hunter and Twin Islands.

🚌 *By bus:* In summer, buses drop off passengers at the Orchard Beach parking lot. From the Bronx, take the BX5 or BX12. From Manhattan, take the 6 train to Pelham Bay Park and change to the BX5 or BX12 bus. From Queens, take the QBX1 to Pelham Bay Park and change to the BX5 or BX12. From the parking lot, walk to the boardwalk and turn left to Hunter and Twin Islands.

Between Labor Day and Memorial Day, you must take the BX29 to the City Island traffic circle and then walk northeast for fifteen minutes to Orchard Beach.

For further travel information, call the **parks department** at (718) 430-1890.

9. Hart Island

"Far from being like some black hole in space into which all entities and identities disappear, the island is more akin to a lighthouse holding forth a frail but faithful flicker of hope for reconnection, for reunion, for being claimed at long last."

—THOMAS MCCARTHY, DIRECTOR OF HISTORICAL
SERVICES, NYC DEPARTMENT OF CORRECTION

Hart Island

THERE'S AN OLD SAYING that any publicity is good publicity as long as your name is spelled right. Well, no island gets more press for less appealing reasons than Hart Island, yet its simple appellation is misspelled more frequently than any other member of New York's archipelago—countless articles and documents mistakenly render it as Hart's Island. While many islands are named for former owners, a Mr. Hart never owned this one. The moniker, commonly thought to derive from the island's early animal life—*hart* is Middle English for "deer"—is more likely a corruption of Heart Island. British cartographers, believing it was shaped like the organ, first gave the island that name in 1775. Within two years, it was appearing on maps as Hart Island.

This 101-acre island, a half mile west of City Island in the Bronx, is a media darling because it's home to the city's potter's field, a forlorn reminder of how brutal and anonymous life in modern Gotham can be. Every year, another reporter or columnist can't resist the images: a white monument built by jail inmates in 1948, bearing the simple imprint PEACE, inscribed in gold; New York City inmates digging graves to bury society's outcasts—the poor, the forgotten, the loners.

Hart Island was not the city's first potter's field. In the eighteenth century, burial grounds for the unknown and indigent were established in Lower Manhattan near what is today the Surrogate Court building on Chambers Street. As the city expanded northward, the potter's field began its procession uptown, first to what is now Washington Square, then to Madison Square, Bryant Park, and the site of the Waldorf-Astoria, before being pushed off Manhattan Island to Randall's and Ward's Islands in the 1840s. In 1869, the cemetery was sent to its final resting place on Hart Island.

On April 20, 1869, Louisa Van Slyke, twenty-four, who died without family to claim her body, became the first person buried at Hart Island's potter's field. Born at sea, she died in New York's Charity Hospital on Welfare Island. Storytellers often adopt her bare-bones tale as the island's defining symbol, obliging Van Slyke to carry the weight of the eight hundred thousand who have followed.

The phrase *potter's field* comes from Matthew 27:3–8 in the New Testament, which describes the aftermath of Christ's crucifixion: "Then Judas, which had betrayed Him, saw that he was condemned, repented himself, and brought again the thirty pieces of silver to the chief priests . . . and they took counsel, and bought with them the potter's field to bury strangers in."

Burials on Hart Island were once confined to two plots, since unembalmed bodies disintegrated more quickly than embalmed bodies. The fields were then turned over and reused to bury a new crop of corpses. In recent decades, the practice was dropped. The cemetery today is spreading across the island, with inmates clearing land for new trenches.

The field is dotted with stumpy white markers, each denoting 150 bodies buried three deep in two rows. The plain boxes are staggered in the trenches to make for easier removal, since bodies are sometimes disinterred after relatives or friends come forward to claim them. A body can be retrieved for up to eight years, before the box deteriorates; sixty-one were removed in 1999. Approximately one-tenth of the adult burials are John and Jane Does; the rest are have-nots who simply couldn't afford a funeral. Amputated limbs, gallbladders, and other medical waste are buried in a separate hole.

The dead arrive by truck four times a week and are ferried over from City Island. In 1999, 1,011 adults and 671 children, babies, and stillborns were interred on the island. The young are memorialized by a 1902 granite cross reading HE CALLETH HIS CHILDREN BY NAME. There are virtually no Jews in potter's field; local Jewish organizations bury their indigent dead in private cemeteries.

Hart Island's grave diggers are inmates from nearby Rikers Island, and the "Ghoul Squad" considers the outdoor work a plum assignment. The nonviolent misdemeanants are paid fifty cents an hour for their labor.

While most of those interred on Hart Island took their stories to the grave, some memorable—possibly apocryphal—anecdotes survive: The so-called Crypt Swindler, Robert Mowatt, was buried there in 1933, after a life of selling phony deeds for crypts in New Jersey mausoleums; one man was there thirty-three years until his son struck oil, became a millionaire, and had his father's body reinterred in a cemetery; a World War I veteran given a pauper's burial was disinterred after French nuns—to whom he had sent small donations for nursing him during the war—learned of his fate. His body was flown to France and buried in the convent cemetery.

All of Hart Island's dead now have someone to remember them: Since

1991, a prayer group affiliated with St. Benedict's Parish in the Bronx has traveled to the island each May, on Ascension Thursday, to say prayers for this city of the dead. The community—which has a population greater than all but ten American cities—can accommodate perhaps another two decades of burials before the idea of reusing the land resurfaces.

While the morbid details are undeniably compelling, there is more to the history of Hart Island than its potter's field. Hart Island was sold by the Siwanoy tribe to Thomas Pell in 1654. During the first half of the nineteenth century, the island became "a favorite pugilistic hideaway," according to Elliot Gorn's 1988 book, *The Manly Art.* (Although bare-knuckled boxing was legal in the state, fights were often subject to raids by policemen searching for gambling, drunkenness, and hooliganism.) Hart Island's biggest bout was a grudge match held in 1842 between Irishman James "Yankee" Sullivan and Englishman Billy Bell for a $300 purse.

More than six thousand people sailed out to the island, or, as the *New York Daily Express* put it, "A gang of loafers and rowdies went out of the city yesterday to see a fisticuffins." They witnessed a brutal twenty-four-round, thirty-eight-minute slugfest dominated from start to finish by the 150-pound Sullivan. According to legend, the city's crime rate dropped during the fight.

Part of Hart Island was then bought in the 1860s by the federal government for a Civil War training ground; more than fifty thousand Union soldiers were instructed and a full-dress parade was held for the public every day.

Hart Island became the potter's field after the city paid the Hunter family (which had also owned Hunter Island) $75,000 for part of the island in 1868. On the remaining acreage, a diverse array of institutions—including an industrial school that took boys off the streets and trained them for the merchant marine and navy, a lunatic asylum, an almshouse, and a school for traffic violators—came and went during the next century.

Life and death peacefully coexisted, albeit in unusual fashion. The *New York Times* wrote in 1880 that when students at the industrial school "behaved themselves well through the week and the weather is fine, the teachers let them have a half-holiday on Saturday afternoons and go out and play among the graves."

In 1895, the department of corrections established a jail workhouse on the island for aged and infirm inmates, misdemeanants, and drug addicts. A youth reformatory was added a decade later, but was subsequently relocated to prevent youngsters from being corrupted by older inmates.

The oddest potential juxtaposition for Hart Island was shot down in 1925 when the potter's field and the jail were almost joined by an amusement park. Solomon Riley, owner of Spectacle Realty, owned four acres of the island and set about building a playland for Harlem blacks barred from "whites-only" amusement parks in Rye and Dobbs Ferry. Riley planned to bring customers to the island using a fleet of sixty motorboats, and to build the park without a fence right next to the prison. This didn't sit well with corrections officials, who feared the great influx of visitors and their proximity to the prison would cause a rash of escapes and contraband smuggling.

Riley planned, nonetheless, to open his amusement park on July 4. His workmen constructed two hundred feet of boardwalk, a dance hall, and eight boardinghouses, and began remaking an old ice boat into a bathing pavilion. Newspapers dubbed the affair "Hylan's Folly," because Mayor John Hylan had passed up the opportunity to purchase the tract from the Hunter family when they sold it in 1922. The city ultimately halted the project because of the prison security issue, and paid Riley $144,015 for the land he had bought for $35,000.

During World War II, the 535 workhouse prisoners were moved to Rikers Island so the navy could use Hart for disciplinary barracks. After the war, overcrowding on Rikers Island forced the run-down Hart workhouse—some buildings dated back to the Civil War—to reopen. Except from 1951 through 1954, when the city housed the homeless there over the loud protests of City Island residents, the Hart Island workhouse operated until 1966.

There were two noteworthy additions to the island during the 1950s and 1960s. The army installed its first Nike missile base—the country's principal defense against air attacks—in 1955. The twenty-one-foot missiles traveled at supersonic speeds, and were capable of destroying any plane within thirty miles. They were stored underground and required the installation of a generator powerful enough to provide electricity for a town of ten thousand. Only six years later, the army—in response to rapidly changing technologies and defense strategies—removed the missiles and pulled out.

The other newcomer was far more benign. In 1960, developer Marvin Kratter donated lights and twenty-two hundred seats for a workhouse ball field. These were no ordinary lights and seats. They were historical artifacts salvaged from Brooklyn's Ebbets Field before Kratter's wrecking ball struck. At the May 27 dedication of Kratter Field, 1,340 inmates watched their Wildcats take on soldiers from the missile base. The game ended in a 5–5 tie at 3:50 PM, because it was time for a prison headcount.

In 1967, after the prison closed, Phoenix House opened a drug rehabilitation program on Hart Island. In a small way, Phoenix House fulfilled
Solomon Riley's dream of entertaining the masses on the island, by sponsoring annual drug- and alcohol-free festivals featuring carnival rides, old
movies, and big-name musicians like the Velvet Underground and Janis
Ian. The events drew crowds of ten thousand. But in 1976, Phoenix House
moved back to Manhattan, a decision based on the cost of ferry transportation and a philosophical shift toward integrating participants in the
larger community.

Since Phoenix House's departure, life has been fairly quiet on the
island. In 1982, Mayor Ed Koch established a small work camp for misdemeanants, but was unable to persuade judges to sentence enough prisoners there. Six years later, he tried reviving both a prison and a homeless
shelter but was shouted down by homeless advocates opposed to the isolation, and by City Island residents who feared more traffic, sewage, and
water-pressure woes for their community.

In the meantime, Hart Island remains a paradox: Standing in the green
fields flecked with gulls, geese, and wildflowers, surrounded by groves of
trees and a spectacular view of the Sound, it is difficult to reconcile the
vitality of nature with the constant specter of death.

Death, even symbolically, looms everywhere on Hart Island. Except for
a small compound for officers and inmates, the island is littered with abandoned structures: Gutted jail administration buildings greet the ferry on
the eastern shore; a greenhouse once operated by recovering drug addicts
is overrun with weeds; a Catholic church, built in 1939 and emptied of its
stained-glass windows, altar, and pews, feels cavernous, dwarfing the figure of a saint left in a nook by a visiting member of St. Benedict's.

An anonymous street is lined with crumbling remains—one building is
filled with rusted machinery, while its neighbor is stuffed with cartons
labeled with bureaucratic epitaphs like 1992 FUNDS and PROPERTY
RECEIPTS. Empty Nike missile silos on another road sit across from the
thirty-foot-high monument erected in 1948, its white paint flaking and its
golden inscription, PEACE, fading.

On the island's picturesque western shore, large white stones embedded
in the grass in the form of a cross slope down a hill toward another set of
white markers denoting the infant dead. An elaborate stone fence sur-
rounds a sixteen-foot obelisk dedicated to Union soldiers who died there.
The men perished from disease, not combat. Their corpses were exhumed
in the twentieth century and reburied in formal cemeteries.

This is the island to which the ferry, without fanfare, conveys the plain white truck bearing the words NEW YORK CITY HEALTH AND HOSPITALS CORPORATION. Inmates in green and gray prison jumpsuits, some wearing masks to ward off the fetor of corpses, work seriously and efficiently. (Along with six officers, twenty-five inmates work on Hart Island, about a dozen on this detail, the others on maintaining the grounds.)

They unload each pine crate from the truck, scrawl a number and surname—Hernandez, Moratio, Smith, Lorenzo—onto the box with black crayon, and then drill the numbers into the wood for good measure. The primitive caskets are lowered into a long mass grave and covered with dirt.

"It's like a warning for people who want to do better for themselves," explained one inmate while working on the island. "I've seen my last name on one box. It's kind of scary, it makes you think. I don't want to wind up here."

10. Forgotten Islands of the Bronx

High Island • Rat Island • Hog Island • East and South Nonations •
The Blauzes • Chimney Sweeps • Cuban Ledge • Codling Island •
Blizzard Island • Wright's Island

Forgotten Islands of the Bronx

High Island

IT WAS, TO SAY THE LEAST, an inauspicious debut. In 1967, CBS was set to kick off a new venture, WCBS NEWSRADIO 88. The station would transmit from a soaring 541-foot radio tower on tiny High Island, just north of City Island in the Bronx, owned by WCBS and WNBC.

But the day before the launch, a small, private Piper Cherokee plane crashed into the tower. The plane, flying from East Hampton to La Guardia Airport in a blinding storm, was unauthorized to fly that day and plunged into Long Island Sound, killing all six on board. The crash demolished all but the bottom sixty feet of the tower's steel frame, squelching transmission. Remnants of the smashed antenna are still strewn about the island.

Fortunately for CBS, several competitors loaned the station transmitters until a two-hundred-foot antenna (now the backup) was hastily erected three days later. Eventually, a 529-foot tower was built as the main transmitter. (Today both WCBS and WFAN 66, a sports station, broadcast from these towers.)

Of course, the tower wasn't the only High Island structure knocked down in the 1960s. To make way for the new radio stations (and their towers), numerous bungalows and trees on the island had to be cleared. The island had housed a small summer community created in 1913 when Nora and Jack Beatty, the island's caretakers, began renting out campsites to earn extra money. (The Beattys lived in a two-story wooden farmhouse on the six-acre island.) In 1925, a new family bought the island and built twenty bungalows, providing summertime refuge to about one hundred people.

The island retreat had none of the luxuries or distractions of the mainland. Before a footbridge was built in 1928, residents walked from City Island to High Island via a sandbar at low tide or took a boat or a ten-cent ferry at high tide. (A steel footbridge was built in the late 1990s when the wooden one burned.) Later, residents parked their cars on City Island, transporting furniture, groceries, and other necessities to the island by wagon. About eight families became so attached to the bungalows that they stayed year-round. In 1960, they unsuccessfully fought a city zoning change that enabled the radio stations to buy the island and relocate their towers from a remote Westchester islet that required costly round-the-clock ferry service.

Today, the only vestige of the old community is the wooden farmhouse, occupied by radio station employee Mike Bierman, the island's caretaker. Bierman, fifty-four, is a former parking garage attendant who moved to High Island from an apartment in Queens in 1997 with his wife and two sons. The change from working and living around people to this splendid isolation was quite dramatic. The family was spooked at first by the quiet; geese landing on the roof sounded like an armed invasion, and Bierman missed the social side of his former job. "I was a little depressed," he says. "It was a tough time for about a year and a half."

But Bierman has adjusted. He cleared land to create a private beach and, with his son, is building a gazebo from felled trees. "I feel like Paul Bunyan," he notes. And he has grown to love the privacy this spot affords him. Says Bierman, "Who else has got their own island they can live on?"

Most of the following information on tiny isles of the Bronx, past and present, comes from John McNamara, an octogenarian historian who spent years kayaking the region's waterways and writing about Bronx history.

Rat Island

As unlikely as it seems, this two-acre rock halfway between Hart and City Islands was a mini-colony for writers and artists early in the twentieth century. It was also a resting place for convicts escaping from Hart Island, and in the nineteenth century, it briefly hosted a hospital during a yellow fever scare in Pelham.

Hog Island

This L-shaped island just south of the Westchester County border was usually sold as a package deal with Hunter Island. The city bought Hog Island in the late nineteenth century, and a beachcombers' colony sprung up. One woman, Marion Laing, claimed squatter's rights, staying there until her death on September 12, 1930. A tablet to her memory was placed on the island, reading THIS ISLAND WAS HER PARADISE.

East and South Nonations

Legend has it that Dutch and English colonists were unwilling to fight over these two adjoining reefs in the Sound, north of Hart Island, so they became islands owned by no nation. Others say they were originally spelled "Notations," meaning a footnote, or abbreviation.

The Blauzes

The name of these mussel-colored reefs west of Hart Island derives from either the Dutch *de Blauwtjes,* meaning "little blue ones," or the Old English word *blazer,* meaning "marker." Early mariners may have used the reefs as guides into City Island; less observant sailors wrecked their ships there.

Chimney Sweeps

Like The Blauzes to their north, these two tiny reefs caused many shipwrecks. Positioned side by side like two stones tied together, these isles resemble a primitive cleaning tool once used by chimney sweeps. Another explanation for the appellation is that the gray humps are as dingy looking as a soot-covered sweep. In the early 1900s, a German family lived on the islands, where they built a tavern attracting boaters eager for refreshment.

Cuban Ledge

South of Rodman's Neck in Eastchester Bay, this islet can be seen only at low tide. Several legends attempt to explain its name, one originating in 1898, when a crew threw its cargo of rocks overboard after learning that the USS *Maine* had been blown up in Havana Harbor. The sailors went ashore and enlisted in the Spanish-American War, leaving the rocks to form a reef or ledge. Others say the islet is cigar-shaped like Cuba, while a different tale says the island was so named when the intoxicated crew of the *Cuban Lady* ran aground there in the 1880s.

Codling Island

This former island, in what is today Eastchester, was created around 1880 when a portion of the Hutchinson River was straightened, severing and isolating a piece of mainland property belonging to George F. Codling. The old channel fell into disuse and silted up, connecting the island to the mainland by 1900.

Blizzard Island

Located in the mouth of the Hutchinson River, this low, rocky ledge was named for David Blizzard, who in the 1860s rented boats and sold tackle directly opposite the island on Tallapoosa Point. Blizzard Island once supported the eastern arch of the original Pelham bridge, built in the late 1880s. The island, eventually joined with landfill to the mainland, is today part of Pelham Bay Park just east of Shore Road.

Wright's Island

Known as Horse Neck in the seventeenth century and Locust Island a hundred years later, the island became known as Wright's Island after Captain George Wright purchased it in 1830. Three generations of Wrights lived on this fifteen-acre island until 1920. The family attached it to the mainland in the 1880s by a narrow causeway. The island was renamed Locust Point (for the swamp trees that grew there) in the 1920s, when it was sold and broken up into residential lots. Marsh draining and landfill operations eventually connected it to the mainland. The approach to the Throgs Neck Bridge, which opened in 1961, is today on what was Wright's Island.

Part IV

East River

ROOSEVELT ISLAND • RANDALL'S AND WARD'S ISLANDS •
RIKERS ISLAND • NORTH AND SOUTH BROTHER ISLANDS •
FORGOTTEN ISLANDS OF THE EAST RIVER

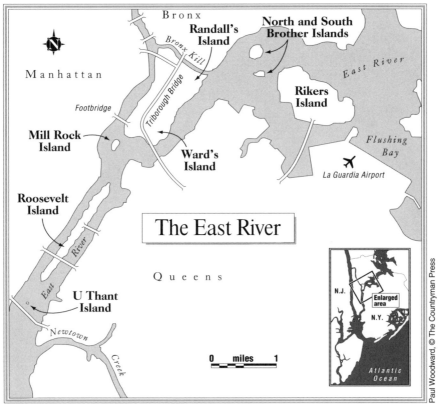

Paul Woodward, © The Countryman Press

Despite the name, the East River is technically a saltwater estuary or tidal strait, linking Upper New York Bay with Long Island Sound. The sixteen-mile stretch, which separates Manhattan from Brooklyn and Queens, is densely populated. From the Brooklyn-Battery Tunnel to the Throgs Neck Bridge, there are eight bridges, eleven tunnels (for cars and subways), a footbridge, and a tram. Notorious for its roiling currents, the water is home to seven islands. Newtown Creek, which branches out from the East River and ends in Maspeth, bisects Brooklyn and Queens.

11. Roosevelt Island

"Is it possible to rescue Blackwell's Island from prosaic prisoners, unappreciative idiots and small-pox patients, careless of scenery and heedless of aesthetics? Perhaps not within the present decade, but when the population of New York shall have outgrown its present limits, and shall clamor for other islands to conquer, the paupers and convicts of Blackwell's Island will no longer be allowed to monopolize that charming spot."

—*NEW YORK TIMES*, JUNE 1, 1872

Roosevelt Island

THE NINETEENTH-CENTURY Gothic lighthouse at the northern tip of Roosevelt Island no longer guides ships through the East River. And the island quarry that provided the beacon's gray Fordham gneiss was exhausted more than a century ago, spent on a plethora of institutions that once dominated the landscape. Two remain on the island's southern end—the Smallpox Hospital and Strecker Laboratory. They're American ruins now, relics of a time when islands were given over to outcasts, thugs, and the infirm.

The rest of Roosevelt Island—save a few landmarks and hospitals—is evidence that attitudes toward island life have changed. Today, people *want* to be on this two-mile-long, eight-hundred-foot-wide strip, which parallels Manhattan from Forty-eighth to Eighty-fifth Streets. Vast residential structures project skyward as monuments to the living. Green spaces are alive with neighborhood soccer games, picnics, and a community garden. Joggers, walkers, and cyclists cruise the promenade hugging most of the island's periphery. Some sit on "meditation steps" overlooking the East River's west channel and absorb the city skyline from a comfortable three hundred feet away.

Roosevelt Island is a young community—it didn't exist until 1975, when urban planners, architects, and the government opened their "New Town in Town." But unlike much of the city, which often bulldozes its history, Roosevelt Island—population about 8,500—willingly keeps company with its checkered past.

Roosevelt Island's aboriginal name is unclear. Many sources call it Minnahanonck, but Stokes's *The Iconography of Manhattan,* perhaps the most comprehensive source on early New York, says Minnahanonck was actually Randall's Island. Dutch settlers referred to Roosevelt Island as Varckens, or Hog Island, and farmed it as early as 1639. After the English captured New York, King Charles granted the island to Captain John Manning, sheriff of New York in 1668, but this reward for his loyalty later became a hideaway of disgrace.

In 1673, England and Holland were at war, and Manning was com-

Roosevelt Island

1. Smallpox Hospital ruin
2. Strecker Laboratory ruin
3. Tram dock
4. Subway station Q & B
5. Meditation Steps
6. Blackwell House
7. Chapel of the Good Shepherd
8. Octagon Park
9. Octagon
10. Lighthouse Park
11. Lighthouse

Manhattan

East River — West Channel

Island

MAIN STREET

36th AVENUE
BRIDGE

AERIAL
TRAMWAY

East River — East Channel

Queens

Roosevelt

QUEENSBORO
BRIDGE

N

N.J.

Enlarged
area

N.Y.

Atlantic
Ocean

0   miles   1/2

manding Fort James (formerly Fort Amsterdam) when he noticed a fleet of Dutch vessels approaching from Staten Island. With only eighty soldiers available, Manning tried negotiating to buy time, but the Dutch bombarded the fort and Manning hastily surrendered. The war ended the following year, the English regained New York, and in 1675 Manning was put on trial for giving up Fort James. With his life at stake, Manning pleaded guilty to cowardice and treason, but beseeched King Charles for leniency. At city hall, Manning was publicly stripped to the waist and his hands were bound with irons. Ten musketeers stood ready awaiting the command to fire. But at the last minute Manning was spared execution. Instead he was condemned to suffer humiliation and disbarment; his sword was broken into three pieces over his head and he was banned from serving the Crown.

The exiled captain lived out his final ten years entertaining friends on his East River island. "His house became a synonyme of hospitality; his wit was a proverb, and he was pronounced the most elegant and agreeable of hosts," wrote Felix Oldboy in 1893 in *A Tour Around New York and My Summer Acre.*

When Manning died in 1685, his island passed to his stepdaughter, Mary Manningham, and her husband, Robert Blackwell, a merchant from Elizabethtown, New Jersey. In 1784, the island was put up for sale by James and Jacob Blackwell, who advertised it as "agreeably situated," and "one of the most healthy situations in the state." Fish and fowl were plentiful; there was an orchard with 450 fruit trees, two small houses, a barn, bakery, fowl house, and cider mill.

There were, however, no takers. Jacob tried persuading the city to buy the island for a potter's field in 1797, but couldn't close the deal. The Blackwell family was stuck with the island until 1823, when it was sold to James Bell. Even this arrangement was short lived. Bell died there two years later and, by mortgage foreclosure, the island reverted to the Blackwells . . . until the city found a use for it.

As New York's population exploded and social problems became a pressing issue, the city turned to institutionalization to preserve order in society. Close at hand yet isolated, the city's islands were perfectly suited for segregating outcasts. Authorities emphasized the benevolence of their deed, maintaining that these beautiful islands offered a healing environment for the sick and a place of reflection for the vicious.

The city, which was just developing Fourteenth Street, purchased Blackwell's—its first East River island—in 1828 for a new prison. The

island was reached by traveling north on the old Boston Road, which
began where Park Row is today, up the eastern side of Manhattan Island.
The road was often muddy and inaccessible. Then came an arduous climb
down a steep bluff to the river from which a ferry journeyed to the island.

The prison—with 500 cells for males and 256 for females—was built
in the center of the island. When its cornerstone was laid on September
10, 1828, there was already talk of adding facilities. "A more eligible spot
for health, cleanliness and safety could not have been selected for the
erection of all public buildings, which are supported at the public
expense," the *Evening Post* reported the Committee on the Almshouse as
saying. "We hope in a few years to see the madhouse and hospital
removed to the island."

The city lunatic asylum opened in 1841, followed by the almshouse in
1847 and, in 1849, the island's first hospital. Penitentiary Hospital treated
both law-abiders and convicts, most of them afflicted with infectious conditions, especially venereal disease. The hospital's sinister name was
changed to Island Hospital in 1857. A workhouse was added to the prison
in 1850.

But the government's claim of an island oasis for the needy proved hollow. In 1842, Charles Dickens visited several of the institutions, including
the lunatic asylum. While impressed with its "handsome" architecture,
especially its octagon tower and elegant five-story spiral staircase, Dickens
was disturbed by the disorder and overcrowding.

"The moping idiot, cowering down with long dishevelled hair; the gib-
bering maniac, with his hideous laugh and pointed finger; the vacant eye,
the fierce wild face, the gloomy picking of the hands and lips, and munch-
ing of the nails: there they were all, without disguise, in naked ugliness and
horror," he wrote in *American Notes*. "The terrible crowd with which these
halls and galleries were filled so shocked me, that I abridged my stay within
the shortest limits, and declined to see that portion of the building in which
the refractory and violent were under closer restraint."

The island's rural character had evolved into a nightmarish netherworld
crowded with institutions built by inmate labor from granite quarried from
the island's bedrock. And there was more to come. In 1858, Charity (later
City) Hospital opened, replacing the flimsy Island Hospital, which had
been destroyed by fire. City Hospital was designed by James Renwick Jr.,
architect of the island's Smallpox Hospital and St. Patrick's Cathedral in
Manhattan. Built in the French Second Empire style with a distinguished
mansard roof and two wings flanking the center, City Hospital was the

largest hospital in the country—three stories high, 354 feet long and 122 feet wide, with a capacity of twelve hundred patients.

Despite its magnificent architecture, City Hospital added to the island's ugly reputation. The nurses and servants were mostly workhouse prisoners who often stayed after their terms ended, "receiving no wages but a pretty liberal allowance of whiskey, the bung of the whiskey barrel being under the control of the physicians," according to a City Hospital history published in 1904.

Among the other hospitals opened between 1856 and 1867 was one each for the treatment of fever, smallpox, epilepsy, paralysis, and "incurables." All told, there were eleven institutions by 1872. Patients were often referred to as inmates although their only crime was being poor or sick. Many were foreign-born and from the city's ghettos, where disease, poverty, and crime prevailed. Women in the insane asylum outnumbered men two to one, in part because husbands frequently punished insubordinate wives by having them temporarily committed.

It was no secret that Blackwell's Island was a rude purgatory of sorrow and suffering. In 1878, a city investigation revealed severe overcrowding in many of the institutions. A year later, after a probe into mistreatment by nurses in the lunatic asylum, the board of physicians and surgeons called for a complete reorganization of the asylum. But little changed.

Blackwell's Island "is a city in which all the misery, despair and viciousness of the metropolis are epitomized," wrote the *Daily News* in 1884 (no relation to the current tabloid). "Within its granite walls the pauper and madman, the wrecked creature whose life is wasting on a hopeless sick-bed and the moral leper, who were better dead, lie cheek by jowl, wards of the community which casts them out but cannot rid itself of them."

Three years later, some reforms were made after fearless reporter Nellie Bly exposed abuses in the asylum (see *Historical Detour: Nellie Bly—Committed to the Truth*). In 1890, a follow-up investigation by the city found the asylum orderly, but still overcrowded. (It also discovered prison inmates sharing cells a mere three and a half by seven feet in size.) The asylum was moved to Ward's Island in 1894, and a year later Metropolitan Hospital occupied this magnificent building with the octagon tower.

By the time the Strecker Laboratory—the country's first center for studying pathology—opened on the island in 1892, most of Blackwell's older buildings were antiquated, especially the crowded penitentiary. To improve prison conditions and remove the unfair criminal stigma borne by patients in the charitable institutions, the city planned to relocate the new peniten-

Designed by James Renwick Jr., the nineteenth-century Smallpox Hospital is a ghostly reminder of Roosevelt Island's institutional past. Friends of Roosevelt Island Landmarks is working to stabilize the ruin so that visitors can see the historic monument up close.

tiary to Rikers Island and turn Blackwell's Island into a hospital compound. The talk produced little action, however, and in 1921, with the hospital park still unbuilt, the city changed the island's name to Welfare Island in an effort to erase its horrific reputation.

Before the prison was finally shoved off to Rikers in 1935, one last showdown at the penitentiary uncovered a tightly guarded Pandora's box of graft and corruption. When reform-minded Fiorello La Guardia became mayor, ending Tammany Hall's reign, he appointed Austin H. MacCormick commissioner of correction. On January 24, 1934, MacCormick and his men made a surprise raid on what MacCormick called "the worst prison in the world," cracking a highly organized system of drug smuggling and mob domination. "Boss gangsters lived in luxury, swaggered around, and at the same time there was an almost incredible condition of misery and degeneracy," wrote the *New York Herald-Tribune*.

Racketeers and their cronies—about 500 out of the prison population of 1,658—feasted on steaks, chops, and fine desserts in relatively lavish

Historical Detour: Big Guns in the Big House

One was corpulent, the other voluptuous, but both did time in an island prison. Tammany Hall leader William Marcy "Boss" Tweed went to the Blackwell's Island Penitentiary in 1874. Actress Mae West was confined to the Welfare Island workhouse in 1927. Neither personality lived the rigorous life of a convict, however. They were jailed in style.

After Tweed and his ring defrauded the city of millions of dollars, the 280-pound politician was sentenced to twelve years in the Blackwell's Island Penitentiary. He was furnished a room away from the main cellblock—a relatively luxurious "apartment" with a desk, library, and other frills, including a six-by-eight-foot window facing south, from which Tweed observed the city he had plundered. He received many visitors, including his private secretary, who continued working for him. The apartment entrance was unlocked and there was rarely a guard within fifty feet of the front door.

Even after newspapers reported Tweed's preferential treatment, little changed. Six months later, the warden ordered Tweed to wear prison garb and suffer the same food and lodging as the other prisoners, but he was released soon afterward, having served only one year. He was later arrested on civil charges and sent to Manhattan's Ludlow Street jail, where—except for an escape to Spain—he again enjoyed a privileged existence until his death in 1878.

Mae West was jailed for ten days for obscenity after starring in a play she had coauthored called *Sex*. She was spared from dormitory life and given a private cell and a job sweeping and making beds—a relatively easy assignment. Her biggest complaint, however, was with the clothes she had to wear.

"For Miss West the change from the silks and crepes and sheer stockings of the average well-dressed woman about the city to the prison outfit was a shock," wrote the *New York Times*, "but she suppressed her instinctive recoil and resolutely slipped into the uniform." West wore the coarse blue cotton dress and heavy cotton stockings, but eventually purchased a pair of white stockings at the workhouse commissary. She wrote a poem about the uncomfortable, fuzzy prison underwear and dedicated it to Warden Harry Schleth.

When she was released, West donated to the workhouse $1,000 she had earned writing a magazine article about her experience. The money went to the Mae West Memorial Prison Library.

cells. Joseph Rao, the Italian leader, Harlem racketeer, and alleged henchman of "Dutch" Schultz, ruled from headquarters he had established in the administration building's hospital quarters, where only six of fifty "patients" were actually ill. Rao had a garden and pet milk goat and enjoyed expensive cigars, silk robes, lilac toilet water, and monogrammed stationery. The Irish mob leader, Edward Cleary, was less ostentatious. He kept a German police dog he called Screw-Hater (slang for "guard hater") in his dormitory hospital cell, along with a cache of smuggled goods, including fresh cranberries, pickled herring, potatoes, milk, and liquor. Both kingpins kept large cotes filled with homing pigeons believed to have trafficked notes and drugs into and out of the prison. Cleary's cote was built right into his hospital room. The bulk of the prisoners were forced into servitude. They often waited on the big shots, were fed bland stew in the mess hall, and shared cells because of overcrowding.

The two mob leaders and sixty-six cronies were arrested in Mac-Cormick's sweep and put in solitary confinement. Warden Joseph C. McCann was suspended, but permitted to resign without facing a departmental trial. The court dismissed criminal charges, ruling that McCann's incompetency and neglect of duty did not constitute a crime.

Before the penitentiary was demolished in 1936, a debate ensued over the island's future. Parks Commissioner Robert Moses advocated utilizing the land for a public park, a concept that dated as far back as 1867, when the *New York Herald* recommended razing the buildings to create an "island paradise." Dr. S. S. Goldwater, commissioner of hospitals, however, supported the old hospital park idea and called for a much-needed centralized care facility for the chronically ill. He planned to double the island's bed capacity by knocking down the five old institutions remaining and replacing them with seven modern ones. Since Moses was already building parks on Randall's and Ward's Islands, Goldwater won the debate.

Once again, the hospital park didn't fully materialize. A nurses' residence opened in 1938, and Welfare Hospital for Chronic Diseases (later Goldwater Memorial Hospital) opened the next year. World War II post-poned further construction, and afterward, priorities shifted. While the hospital shortage continued, the city poured its money into housing, mass transit, schools, and—out of proportion to actual needs—into the roadways and spans designed by Robert Moses and his Triborough Bridge and Tun-nel Authority. Only one more chronic-care facility opened on the island, Bird S. Coler Hospital, in 1952. (Goldwater and Coler merged in 1996, forming what is now called Coler/Goldwater Special Hospital and Nursing Facility.) The city finally abandoned the hospital park concept and closed or relocated Welfare Island's ancient institutions—Metropolitan Hospital moved to Harlem and City Hospital to Elmhurst, Queens, leaving the for-saken asylums and hospitals to decay.

With most of Welfare Island lying fallow, architects and city planners searched out a constructive use for the neglected 147-acre strip. Numerous plans were proposed in the 1960s, including a twenty-thousand-unit resi-dential community of fifty-story buildings. The American Institute of Architects, influential urban writer Lewis Mumford, and Parks Commis-sioner August Heckscher advocated preserving the space as a park. In 1965, after the Metropolitan Transit Authority promised to link the incon-veniently located island to the subway system within ten years, new sug-gestions flooded in, including one proposing to reconstruct the Metro-politan Museum of Art's Temple of Dendur on the island's southern tip. Even more unusual was a plan to dig up bodies from Queens and Brooklyn cemeteries and reinter them on Welfare Island, freeing up borough land for housing.

Mayor John Lindsay established a committee of citizens and city offi-cials, who ultimately recommended a multi-use plan designed by archi-tects John Burgee and Philip Johnson. The plan was socially idealistic—a mixed-income, mixed-race, handicapped-accessible new town of twenty thousand. The community was to have two neighborhoods—Northtown and Southtown—with low-rise apartment buildings tightly clustered to allow for ample park and recreational space and water views. It would be a walk-ing and cycling town, with a four-mile promenade along the island's perimeter and a pedestrian Main Street, from which cars would be banned. (They'd park in a garage near the Thirty-sixth Avenue Bridge linking the island to Queens.) The project promised to restore seven historic land-marks, retain Coler and Goldwater Hospitals, and build facilities like a school, a hotel, shops, and an office building.

In 1969, the city leased the island to the state for ninety-nine years, allowing the new Urban Development Corporation (UDC) to take control of the project. Created by Governor Nelson Rockefeller to expedite housing renewal, this public authority was given power to float bonds and override local zoning regulations. UDC installed its own team of architects, each working on a separate segment of the project. It also altered the Burgee-Johnson plan to include fewer but significantly taller buildings and a smaller town population. In 1973, the island was renamed to honor President Franklin Roosevelt.

Most of the original plan was ultimately retained, but UDC ran into problems. Without a leader, communication between projects broke down. And when the city's fiscal crisis delayed construction of the subway stop, the state was forced to come up with an alternate means of transportation—a commuter tram to Manhattan. Meanwhile, UDC found itself operating in the red and unable to repay loans and bonds, so when Roosevelt Island welcomed its first tenants in 1975, only 40 percent of the project was completed. These government-subsidized, low- to middle-income buildings were twenty-one stories tall. UDC subsequently left the housing business, passing responsibility for Roosevelt Island to the state division of housing and community renewal. In 1984, the Roosevelt Island Operating Corporation (RIOC) was established, becoming the first independent agency charged with developing and operating the island.

Further development was stalled for more than a decade until 1989, when a high-rise luxury rental with free-market units and a smaller subsidized building for low-income, disabled, and elderly residents opened. The subway also opened that year, sending the tram into a deficit. And now it appears that the island's southern portion, phase three, will finally be developed. According to RIOC, ground will soon be broken on the two-thousand-unit Southtown residential community, a complex of nine buildings ranging from sixteen to twenty-eight stories. Two-thirds of the tenants will be employees from three hospitals located on the Upper East Side. A controversial high-rise hotel and convention center has been proposed for Southpoint, ten acres on the island's southern tip. There are also plans to build low-rise, subsidized housing, perhaps for artists or graduate students, as part of the restoration of the old Octagon Tower, as well as senior housing and luxury condominiums elsewhere on the island.

Roosevelt Island's earliest residents possessed a frontier spirit. Paul Claudatto was the first tenant, moving into Island House from the Bronx in

May 1975. Although there was a buzz of activity from construction workers and hospital employees, the island's first fifty families enjoyed a "glorious isolation," recalls Claudatto, who now lives in Queens. It was three
months before Claudatto even heard a noise in the hallway. A neighbor! "I
felt like Robinson Crusoe finding the footprint in the sand."

Claudatto enjoyed wandering among the island's ruins, their romantic
Gothic quality in stark contrast to the United Nations, Sutton Place, and Turtle Bay across the river. This was about the only place to ramble. Main Street
wasn't finished, and there was no shopping. To keep new residents happy, a
stretch limousine took Island House tenants to a supermarket in Queens.

Once the tram arrived in 1976, the island evolved into a full-fledged
small town, albeit with New York diversity. In Genesis-like fashion,
islanders created what had not existed before—a library, Little League,
garden club, theater troupe, and other volunteer organizations. (Today, the
island has about sixty volunteer groups, most surviving since the early
days. And at long last, the library has become part of the New York Public
Library system, providing better hours and more selection for residents.)
Shopkeepers moved in, parks were built, and some landmarks were
restored or stabilized. By 1980, seven thousand people lived on the island.

The island also delivered on its promise to be an economically and
racially mixed, family-oriented community. There are now approximately
eighty-five hundred residents, many of whom are foreign-born, including a
large number of UN employees. Children from about three dozen nations
mingle in the public school. The island has both a high median income
($44,518 in 1990) and a relatively high number of residents living in
poverty (one in six in 1990). While the city's other island communities—
City Island and Broad Channel—are largely white, Roosevelt Island is
fairly evenly balanced between whites and minorities. But unlike City
Island or Broad Channel, Roosevelt Island, with its transient UN population and young singles, who live mostly in the island's free-market building, has a fair amount of tenant turnover.

In design and ambience, the island evokes a collegiate intimacy. The
city's 114th Precinct occasionally patrols the campuslike island, but most
law enforcement is supplied by RIOC's unarmed peace officer force. "It
feels pretty small-town to me. Everyone knows everyone, if not by name
then by sight," says Janice Taylor, who moved to the island in 1978 and
lives there with her husband and two children. "When I go out for the
paper on a Saturday morning, it might take a half hour because I stop to
say hello to so many neighbors on the street. And I love that the bus driv-

ers wait for you—these guys see you coming out of the building and they wait. It's so laid-back and civil."

Best of all, residents say, is that they have all the benefits of island life and yet are close to everything the city has to offer. (The island is part of Manhattan even though the only bridge access is from Queens.) By train or tram, it's Bloomingdale's in five minutes and Lincoln Center in twenty minutes. "You're literally in a suburb that is three hundred yards from Manhattan," says sixty-seven-year-old H. Patrick Stewart, who has lived on the island for eighteen years.

Even the estimated two thousand long-term and chronic-care patients in the city-run Coler/Goldwater Special Hospital and Nursing Facility find the island a liberating experience, since it is completely wheelchair-friendly.

While most residents are less concerned with the island's aesthetics than its atmosphere, outsiders may be struck by the gloomy and monotonous architecture. Because the apartment buildings tier down to the water, the tallest portions flank Main Street, making it dark and dreary. (The design, however, provides most residents with river views.) The downtown's drab appearance is heightened by the generic red-and-white signs identifying each shop: COCKTAIL LOUNGE, FISH STORE, GENERAL STORE. But what really irks the residents are the stores' high prices and limited selection, which send them off-island to shop; with a captive but limited customer base, merchants have no incentive to compete.

The limited customer base also makes it difficult to financially support many of the island's small businesses. In fact, since Governor George Pataki cut all funding to the island in fiscal year 1996–97, the island has been forced to find other ways to make itself self-sufficient. Stewart credits Robert Ryan, who in the late 1990s replaced the unpopular Jerome Blue as RIOC president and chief operating officer, with looking for creative ways to help Roosevelt Island, such as applying for grant money. "He is doing as good a job as he possibly can under the circumstances, and the circumstances are not easy," says Stewart, former president of the tenants' association and a resident member of RIOC's board.

But grant money is not going to float Roosevelt Island. In order to survive, RIOC is going to have to generate its own capital and operating budget by encouraging further development of the island—which was planned for but never completed. Some residents, particularly old-timers accustomed to the island's relatively small population, are opposed to the size and scope of some of those plans, particularly the Southpoint complex. Southpoint, with its proposed 350 hotel rooms and fifty condomini-

Historical Detour: Nellie Bly–Committed to the Truth

In 1885, when she was about to turn twenty-one, fortune smiled on Elizabeth Cochrane. Raised in Pennsylvania mining towns and frustrated by her inability to find employment in Pittsburgh, Cochrane had written a blistering rebuttal to a chauvinistic *Pittsburgh Dispatch* columnist's pontifications on women and work. Her letter caught editor George Madden's attention, and he asked Cochrane to write a story on the subject.

After the success of that piece and another on the taboo subject of divorce, Madden offered Cochrane a full-time job . . . and a pseudonym, since journalism wasn't considered a proper vocation for a lady. The name they chose, from a well-known song, was Nellie Bly. Bly wrote features about the Pittsburgh slums and women in factories before traveling to Mexico, where she sharpened her skills as a muckraker by reporting on poverty and corruption. Bly's talent and instinctive sense of adventure proved indispensable for the story that would earn her national recognition—an inside look at life in the dreaded lunatic asylum on Blackwell's Island.

It wasn't easy being a "girl reporter" in the nineteenth century, and when Bly moved to New York in 1887 looking for a job, she found journalism's boys' club closed to her. She got her foot in the door after interviewing all the top editors for a *Pittsburgh Dispatch* story about women in journalism; their shameless sexism created quite a stir and won Bly an interview at the *New York World*. Impressed by her moxie, and anxious for an extraordinary probe of the notorious bedlam on the East River islands, the *World* assigned her to an undercover investigation of alleged abuses at the asylum.

Bly checked into the Temporary Home for Women at 84 Second Avenue, claiming to be Nellie Brown from Cuba. She jabbered nonstop and feigned irrational behavior; the police were eventually called in and Bly was sent to court. A few reporters on the court beat took notice of the attractive, well-dressed redhead and filed stories. The *New York Sun*'s front-page headline asked, "Who Is This Insane Girl?" while the *New York Times* described Bly as the "mysterious waif" with a "wild, hunted look in her eyes." The *World* remained silent as Bly was remanded to Bellevue Hospital for an examination and, finally, ferried to Blackwell's Island.

Bly was appalled by the detestable conditions she found there, and when a *World* attorney obtained her release ten days later, Bly wrote a series of stories detailing her harrowing experiences. The first ran on October 9, 1887, and Bly was given a byline—a rare honor in those days. She told of inedible food, insensitive doctors, nurses who savagely beat patients, and foreign women committed to the asylum because nobody could understand them.

"We were taken into a cold, wet bathroom, and I was ordered to undress," described Bly. "I noticed one of the craziest women in the ward standing by the filled bathtub with a large, discolored rag in her hands. She was chattering away to herself and chuckling in a manner which seemed to me fiendish . . . They began to undress me, and one by one they pulled off my clothes . . . I gave one glance at the group of patients gathered at the door watching the scene, and I jumped into the bathtub with more energy than grace.

"The water was ice-cold, and I again began to protest. How useless it all was! I begged, at least, that the patients be made to go away, but was ordered to shut up. The crazy woman began to scrub me . . . From a small tin pan she took some soft soap and rubbed it all over me, even all over my face and my pretty hair . . . My teeth chattered and my limbs were goose-fleshed and blue with cold. Suddenly I got, one after the other, three buckets of water over my head—ice-cold water, too—into my eyes, my ears, my nose and my mouth. I think I experienced some of the sensations of a drowning person as they dragged me, gasping, shivering and quaking, from the tub. For once I did look insane. I caught a glance of the indescribable look on the faces of my companions, who had witnessed my fate and knew theirs was surely following."

The *World* hammered home Bly's reportage with front-page commentary about the despicable abuses. The story of her escapade caused a national sensation and ushered in a new era of crusading investigations into sensationalistic topics. When Bly returned to the island later that month with the assistant dis-

trict attorney and grand jury, many of the violations had been
tidied up. The jury nonetheless recommended reforms and
increased funding, which was approved by the city. Already
starting to face up to the island institution's problems, the city
had been contemplating change. Bly's in-depth exposure en-
sured there was no turning back.

In 1895, Bly married seventy-year-old millionaire Robert
Seaman just days after they met on a train to Chicago; a year
later she gave up her career. After Seaman died in 1904, she ran
his Iron Clad Manufacturing Company until it went bankrupt in
1912—in part because Bly was robbed by employees. She then
lived in Europe for six years, occasionally working as a war cor-
respondent for the *New York Evening Journal*. She returned to
New York as a *Journal* columnist in 1919, but died of pneumonia three years later at the age of fifty-seven. Bly was honored in
her *Journal* obituary as "the best reporter in America."

ums to be housed in two twenty-six-story towers with views of Midtown
Manhattan and the United Nations, is far from the existing tram and subway, and would be linked to Manhattan and La Guardia Airport by ferry.
The developers would also be asked to help fund the long-planned-for
Roosevelt Memorial as well as preserve the landmark smallpox hospital
ruin. (Preservation in this case may mean incorporating the building's
Gothic frame into an ultramodern edifice, which is anathema to many
preservationists.) Some development opponents contend that the site was
promised as parkland; others say the project is simply out of place. RIOC
maintains that Southpoint is necessary because it will provide some of the
revenue—$2 million annually—to help the island support itself.

"As long as the island is developed appropriately, that's fine with us,"
says Stewart. "I just don't think it makes sense to have a development
down there that needs the logistical support a hotel would need."

Some residents are also itching to break free from the state altogether,
hoping to persuade the state to pay off its debts and make the island just
another city neighborhood, eligible for basic funding and services. In
1999, Mayor Rudolph Giuliani—who has been constantly at odds with
Governor Pataki—came to the island and told residents, "I would be very,
very happy to work with you to liberate Roosevelt Island."

In the meantime, some islanders complain that RIOC doesn't listen to them and maintains a totalitarian attitude that deprives residents of the democratic process most city residents enjoy. (Residents do, however, hold four seats on RIOC's nine-member board.) In particular, islanders are furious at Governor Pataki's budget cuts and say inadequate attention is paid to quality-of-life issues on the island, such as the decline in the quality of the public school. The island's infrastructure also has not been maintained for five years, due to budget cuts, says Stewart.

"They're a state bureaucracy that's incurable," says Judy Berdy, president of the historical society. Ryan contends, however, that "RIOC is always working to improve its relationship with residents."

Some say the pioneer spirit has dimmed on Roosevelt Island. Though a core group of residents remains civic-minded, this expanding community has lost some of its intimacy. Many of the original homesteaders have moved away, making room for newcomers who lack the time and passion for building a Jamestown on the East River. But for those attracted to the island's experimental community, and for those who simply want respite from the madness of Manhattan, Roosevelt Island remains the ideal abode.

"We may have our local conflicts," adds Berdy, "but we like living here. It functions, but Roosevelt Island is sort of dysfunctional. We're eternal optimists."

Exploring the Island

A unique residential community, Roosevelt Island offers four public parks and six New York City–designated landmarks, four of which can be seen during a leisurely stroll. The island is almost entirely ringed by a paved esplanade, which when completely built will offer a four-and-a-half-mile scenic loop.

From the tram or subway station, walk north, veering right onto an artery of Main Street. The **Blackwell House** to your right was built in 1796 by James Blackwell and is the sixth oldest house in New York City. Unfortunately, it is not open to the public. According to RIOC's Robert Ryan, RIOC is waiting for some grant money to refurbish the building.

Continuing down Main Street, you come upon the **Chapel of the Good Shepherd,** the only refreshing piece of architecture in the town center. This stone-and-brick Victorian Gothic church was built in 1889 by English architect Frederick Clarke Withers, who was one of the first members of the American Institute of Architects. The church was commissioned by the New York Episcopal Mission Society to minister to residents of the island's institutions; it was renovated in 1976 and is now called the Good Shepherd Community Ecumenical Center. The church's bronze bell, cast in 1888, is exhibited in the plaza.

Farther north on Main Street is a community garden to your left. Past the tennis courts and Octagon Park is **Octagon Tower,** which is all that remains of the lunatic asylum. The tower's two wings were demolished in 1970; in 1982, a fire destroyed the tower's Victorian cupola, exposing the inside to the elements. Then, in 1999, yet another fire demolished much of the building's upper portion and severely damaged the interior. The building is fenced off from the public. There has been a proposal to refurbish the tower as part of a development plan that calls for the construction of low-rise residential units on the footprint of the old Octagon wings.

Head to the west side of the esplanade, then veer north until you reach **Lighthouse Park,** the island's most picturesque spot, with views of Mill Rock and Ward's Island, the Triborough Bridge, and Manhattan's Upper East Side. "It's like being on the front of a boat in the middle of the river," says John Mullaly, a visitor from Long Island City, Queens. "You're always going to get a nice breeze." The fifty-foot Gothic lighthouse sits on the northern point. Designed by James Renwick Jr. in 1872, it replaced a fort constructed in the previous decade by a patient in the lunatic asylum who feared a British invasion. According to an 1866 *Harper's New Monthly Magazine* article, officials let the patient—who styled himself "Thomas Maxey, Esq., architect, mason, carpenter, civil engineer, philosopher, and philanthropist"—build the four-foot-high clay and grass garrison with a house inside the parapet because, in the adrenaline rush of his work, Maxey also cleared acres of marsh, making the land useful. Officials even gave Maxey some old Civil War cannon, which he stuck through the walls of his fort.

Similarly, a patient named John McCarthy is said to have helped build Renwick's lighthouse. A plaque supposedly carved by the patient and affixed to the lighthouse proclaimed: "This is the work done by John McCarthy, who built the lighthouse from the bottom to the top; all ye who pass by may pray for his soul when he dies." It mysteriously disappeared in the 1960s.

On your way back to the tram or subway, you may want to relax at the observation pier or meditation steps along the esplanade and contemplate Manhattan's skyline, including the UN, Chrysler, and Empire State Buildings. The Queens landscape, seen from the island's eastern edge, is far less appealing—the focal point is the monstrous Con Edison generating plant known as Big Allis.

Two other landmarks, the ruins of the **Smallpox Hospital** and **Strecker Laboratory,** stand within a fenced area at the island's southern end. At night, the castlelike hospital is bathed in floodlights. RIOC hopes to allow access when the ruins are stabilized as part of the Southpoint development.

Tours of the island are offered by various groups, including **Historic New York Tours,** (718) 729-4055; **Adventures on a Shoe String,** (212) 265-2663; **Big Onion Walking Tours,** (212) 439-1090; and **New York City Cultural Walking Tours,** (212) 979-2388.

Where to Eat

Roosevelt Island is not a culinary paradise. "We have five restaurants that add up to one star," quips resident Judy Berdy. And the word *restaurant* is used loosely on Roosevelt Island. For a bite to eat, try **Trellis Diner,** 549 Main Street, (212) 752-1517, although picnicking or barbecuing in the parks is your best bet. There are public rest rooms at the tram station and at Octagon Park.

Island Hopping

By tram: More than a mode of transportation, this urban gondola is a tourist attraction in itself, affording dazzling views of Manhattan, the island, and the East River. After leaving the tramport at Second Avenue and Sixtieth Street, the Swiss-built machine, which accommodates 125 people and is the only commuter tram in the country, travels high above the city at about sixteen miles per hour. At its peak, it climbs 250 feet above the river. The ride from Manhattan to the island—a whopping thirty-one hundred feet—takes five minutes. The hostage scene in Sylvester Stallone's movie *Nighthawks* was filmed on the tram. A red Roosevelt Island bus meets the tram and takes passengers throughout the island. For information call RIOC, (212) 832-4540.

By subway: From Manhattan or Queens, take the Q or B trains to Roosevelt Island. The B train runs evenings and weekends.

By bus: The Q102 to the island can be caught at Queensboro Plaza.

By car: Take the Thirty-sixth Avenue Bridge from Queens, and park in the Motorgate garage on the right as you enter the island. Private vehicles are restricted. If you want to save money, park on the Queens side of the bridge and walk over.

12. Randall's and Ward's Islands

"I never visit these islands without a sentiment of admiration, excited by the beauty of their position and adaptedness to the purposes to which they have been appropriated."

—Robert Kelly, president of the Society for the Reformation of Juvenile Delinquents, which ran the House of Refuge in 1869

Randall's and Ward's Islands

MOST NEW YORKERS ONLY experience Randall's and Ward's Islands peripherally, by train whooshing across the Hell Gate Bridge, or by car inching toward the toll plaza of the Triborough Bridge. Travelers are not drawn to explore what goes on beneath these massive spans, partly because the islands have been plagued by an incoherent identity created by the government's mix-and-match urban planning.

Arches and abutments dominate the landscape, casting long shadows and dividing this hodgepodge of recreational areas and government institutions into large chunks and narrow slices. Randall's Island has ball fields, tennis courts, soccer fields, and a driving range; but much of the space has long been occupied by a slew of city agencies: the parks department garage and maintenance area, Triborough Bridge and Tunnel Authority headquarters, training facilities for the fire and sanitation departments, the police harbor division, and a separate detectives unit.

Ward's Island is home to an equally incongruous combination: ball fields, a barbecue area, sewage disposal and sludge treatment plant, psychiatric hospital, and homeless shelter.

In addition to this unlikely commingling of elements, the islands maintain distinct names even though the Little Hell Gate waterway between them has been mostly filled in, creating a single island between East Harlem and Astoria ,Queens. Randall's Island is just south of Mott Haven and Port Morris and segues into Ward's Island at a point parallel to Manhattan's 115th Street; Ward's continues down to Ninety-ninth Street.

Today, this 486-acre mass is being plucked from obscurity thanks to the dream of one visionary woman. In 1992, frustrated by the city's unwillingness to spend on its parks and its children, Karen Cohen founded the Randall's Island Sports Foundation. By blending public and private funding while working with the parks department—which owns virtually all the land there—she hopes to recast the island as the center of the city's sports and entertainment scene.

"It's a win-win situation," she says. "We'll get money for the city and provide places for children to play—and it's beautiful. The city needs this so desperately."

Cohen, a former interior designer who has served on many philanthropic boards, spent years watching her own children play on the island. Each round of city budget cuts brought "more garbage and more condoms and more drugs," she says. Finally, this well-connected Upper East Sider was impelled to action, not only for her own kids (now grown), but also for those in neighborhoods like East Harlem just across the river, which lack proper recreational spaces. "This is their backyard," she says.

Raising money for the Randall's Island Sports Foundation initially aroused different reactions than, say, the Statue of Liberty–Ellis Island Foundation. Common responses to Cohen's early pleas for support were "You mean Rikers Island?" or "What are you talking about?" Despite the island's identity crisis, she persevered and made small improvements.

Much of the island is still dominated by entrenched institutions. In the years that followed, Cohen's initial plans underwent numerous changes, and she has stepped back from day-to-day responsibilities as the foundation's staff and board have come into their own. After nearly a decade, it seems as if the island will finally be reborn with a new image, a Herculean accomplishment even Robert Moses couldn't fully achieve in a twenty-year battle at the height of his power.

Before Moses became parks commissioner in 1934, these lush green islands had never been available to the public as a communal backyard. Between Dutch Governor Wouter Van Twiller's 1637 purchase of Minnahanonck (Randall's) and Tenkenas (Ward's) from Native Americans and the end of the American Revolution, several owners established homes on these islands, located near the village of Harlem but far removed from New York, which had not yet developed past Canal Street. Ward's was known as Great Barn Island, Randall's as Little Barn, Barn probably being a corruption of Barendt, a former Dutch owner's name. The most notable event of these early days occurred in 1696 when stones for the original Trinity Church were quarried on Little Barn and hauled by sloop to Lower Manhattan.

In 1772, Captain John Montresor bought Little Barn and settled in with his family. Prominent in the British military, Montresor secretly surveyed New York and the harbor islands before the Revolution and advised British army chief General William Howe on New York invasion sites. (Montresor also inadvertently helped make a hero of spy Nathan Hale. Montresor witnessed Hale's execution and recounted it to Hale's friend Captain William Hull, whose memoirs made famous Hale's last words, "I only regret that I have but one life to lose for my country.")

Early in the war, the colonists controlled New York, and General George Washington established a smallpox quarantine on Montresor's Island in the spring of 1776. In early September, after triumphing at the Battle of Brooklyn, the British, who viewed the islands as key strategic points, drove the Americans from Blackwell's, Montresor's, and Great Barn Islands. Great Barn became an army base, while an officers' hospital was established on Montresor's Island, with Montresor's wife, Frances, serving as matron.

The Americans, meanwhile, held positions in what is now the south Bronx, just across a narrow kill north of the island. Skirmishes broke out between American and British sentries. When a British officer was shot, the redcoats threatened to bomb the Yanks. Instead, the two sides agreed to a cease-fire and became so friendly that they traded tobacco and other goods. Hostilities recurred once, at dawn on September 22, when American General William Heath sent 240 men in three flatboats to attack Montresor's Island. The offensive failed when many soldiers refused to attack. Heath court-martialed the insubordinates.

Montresor later blamed the Americans for burning his house and barns in early 1777. Heath contended, however, that after the British witnessed Yankee troops faking preparations for a large-scale invasion, the British panicked and set fire to their countryman's island before fleeing. Montresor moved back to England the following year.

A farmer named Jonathan Randel bought the island in 1784 and tilled the soil there until he died in 1830. His heirs sold the island, along with Sunken Meadow, a sandy fifty-acre isle just to the east, to New York City in 1835. (Randall's current name derives from a spelling error by the city.)

Meanwhile, Jaspar and Bartholomew Ward bought Great Barn Island to the south. The brothers' efforts to develop a farming community there around 1807 failed, but they later operated a cotton mill on the island. The Wards, along with a man named Phillip Milledoer, also built the first bridge from Harlem to the island—wooden in some accounts, stone in others. Neighbors across the river hated it, claiming its pilings created dangerous obstructions and currents in the water. A storm destroyed the bridge in 1821.

After the city established a penitentiary on Blackwell's Island, government officials vigorously pursued the strategy of turning more of the city's islands into dumping grounds for social outcasts. In 1843, a new potter's field opened on Randall's Island. Some one hundred thousand bodies were also exhumed from a Manhattan potter's field and reburied on Ward's Island. Then in 1845, an almshouse opened on Randall's, followed by a children's hospital three years later. The State Emigrant Refuge, for "sick and destitute aliens," opened on Ward's in 1847, after officials rejected Ellis Island as a site. The busy facility also supplemented the often overwhelmed Castle Garden immigration station from 1860 until Ellis Island opened in 1892.

In 1854, the House of Refuge, run by the Society for the Reformation of Juvenile Delinquents, became Randall's most prominent resident after outgrowing its East Twenty-third Street site. Randall's was also eventually burdened with the Idiot Asylum, while Ward's subsequently accommodated a homeopathic hospital, the Inebriate Asylum, a rest home for Civil War veterans, and the city's insane asylum.

Much of the architecture, especially at the House of Refuge and the insane asylum, was impressive in a forbidding way. In 1880, the *New York Times* described the asylum as "one of the ornaments of the City. It looms up like a mountain. It is built of brick, with stone trimmings, and has a great many wings all highly ornamented."

But inside, these intimidating institutions were impersonal at best, tyrannical at worst. Discipline at the House of Refuge was extremely strict. "The boys have a cowed way about them that is anything but pleasant," wrote the *Times*. Criminals were housed separately from street urchins. Both groups consisted mainly of teenage Irish boys (and a few girls) with little schooling. The average number of children there through the end of the century was between five and six hundred, although in the 1860s and 1870s, nearly a thousand were often crammed in.

Children spent four hours a day in religious and secular instruction and six and a half hours in industrial employment, caning chairs and making shoes for outside contractors. After their stay, some were released to family or friends, but most girls were indentured as housekeepers and most boys as farmers. (This practice gradually died out after the immigration flood of the 1880s supplied even cheaper labor.)

While society officials nobly proclaimed this ascetic lifestyle the path to salvation, they were oblivious to the reality at the refuge, where a pitiless sweatshop existence was inflicted by taskmasters who savagely beat children for failing to keep up, and hung them by the thumbs for misbehaving.

There were periodic state investigations, and longtime superintendent Israel Jones was accused in an 1872 state report of being "a man wholly unfit and unworthy of the position and whose administration is characterized by brutality and neglect." Yet nothing was done until 1887, when businesses forced the state to prohibit their competition from using refuge inmates for cheap labor. Work was replaced by military drills; beatings

lessened and overall conditions improved slightly. But investigations at
the turn of the twentieth century still revealed underfed, poorly clothed
boys who were often mistreated by drunken officers. Boys were subjected
to such discipline as weeks of standing handcuffed to a cell for up to nineteen hours a day. Not surprisingly, the refuge was beset by armed revolts
and arson throughout its existence.

Treatment was not much better elsewhere on the islands. An 1887 state
investigation declared that the insane asylum "should be condemned as
uninhabitable." It was operating at twice its thousand-person capacity, its
patients huddled together in filthy wards. The dismal conditions attracted
only the least qualified attendants, exacerbating the situation. In 1896, the
city turned the asylum over to the state, which simply continued the warehousing policy. By 1899, the Manhattan State Hospital had become the
world's largest mental institution, with 4,393 patients; the state continued
piling more people in until the population peaked at 7,000 in 1926.

In 1934, Robert Moses took over the parks department and the Triborough
Bridge Authority (now the Triborough Bridge and Tunnel Authority). For
Moses, Randall's and Ward's Islands were vital to a long-unrealized plan
linking Manhattan, the Bronx, and Queens by bridge, which would provide
city dwellers access to Moses' new system of parkways on Long Island.

To this project Moses added a sports complex featuring a stadium, ball
fields, and parks for Randall's and Ward's Islands. (The parks department
had been contemplating the concept since 1916.) However, the islands
were still monopolized by various government institutions. To achieve his
goals, Moses had a bill rammed through the state legislature forcing the
institutions out within a decade. The House of Refuge and most of the others were demolished by 1937. In some cases, patients were forced to transfer to overcrowded institutions.

As head of the Bridge Authority, Moses also snagged federal funding for
his parks department project by claiming that the new recreational facilities would attract toll-paying drivers across the new bridge and to the
islands, which had previously been accessible only by ferry.

By 1936, the Triborough Bridge—seventeen-plus miles of four con-
nected bridges supported by Randall's and Ward's Islands—was complete.
An engineering marvel, the twenty-five-cent toll bridge, designed by O. H.
Ammann and Aymar Embury, opened to gushing admiration on July 11.
Within six weeks, drivers taking the bridge from the city and Westchester
were causing the worst traffic jams in Long Island history. (To relieve the

crush of cars, Moses, who disdained mass transit, later built the Long Island Expressway.) The Triborough Bridge carried eleven million vehicles over the islands in 1941. That total more than doubled by 1949 and again by 1960; in 1999, 61.9 million drove across the bridge.

Although unable to fund his envisioned seventy-thousand-seat arena, Moses did build the twenty-one-thousand-seat Municipal Stadium, which opened the same day as the Triborough Bridge. (The stadium was renamed in 1955 in memory of John Downing, a former recreation director who worked forty-one years for the parks department.)

Over the next three decades, Moses had the land between Randall's, Ward's, and Sunken Meadow filled in, allowing him to build dozens of ball fields and tennis courts. Moses also built a footbridge connecting Ward's Island to 103rd Street in East Harlem. While it had been planned since 1938, Moses didn't follow through until 1949 when he helped Mayor William O'Dwyer defeat Newbold Morris, who was championing new parks for the poor neighborhoods of Harlem. Moses, uninterested in creating parks for the poor, defused the issue by announcing that he would link the community to Ward's Island. The bridge opened in 1951.

Moses' vast sports complex, however, was never fully completed, because the island was never entirely his domain. In 1937, a sewage treatment plant opened on the one section of Ward's Island not owned by the parks department. More significantly, the Manhattan State Hospital refused to leave. Although its buildings were decrepit and conditions depressingly reminiscent of 1887, the state law mandating its shutdown by 1943 was ignored due to overcrowding elsewhere. Moses continued his battle, but in 1954 voters approved a $350 million bond issue to build new mental health facilities on the island.

The vote of confidence and three new buildings didn't end the hospital's troubles, however. In the late 1960s and early 1970s, after decentralization had split the institution into three distinct hospitals, fear invaded the complex. Patients and staffers were robbed and raped on several occasions, usually by outsiders who had slipped past lax security. In 1974, the *Times* reported that sixty-three retarded patients transferred from Staten Island's notorious Willowbrook mental hospital sat idly in empty rooms while expensive equipment—designed to teach them balance, dexterity, and other skills—stood unused nearby due to understaffing and mismanagement. Three years later, Congressman Ed Koch, a mayoral candidate, slammed the hospital's unsanitary conditions, poor record keeping, and careless dispensing of drugs.

Historical Detour: Training for the Devil

There is one place in New York where starting fires is legal, and, in fact, essential: the Fire Department Training Academy on Randall's Island. (The academy moved to Randall's from Roosevelt Island in 1975.)

Although Deputy Chief George Bauer says "There's nothing like going into a long hallway with the devil dancing all around you," the academy's rigorous twelve-week program skillfully re-creates the challenges of fire fighting. Each year, about five hundred "probies" (probationary firefighters) rappel down buildings, grope blindly through a maze in a race against time, and, of course, face the flames.

The academy's stodgy brick buildings and junkyard autos have all the ambience of an abandoned factory town. This is where probies learn to work the hoses as a team and rescue mannequins from subways, overturned cars, and smoke-filled apartments. In the burn building, where everything is steel—even the kitchen sink—computers control the duration and intensity of propane blazes that can reach twelve hundred degrees.

The academy is often visited by movie and video directors who use the props or set up their own buildings to burn under the firefighters' watchful eyes. Within this controlled environment are reminders of fire's real dangers; the street names, such as Kehayas Court, are named for firefighters who died in a 1966 conflagration.

Yet Mayor Koch continued using the islands to isolate outcasts. In 1979, the city opened what it referred to as a temporary emergency shelter on Ward's Island for two hundred homeless men. But *temporary* is a relative term in politics, and today the Charles Gay Homeless Shelter remains in operation, despite a long history of protests. The East Harlem community felt the shelter was too near the pedestrian bridge linking the island to their neighborhood, while the mental hospital sued to keep these unmonitored newcomers from settling down virtually next door to their children's complex. Newspapers like the *Daily News* editorialized that while group homes were politically unpopular, they were a good alternative to these large, impersonal shelters. Hoping to produce a more compassionate refuge, the city later turned shelter operations over to the Volunteers of America (VOA), making it the city's first privately run shelter. By 1981, the shelter had five hundred male residents, many of whom essentially made it their permanent home.

More than 950 men live there today, and the homeless consider it a well-run shelter, clean and generally safe, with a wide array of services. In the early 1990s, the shelter had been a continual source of controversy—the adjacent hospital accused the residents of stealing, trespassing, and exposing themselves to children, while East Harlem saw its Ward's Island bridge deteriorate into a menacing lair for crack dealers and addicts. But the atmosphere around the shelter has improved dramatically, thanks largely to the Randall's Island Sports Foundation and the parks department. When an army-run, inner-city youth program needed a project, kids were put to work clearing overgrowth that was choking century-old trees and providing cover for illicit activities. The foundation and parks department also cleared overgrowth near the footbridge to East Harlem (the bridge is now raised in winter to reduce unsavory traffic) and pressured the VOA into installing guards and fences at the shelter's border. Since the mid-1990s, relations between the shelter and its neighbors have been "stable and steadily improving," says Amy Bodin, the city's administrator for the islands' parks and executive director of the Randall's Island Sports Foundation.

Even the hospital—reconsolidated in 1979 into the Manhattan Psychiatric Center—is better managed than the institutions of old. Today, it offers several innovative programs, including a patient-run pizzeria and an art program that has led to showcases of patients' art in a Soho gallery. More than half the patients work and all spend time learning community skills, says Deputy Director Joel Silbert. "We are a more active and functional rehabilitative hospital than ever before."

Yet as society has embraced deinstitutionalization, the hospital's population has shrunk dramatically from its high of seven thousand in 1926. Inexplicably, in an era when most patients would be better—and far less expensively—served in group homes or supervised residences, the state renovated the compound in 1988 at a cost of $120 million. By 1995, there were only 900 patients, and five years later, the total was down to 400, with future reductions down to 250 a possibility; virtually all the patients still there could function in group homes or supervised residences. Meanwhile,

Historical Detour: A View from the Cheap Seats

After six decades, Downing Stadium has finally gone the way of the Polo Grounds and Ebbets Field. It was demolished in spring 2001. And while this old arena—which hosted everything from semipro soccer leagues to jazz concerts featuring Duke Ellington and Dizzy Gillespie—lacked the lustrous history of the old ballparks, there are memorable moments (some wonderful, some bizarre) worth preserving.

When the twenty-one-thousand-seat stadium opened with Olympic tryouts on July 11, 1936, the occasion was overshadowed by the Triborough Bridge dedication and undermined by a malfunctioning public address system that created chaos among athletes. No one knew when to report for events, and spectators often couldn't tell who was competing.

In the sweltering heat, only a "pitifully small crowd of 8,000" attended what the *Daily News* called "the most poorly conducted major meet in the history of American track." But they got to see Ohio State star Jesse Owens earn two Olympic slots, with victories in the hundred-meter dash and broad jump. The next day, he won the two-hundred-meter dash in twenty-one seconds, a new world record. Owens later won four Olympic gold medals in Berlin.

In 1944, at the Outdoor Track and Field Championships, six runners lined up for the finals of the hundred-meter dash, but nobody reached the finish line. Race official Jack Lavelle disqualified the six sprinters on false starts and recalls, then declared, "There will be no hundred-meter champion this year." Meet directors protested, but Lavelle, a popular local sports figure, would only stage the new race as an exhibition. Officials, however, later added the winner, Buddy Young, into the record books.

But Downing Stadium wasn't only about sports, it was about music, too—from opera and jazz to the disastrous New York Pop Festival held the weekend of July 19, 1970. When they weren't paid up front, Delaney and Bonnie, Ravi Shankar, and a band combining Miles Davis and Eric Clapton all canceled. When Joe Cocker pulled out, Sly and the Family Stone were hired, but they already had a gig in Minnesota, and so they didn't show up either.

This Woodstock wannabe (minus camping) was further sabotaged when an assemblage of mostly white radical groups tried using the concert for their own purposes. They demanded that concert producers provide bail money for political prisoners and microphone access for speeches, while staging local bands of their choosing. When the producers and radicals reached a compromise, the Young Lords (the Puerto Rican equivalent of the Black Panthers) stepped in with their own wish list. Since this was East Harlem's local park, they said, some of the profit should go toward community TB testing and free breakfasts for kids.

The concert's opening night was delayed two hours when white radicals instigated gate crashing and manhandled concertgoers under the guise of crowd control. *Rolling Stone* reported that "the mood of the audience was strange—like a strangled scream." Nonetheless, Grand Funk Railroad, Steppenwolf, and Jimi Hendrix—in one of his last American appearances—all performed.

The atmosphere worsened Saturday afternoon when the white radicals tore open fences and admitted people for less than the price of a ticket, pocketing the donations themselves. The overflow crowd of fifty thousand restlessly awaited big-name acts that never materialized; without ticket revenue the producers had no money, so all the scheduled bands except Ten Years After backed out. Radio disc jockey and emcee Dave Herman was sent out to calm the audience. "It was a very, very rowdy place," Herman remembers. "There was a sense of tension, that we were on the verge of disaster. This crowd was not a peace and love crowd. There were moments when I was wondering how I was going to get out of there."

After losing $300,000, the producers admitted defeat and invited everyone in free on Sunday to see Mountain and Dr. John. It would be nearly a quarter of a century before rock festivals—in the form of Lollapalooza, the traveling alternative-music tour featuring acts like Sonic Youth and Hole—returned to Downing Stadium.

June 16, 1975, this time for a soccer game. The New York Cosmos, featuring international star Pelé in his first home game, also attracted three hundred reporters and television crews from twenty nations. By 1977, the stadium's limited capacity and unbearable Triborough tie-ups on game days forced the Cosmos to move to the Meadowlands in New Jersey.

After a twenty-five-year hiatus, the Outdoor Track and Field Championships returned to Downing Stadium on June 13, 1991. Only a few hundred spectators—along with several large rats—were in the stands that day to see athletes competing on poorly prepared surfaces.

Attendance improved during the week, however, and the crowds were treated to several compelling dramas: Emerging star Dan O'Brien bested Dave Johnson in the decathlon, finishing with 8,844 points, 3 shy of the world record. In another tight contest, Carl Lewis barely preserved his ten-year, sixty-five-match winning streak in the long jump. On his sixth and final jump of this competition, Lewis leaped twenty-eight feet, four and a quarter inches, beating Mike Powell by a half inch. But Lewis could not keep pace with Leroy Burrell in the hundred-meter dash, finishing second as Burrell broke Lewis's world record with a 9.90-second run. Lewis reclaimed the record two months later, blazing to a 9.86 on the island of Japan.

funding and staffing have also declined, and several buildings are completely closed, as are many floors within operating buildings.

When the Randall's Island Sports Foundation arrived in 1992, Randall's and Ward's Islands supported nearly as many governmental agencies as there had been institutions a century earlier. But there have been inroads in recent years. The foundation has recovered seven acres from the fire department, and both the sanitation department and police detectives unit are leaving. The foundation is also negotiating with the psychiatric hospital and homeless shelter and simultaneously lobbying in Albany, says Board Chairman Rich Davis, hoping to acquire at least some of the institutions' land even before their leases expire in 2012. Bodin says the foundation must "insinuate itself" in the process to stop the hospital from letting unused buildings deteriorate and to avoid a "land grab" by other state agencies.

While shabby treatment of the island caused the use of the parks and stadium to decline, some urbanites never abandoned the site. Corporate softball and youth baseball leagues play there regularly, and Harlem and Bronx residents come to fish and barbecue. Some Bronx residents arrive via stepping-stones in the Bronx Kill at low tide; others cross an informal cement bridge under the Hell Gate train trestle. There have also been some small strides, independent of the foundation, toward maximizing the island's potential. In 1991, a year before the foundation started, the city brought out new faces by licensing a batting and golf range on Randall's Island to a private concessionaire, who also operates express mini-buses from a few Manhattan locations. In the mid-1990s, major events—including the Gay Games, the alternative-rock tour Lollapalooza, and the Irish-inspired Fleadh Festival—returned to Randall's Island for the first time in a generation. (See *Historical Detour: A View from the Cheap Seats.*)

The foundation, however, continues to be the driving force behind the island's rejuvenation, seeking improvements large and small. When Con Edison wanted to run a cable beneath Randall's Island, the company was required to refurbish two soccer fields. And finally, with the dawning of a new century, the foundation seems ready to capture the public's attention. Moses' uncomfortable and unappealing Downing Stadium was demolished early in 2001, and on a nearby site, a new $35 million, 19,500-seat amphitheater with water views is being built. (It's expected to open on Memorial Day 2002 with a Rolling Stones concert.) Another new attraction, a $10 million, Olympic-quality track-and-field center, is expected to open in 2002. The foundation is also separating soccer fields from bat-and-ball fields, so soccer players will no longer run through the Little League's outfield. The new "Sports Lawn" on Randall's Island will have fields for baseball, softball, cricket, and Kabbadi (an Indian sport), while Ward's Island will have more soccer fields. The tennis courts, known for horrific parking and facilities, will get a new home. On a smaller scale, shoreline and wetlands are being restored, while a waterfront walking path and boardwalk across from the Hell Gate Inlet are being built.

"By 2002, you will see a major, major difference," Cohen says, encouraging even more investment. "That should make the rest of this fly."

Next up, possibly as early as 2003, will be a family-themed water park. "It will be like Great Adventure on a kiddie scale," says Bodin, adding that it will be themed and marketed specifically to be "uncool" so that teenage boys will not descend upon it in hordes. The park will occupy fifteen acres and require an investment of more than $50 million.

Davis also expects to undo part of Moses' legacy—poor access, especially for those without cars. The Triborough Bridge is undergoing a multi-billion-dollar overhaul, part of which includes building additional ramps onto the islands, but the foundation is also hoping to persuade the car-oriented Triborough Bridge and Tunnel Authority to improve bike and pedestrian access. There will also be ferry service and increased bus service from Manhattan and Queens—and perhaps, Davis says, more footbridges in the long term.

"It took much, much longer than I expected," Cohen notes, adding that she still has ambitious dreams, such as converting the empty Washburn Wire Center across the water in Harlem into an indoor sports center and then building a bridge connecting it to the island. "People are just now catching on to the need for recreation spaces in New York. It's going to be a great future."

Exploring the Island

For information about the ball fields, amphitheater, track center, and other public amenities related to the **Randall's Island Sports Foundation,** call (212) 830-7719. For the tennis courts, however, call (212) 534-4845. (During summer, a city parks permit or day pass is required. In winter, indoor courts can be reserved for a fee.) The island also features the **Randall's Island Family Golf Center,** (212) 427-5689, which has a driving range, batting range, and miniature golf.

If you're interested in bridge architecture, you'll want to roam beneath the imposing towers and arches of the **Triborough** and **Hell Gate Bridges**—Robert Moses liked boasting that the Triborough tower on Ward's was taller than the pyramids. Photographers will be captivated by the juxtaposition of city infrastructure, institutions, parkland, and waterways. For family outings, Ward's Island has barbecue pits, but the area is often unpleasantly crowded on summer weekends.

Island Hopping

🚌 ***By bus:*** From the East Side, take the M35 from 125th Street and Lexington Avenue. From the West Side, take the M60 from 116th Street and Broadway to the foot of the Triborough Bridge. Change to the M35 or walk over. You can also reach the M35 by subway. From the West Side, take the A, B, C, D, 2, or 3 to 125th Street for the bus. From the East Side, take the 4, 5, or 6 to 125th Street to the bus. **Randall's Island Golf,** (212) 427-5689, offers limited shuttle bus service from the Upper East Side.

👢 ***By foot:*** From Manhattan, walk across either the Triborough Bridge or the Ward's Island footbridge at 103rd Street and the East River. You can also walk across the Triborough Bridge from Queens or the Bronx.

🚗 ***By car:*** From Manhattan, drive north on FDR Drive, south on the Harlem River Drive, or east on 125th Street to the Triborough Bridge. From the Bronx, drive south on either the Bruckner Expressway or the Major Deegan Expressway. From Queens, take the Brooklyn-Queens Expressway or the Grand Central Parkway.

13. Rikers Island

"Those who are laying this cornerstone today do so with mingled feelings of humility and hope; humility because of the realization of the multitude of threads of heredity, environment, education, association, and mental and physical and emotional equipment which go to form the fabric of the offender; and hope that the treatment which these unfortunates will receive in this institution will be the means of salvaging some lives which would otherwise have been wasted."

—Excerpt of text sealed into the cornerstone of the new
Rikers Island Penitentiary, dedicated July 28, 1931

Rikers Island

WHEN IT OPENED WITH much hoopla and hope in 1935, Rikers Island Penitentiary promised a dramatic break from the medieval cellblocks of the Blackwell's Island Penitentiary, where inmates idled the days away in cramped quarters. The city's new $10 million Rikers facility would provide modern accommodations and the latest in rehabilitative services, enabling prisoners to leave as "better citizens, with clear eyes, hard muscles and better mental and moral health as well," Commissioner of Correction Richard C. Patterson Jr. predicted in 1928.

Instead, Rikers Island evolved into a notoriously overcrowded and explosive community filled with young, hot-tempered inmates, including an increasing number of gang members who feast on one another like vultures. Approximately thirteen thousand inmates are crammed into the world's largest lockup, a hodgepodge of ten hastily built jails scattered over a 415-acre complex. It is only in recent years that correction officers have begun to regain full control of the jail and that the government has begun exploring ways to revamp Rikers' infrastructure and replace outmoded jails.

Rikers Island—off the shore of Astoria, Queens, where the East River veers east toward Long Island Sound—was sold by Native Americans in 1664 to William Hallett, sheriff of Flushing. When Peter Stuyvesant, the surly Dutch governor of New Netherland, learned of Hallett's unsanctioned purchase, he sought revenge. In his final official act before surrendering the colony to England, Stuyvesant fired Hallett and gave the island to Abraham Rycken, a respected farmer, whose family later changed its name to Riker. The grant was reconfirmed by English governor Richard Nicolls. In the eighteenth century, the family built at least one house on the island, where they lived into the nineteenth century.

New York's department of public charities and correction bought the island in 1884 for $180,000. (It is unclear whether the island still belonged to Riker descendants at the time.) While many New Yorkers believe that Rikers Island is in Queens—indeed, the jail has a Queens address and is linked to Queens by bridge—it is actually part of the

Bronx. When New York City purchased Rikers, it was in Newtown, Queens, and was annexed to the city's 23rd Ward. After the city was consolidated, the ward and Rikers eventually landed in the Bronx.

The city planned a new prison on Rikers Island to replace the crumbling, overcrowded penitentiary built in 1832 on Blackwell's Island (now Roosevelt Island). The transfer also promised to improve the lives of the poor and the mentally and terminally ill living in Blackwell's myriad institutions in the shadow of the penitentiary. "It has long been a reproach to this city that the sick and unfortunate who are the legitimate objects of charity are sent to Blackwell's Island, which is generally associated in the public's mind with a penal institution," said Mayor Thomas Gilroy in 1893.

Despite the rhetoric, it took decades before the Rikers Island Penitentiary was built. In the meantime, the island became the municipal farm, an adjunct of the main penitentiary, where prisoners were sent to work on vegetable and pig farms. Rikers also became a municipal landfill, allowing New York to end the ocean dumping that had caused refuse to wash up on Coney Island and the New Jersey coast. The landfill also provided the material needed to transform Rikers Island into a larger, more valuable piece of real estate.

While only forty-three of the island's original eighty-seven acres were above the high-water mark, there were seventy-nine acres of shoal ground west of the island and 315 shallow acres to the east. Using prison labor, the city planned to fill the sandbars with city refuse and dirt from the excavation of the Lexington Avenue subway.

Although several prominent physicians advocated incinerating the garbage, Health Commissioner Joseph D. Bryant assured residents that its use would not endanger public health, explaining that once the refuse reached the low-water mark, it would be covered with ashes or fresh earth or otherwise disinfected and sanitized. In 1893, the city began dumping on Rikers a mishmash of trash including street sweepings, horse manure, ashes, rubbish (inorganic material), and garbage (organic material). The dump's untenable odors soon wafted over to northern Queens and the South Bronx, inciting impassioned protests from residents.

Then, in 1895, Colonel George E. Waring Jr. was appointed street cleaning commissioner. Waring became known as the Apostle of Cleanliness for successfully implementing reforms such as recycling and waste utilization. In 1896, the city contracted with the New York Sanitary Utilization Company, a reduction plant on Barren Island that transformed garbage into fertilizer and soap, and until 1919, the Rikers Island landfill received less objectionable debris—primarily ashes and street sweepings that didn't rot and cause odors.

After the Barren Island plant closed and the recycling market collapsed in the 1920s, every kind of refuse was again dumped on Rikers Island, where it often smoldered for years under a blanket of ashes. "From the shores of Queens and the Bronx any day the smoking island looks like a volcano preparing for eruption," the *Times* reported in 1926. By this time, more than 450 prisoners worked there, some of them housed in the island's flimsy, wooden dormitories.

A year later, the state commission of correction advised the city that Rikers Island—its trash mounds swarming with flies and thousands of giant rats—was not an ideal place for a new prison. In 1930, the department of sanitation imported wild dogs to assist rifle-toting workers in their attempts to pare the rat population, but when two hundred dogs "did not find the rats all that they were recommended to be in the way of sport," they killed several pigs from the municipal farm's piggery, the *New York World* reported. This led to a bitter feud between the department of corrections, which wanted the dogs removed, and sanitation workers, who wouldn't go near the dump without canine protection. Several renegade dogs were killed, and the city turned to poison gas to combat the rats.

When the new jail finally opened in 1935, the state commission of correction implored the city to end dumping on Rikers. But it took a combination of citizen complaints, the 1939 New York World's Fair, and Robert Moses to finish off the Rikers Island landfill operation.

Parks Commissioner Moses was charged with helping to ensure that the world's fair in nearby Flushing was a hit. Realizing he couldn't close the dump immediately, Moses—along with Sanitation Commissioner William Carey—screened the island with a small forest so the mounds of refuse, some one hundred feet tall, wouldn't be visible from the fair. By 1940, the island's fifty-acre nursery contained seven thousand trees, used to supply city parks with foliage.

In the meantime, Moses battled with Carey over dumping on Rikers Island. Moses favored incineration and recycling, declaring that dumping was a policy "so stupid, costly and barbaric that neither my friend, Carey, nor any other public official can survive it." Carey argued that landfill created new land without offense to anyone. He also said families shouldn't have to recycle because it was inconvenient. In 1939, a compromise plan transferred dumping operations for several years from Rikers to the east

Bronx to create a park in the neighborhood of Soundview. Tons of Rikers ash were also used as fill for what is now La Guardia Airport. In 1948, the city began dumping garbage in Staten Island's Fresh Kills landfill.

While garbage was piling up on Rikers' southern side, the northern end, or original island, was being readied for the new prison, which had problems even before it opened. In 1934, with the facility 95 percent complete, the city's commissioner of accounts suspended payments to the architect and contractors until leaky walls and roofs and other inferior construction were corrected. The commissioner further alleged that public funds had been squandered by Tammany Hall Democrats during the jail's construction. (Mayor Jimmy Walker served from 1926 to 1932 before resigning under a cloud of corruption charges.)

Inmates from the penitentiary and workhouse on Welfare Island were transferred "up the river" to Rikers in 1935. Unlike the fortress-style prison on Welfare Island, Rikers Island Penitentiary had no outer walls, only a wire fence with guard towers. Additional security was provided by the turbulent waters surrounding the island, which hindered escape attempts. Considered innovative for its time, the prison included eight cellblocks, an auditorium, and exercise space. The prison also boasted employment, education, medical and psychological services, and individualized treatment for its inmates. Not only would offenders—males arrested in the city and serving no more than three years—be incarcerated at the Rikers Island Penitentiary, city officials promised they would be reformed. The prison ran a sixty-acre farm and a piggery that in the early 1940s produced 110,000 pounds of pork annually, feeding residents in many city institutions. And in 1940, Rikers' seven-story, three-hundred-bed hospital became the nation's first prison hospital approved for internship training by the American Medical Association, which praised the hospital's dedication to restoring the health of sick inmates and preparing them for society.

"Such operations as the correction of crossed eyes, the removal of unsightly abnormalities, the correction of badly shaped noses and the elimination of scars are performed with the idea that the individual may be thus released from an embarrassment that might contribute to his anti-social behavior," reported the *Times*.

The prison's accommodations for twenty-two hundred inmates, however, quickly became overcrowded; the population climbed from seventeen hundred in 1936 to twenty-five hundred by 1941. To house the extra inmates, shop buildings were used as dorms. And while inmate population throughout the city system decreased significantly during World War II, between 1945 and 1954 the total number of prisoners at Rikers nearly doubled. By 1954, the island's population had swelled to 3,287, leaving each inmate fewer opportunities for work, recreation, education, and psychological attention.

Rather than build new prisons or confront the social issues causing the increase, the government relied on Band-Aid solutions to this chronic problem. Rikers handled overflow with makeshift cells and by doubling up prisoners; the city also shipped prisoners to the workhouse on Hart Island. A former inmate, who used the fictitious name Stanley Conrad in a 1953 *New York Post* article, called Rikers a "penitentiary laboring under a 1933 system . . . For modern operation, it still has 20 years to catch up."

In the 1960s, the city finally committed to expanding the prison system. New York hoped to save money and improve efficiency by centralizing its facilities on Rikers Island, which still had several hundred acres of isolated land available. This strategy shifted most of the city's detention jails to Rikers; about two-thirds of Rikers' inmates today are detainees.

The first new jail built on Rikers Island after 1935 was the Correctional Institution for Men, which opened in 1964 and was expanded in 1973. Three additional jails were built between 1971 and 1978. In 1966, the island's snail-like and expensive ferry service was replaced by a three-lane automobile bridge linking Rikers to Astoria, Queens. Mayor John Lindsay dubbed it the Bridge of Hope, although by then idealism about the prison system was starting to sound perilously naive.

The late 1960s and early 1970s—a volatile time in American cities—signaled another turning point for Rikers Island. Like other jails, it was plagued by racial violence, overcrowding, and inmate suicides. In 1969, black inmates were attacked after moving into an area of the correctional institution controlled by whites, who made up about 35 percent of its population. (The percentage of white inmates has declined steadily since 1930, when the system was about 85 percent white, in part due to the city's changing racial makeup.) Four months later, more than forty adolescent inmates and five corrections officers were injured during another jail brawl. That year, 152 inmates attempted suicide in city jails.

By 1970, approximately fourteen thousand inmates were housed in a citywide system built to accommodate eight thousand. On March 14, 1970, fifteen hundred Rikers inmates staged a hunger strike and work stoppage protesting a 1967 state law reducing the amount of jail time that could be shaved from a sentence for good behavior. The inmates said the law contributed to overcrowding. A few days later, convicts clashed with officers during a violent mess-hall melee, and in May, corrections officers protested conditions by picketing the city's jails.

"Once again . . . overcrowding is the single greatest crisis in the city prison system," stated the department of corrections in its 1971 annual report. "To ignore this warning is to jeopardize the lives of correction officers, the possibility of intelligent prison administration, and the humane treatment of prisoners . . ."

This era of social unrest affected prisons around the nation. In 1971, some twelve hundred inmates at Attica Correctional Facility in upstate New York held thirty-seven guards and civilian employees hostage for several days while demanding better conditions. When negotiations failed, armed lawmen stormed the prison, leaving forty-one dead, including thirty-one inmates. At Rikers, the most hostile upheaval came in 1975, when sixteen hundred inmates in the House of Detention for Men (originally Rikers Island Penitentiary; now the maximum-security James A. Thomas Center) held five officers hostage for seventeen hours, threatening them with pipes torn from cellblock railings, toothbrush handles embedded with razors, and sharpened tiles ripped from bathroom walls. The inmates took over six cellblocks before a settlement was reached granting them amnesty and the promise of reduced overcrowding—a pledge the city found impossible to keep. By 1981, Rikers' six jails, with seventy-two hundred inmates, were again above capacity.

Throughout the 1980s, Rikers' environment remained turbulent. A city proposal for a state takeover failed. In 1981, Correction Commissioner Benjamin Ward installed security fences and posted armed officers around the island's three-mile periphery to thwart escapes. (Guns are not carried inside the prison for fear inmates will snatch them and turn them on officers. While Rikers Island was originally considered escape-proof, the bridge and a La Guardia Airport runway built within one hundred feet of the island slowed the current of surrounding waters that had served as a barrier.)

To avoid trouble, officers increasingly forged "gentlemen's agreements" with inmates, turning away while inmates engaged in drug use, sex, and violence against other inmates. As Phil Seelig, then president of the Correction Officers Benevolent Association, put it in 1981, "Everyone is conspiring to keep the lid on, and we're paying the price."

But the lid always seemed to pop off at Rikers. On August 7, 1990, Corrections Officer Steve Narby was assaulted in a stairwell in the Otis

Historical Detour: Parting Gifts

Rikers Island parting gifts, circa 1953: "When a prisoner is released from Rikers," an ex-convict using the alias Stanley Conrad told the *New York Post* in 1953, "he is given 50 cents and two baloney sandwiches on white or rye. And some clothes. If he was an inmate of the penitentiary, he gets a thin suit, and if it's subfreezing, a topcoat. If he's released from the workhouse, he gets a blue-grey denim shirt, striped cotton pants, and if necessary, a light cotton sweater. If he's a parole violator, he gets a pair of blue pants and a lumber jacket. The doors open wide for him and he's on his own."

Rikers Island parting gifts, circa 2000: Prisoners are given a Metrocard with $4.50 for three rides and are delivered by bus after midnight to Queens Plaza, where they are often greeted by prostitutes and drug dealers.

Bantum Correctional Center (OBCC), one of two new jails opened in the late 1980s. Six days later, officers blocked the bridge to Rikers to protest overcrowding. After traffic had been halted for thirty-five hours, OBCC inmates began rioting inside. A total of 120 inmates and twenty-one correction employees were injured. A city investigation concluded that the incident was mishandled by department of corrections brass and that corrections officers used unnecessary or excessive force against inmates during the disturbance. The investigation further determined that budget constraints had forced the department to make decisions compromising employee security. Four years later, fifteen inmates and seventeen officers were injured within a week in two serious disturbances at the James A. Thomas Center. Other trials and lawsuits in the early 1990s revealed brutal violence perpetrated against inmates by corrections officers, including the beating of shackled prisoners. Officers subsequently falsified reports.

Today, Rikers Island has ten jails and about thirteen thousand inmates who eke out an existence on this stifling island of bane. It's a curious community, with its own fire department, power plant, infirmary, public school, and annual budget of about $710 million. Each institution, or portion of one, serves a distinct clientele—sentenced inmates, detainees, those who are mentally ill or extremely violent, adolescents, or women. Ninety-three percent of the inmates are black or Hispanic. But many detainees have a common bond: They are poor and can't make bail, and so are incarcerated—sometimes for months—for crimes for which they have not yet been convicted. Often facing felony charges and an uncertain future, detainees are usually far more volatile than sentenced misdemeanants, who will be free in less than a year.

It costs $53,224 annually to house one Rikers inmate, more than twice the cost of residential drug rehabilitation. From 1984 (referred to by one inmate as "B.C." or "Before Crack") through 1994, inmate population increased by 300 percent, with a 500 percent increase in women prisoners to a total of about fifteen hundred. As the crack epidemic has receded and the crime rate plunged, the inmate population has dipped. But tremendous numbers of the inmates still have substance abuse problems, and AIDS remains a major health concern.

Both inmates and staff say escalating violence and gang activity within the jails reflect the lawlessness of the streets. Meanwhile, inmates add that officers dehumanize them, rarely acknowledging their names. "One officer said to us the other night, it's not about faces, it's not about names, it's about bodies," says Anthony, an inmate. Officers admit wearing impersonal demeanors like coats of armor, explaining that eye contact and friendly banter only open the floodgates to emotional involvement and inmate trickery.

Vicious scuffles are routine at Rikers, and the violence has become more organized. One-on-one confrontations still occur, but gangs—which often recruit within the jails—have developed hand signals and other silent forms of communication that allow them to perpetrate their violence en masse and without warning. Hispanic gangs like the Latin Kings and the Netas often vie for turf and privilege with black gangs like the Bloods and Crips. In 1995, a federal judge allowed New York to ban gang-identifying beads and bracelets that the city says contribute to violence.

"Running the jails from the inside is not new," says John Conley, a prison historian and professor at New York's Buffalo State College. "That's been true of prisons ever since we've built them. Now it's being run with a much more violent undertone to it."

Another problem is that inmate services such as drug treatment—which may represent the best chance to reduce recidivism and over-crowding—have been axed by the city. "The problem we're having as a society is that we really don't know what we want our prisons to do," explains Conley. "We built them in the nineteenth century . . . when everybody thought they had the answer to all the social ills of the society.

"But the reality of running a jail," he continues, "and the reality of the population you have, and the reality of the citizens refusing to pay the tax dollars to put on the programs and so on and so on, work against the institution's success—if you expect that institution to do any rehabilitation. What we do very effectively is warehouse people."

While life on the island is still harsh for inmates, in recent years the powder-keg atmosphere has been effectively tamped down, thanks to intensive new efforts by the city. In the mid-1990s, Norman Seabrook, president of the Correction Officers Union, warned that low morale, lack of training, and staffing cuts meant the city was on the verge of another Attica.

Since then, Seabrook says, the city has made major investments on Rikers Island, boosting the number of corrections officers from about eighty-two hundred to more than ten thousand, providing more training and adding a slew of new equipment and aggressive tactics that have resulted in a startling decline in violence on the island. From 1994 to 1999, stabbings and slashings among inmates plummeted by over 90 percent, from more than a thousand incidents to less than a hundred.

The department has also added a unit to monitor gangs and a SWAT team to deal with violent outbreaks. Officers are now given stun shields, pepper spray, mace, and the BOSS chair (a body orifice scanning system that uses magnetic sensors to find weapons stashed inside inmates' bodies). "They help us do our job and motivate us even more," Seabrook says. "We're not as reluctant to do certain things the way they're supposed to be done." Officers conduct far more searches than ever before, particularly at random hours, like 3 AM. "That used to be unheard of," Seabrook says.

As a result, inmates have fewer weapons and are deterred from violence or subdued more easily during cell and personal searches and during confrontations. Also, inmates are now handcuffed behind their back instead of in front, and those who slash other inmates have their hands clamped into "the mitts," foot-long protective tubes. Inmates charged with infractions like punching a guard or weapons possession are now arrested and charged with new crimes rather than merely being disciplined.

The new tools and methods have prompted complaints from inmates and their advocates who call the techniques repressive and say there is too much potential for abuse. Seabrook counters, "We patrol the toughest precinct in New York. We are often assaulted with urine and feces by inmates."

In addition to the new strategies implemented inside the prison, there are also plans to improve the island's facilities, taking a holistic approach. Indeed, one reason for Rikers' problems is that most construction through the years has been carried out only in response to an immediate need for jail space. The result is a jumble of huge, hastily built buildings with modular additions and temporary structures tacked on without regard for overall prison management. "These buildings are like mushrooms—they just pop up because a problem arises," says Paul Silver. In the 1990s, as managing principal of STV/Silver & Ziskind, Silver helped devise a preliminary forty-year master plan to rethink Rikers Island for the city.

Moreover, many of Rikers' jails were built before normative design— which reduces the stress of confinement by eschewing traditional symbols of incarceration like barred cells, sliding gates, and clanking doors—came into vogue. The buildings added later were only peripherally influenced by contemporary prison design, says Silver.

According to preliminary plans, one of the obsolete high-maintenance buildings likely to be replaced is the original penitentiary, built in 1935 and based on a nineteenth-century design. The current system is bogged down by a "complicated network of corridors and access passages," says Silver, who adds that any new plan should not cost more than maintaining the present system, since it will rearrange the inefficient complex layout and establish a cost-effective, more secure route linking the island's various facilities.

Silver believes the new jails will run more efficiently with less stress placed on officers and inmates, but they won't alleviate all the burdens of incarceration, which is the essence of life on Rikers Island. "The loss of freedom is such a profound thing," he says, "and it is such a fundamental loss that one cannot hope to ameliorate it simply with environmental tricks."

14. North and South Brother Islands

"It was one hell of an experience. We made up the laws and rules. It was a pathological zoo."

—FRANK LIMA, FORMER PATIENT AT NORTH BROTHER ISLAND'S RIVERSIDE HOSPITAL, A NARCOTICS REHABILITATION FACILITY FOR TEENAGERS FROM 1952 TO 1963

North and South Brother Islands

IT IS A TALE OF TWO SIBLINGS, islands with lives so drastically dissimilar that no one would ever guess they were related. One has remained small and silent, a wholly private entity. The other, larger island has lived an exceedingly public life defined by tragedy and failed schemes, an inspiration for writers and artists. It is only in recent years, with a flock of new residents, that North and South Brother Islands have finally achieved solidarity.

North Brother Island lies approximately two thousand feet east of the Port Morris section of the Bronx, and twenty-five hundred feet west of Rikers Island. Its twenty acres of overgrown vines and deciduous woods threaten to swallow the skeletons of more than a dozen abandoned buildings. South Brother Island, approximately seven acres of undeveloped brush, is about five hundred feet southeast of its big brother, and about twenty-five hundred feet north of Astoria, Queens. The waters here—where the East River makes a sharp turn before flowing into Long Island Sound—are not as treacherous as those of Hell Gate to the south, but are nevertheless powerful and dangerous.

The islands were claimed in 1614 by Captain Adriaen Block for the Dutch West India Company. Block christened the duo De Gesellen, which translates to "the companions." In 1695, the British government granted the two Brother Islands to a James Graham. Then officially part of Queens, the islands remained undeveloped for nearly two centuries, chiefly because of the surrounding currents. North Brother was sold in 1871 to the town of Morrisania (in the Bronx). South Brother remained part of Queens until 1964, and is the only major island in New York City never publicly owned.

Although many newspaper articles claim that nothing has ever been built on South Brother, in 1894 Colonel Jacob Ruppert, a beer magnate and owner of the New York Yankees during the Babe Ruth era, built a summer home there. He used the retreat until 1907; it burned down in 1909. The land remained untouched until 1944, when Ruppert's estate sold the property to John Gerosa, president of Metropolitan Roofing Supplies. Gerosa generously announced a plan to establish a summer resort for his employees there, but the cottages were never built.

Gerosa sold South Brother Island in 1958; during the 1960s, it was bought by Hampton Scows, a Long Island-based company. The island has since lain fallow for three and a half decades. Hampton Scows has no plans for it, although co-owner James Murphy "is willing to listen to anyone with prospects for it."

Despite this inactivity, the city felt compelled in 1964 to unite the two brother islands by moving the borough boundary to include South Brother in the Bronx. (The island is held in such low esteem that Bronx officials vehemently insist they sent it back to Queens in the 1980s; Queens officials dismiss this claim and deny any affiliation with South Brother.) North Brother probably welcomed the company, having recently been abandoned after eight tumultuous decades of use.

North Brother was utilized like many other city islands in the late nineteenth century—society's castaways were warehoused there in hospitals. But how North Brother joined this league of quarantine islands is shrouded in mystery.

The traditional story presented in most articles and books recalls an island unused except by the lighthouse keeper until 1880, when the local Sisters of Charity or Sisters of St. Stephen built a hospital there. In 1885, the city assumed control of the island, transferring Riverside Hospital there from Blackwell's Island to expand the existing clinic.

In describing the city's construction plans, the *New York Times* reported in 1881 that the lighthouse keeper and his family were the only residents. They cultivated a farm with laborers who resided in what was once the Westchester County pesthouse for smallpox.

But a 1913 city department of health history offers a more dramatic tale. It reports that until 1880 residents of small towns in Westchester, which then included the Bronx, would chase smallpox victims into the city, forcing New York to care for them on Blackwell's Island. New York finally forced the suburbs to build their own hospital—a small shack along the East River. When residents discovered that the one patient there was black, they burned the shack and forced the caretaker and patient into a boat. Set adrift, the duo found refuge in an unoccupied house on North Brother Island. (Who had built the house is unexplained.) Thus, a hospital was born.

The city took over the island in 1885, rushing to complete Riverside Hospital at the height of a typhus epidemic. The Sisters of Charity maintained a tent colony for suspected typhus patients there for six months before the facility was completed.

Whatever its genesis, Riverside Hospital opened on North Brother

Island in 1885 to care for victims of infectious diseases like typhus, cholera, yellow fever, and smallpox. Through the end of the century, Riverside also received immigrants with smallpox from the state quarantine at Hoffman and Swinburne Islands. After New York consolidated in 1898, Riverside was largely used for Bronx residents, except in emergencies.

The hospital complex included a two-story brick building for eighty patients, with plans for three additional frame structures, each with forty beds, for patient overflow during epidemics. It turned out much more was needed. Massive immigration and rapid industrial and urban development provided fertile breeding ground for infectious diseases. The city's public hospitals were flooded with cases. In 1886, five wooden pavilions were added to ease overcrowding at Riverside. Then, in 1892, two structures were built specifically for smallpox patients. A typhus plague a year later forced the hospital to import three portable houses.

By the turn of the twentieth century, the city was awash with another grave peril: tuberculosis. The highly infectious lung disease killed thousands of New Yorkers—more than one in ten deaths were attributed to TB. In 1903, several vacant pavilions were used to forcibly detain infected patients whose willful carelessness posed a danger to their community. When those forty-eight beds quickly filled up, a renewed building frenzy began. During the next decade, the city enlarged North Brother Island with four acres of landfill and constructed many buildings, including four concrete pavilions for 320 new TB patients. While the wealthy sought treatment in sanatoriums, derelicts and the indigent were sent to North Brother's Riverside Hospital. Their care was an extension of government efforts to use science to resolve issues dealing with the poor and immigrants, says Dr. Barron Lerner, historian of medicine at Columbia University. "This solved both a medical and a social problem."

But a more urgent crisis was still to come. Before 1916, poliomyelitis was a relatively rare disease: From 1912 through June 1916, it had killed only 171 New Yorkers. But from July 1 through September 9, 1916, polio fatalities averaged 209 per week. The disease was especially grim because 90 percent of its victims were under the age of ten. The city transformed contagious disease hospitals into polio centers. (The Swinburne Island quarantine served Staten Island.) Riverside Hospital treated 1,211 patients in those turbulent weeks. (Interestingly, children living on islands, and insulated from the greater society, were not affected by the epidemic. There were no polio cases among the eighty youngsters of Governors Island. Even the 350 children on Brooklyn's Barren Island—a poor com-

North Brother Island was dominated by institutions for eight decades prior to its abandonment in 1963.

munity plagued by flies, mosquitoes, and rats, with no sewage or public water—were not infected.)

In 1938, with 350 TB patients and seven typhoid carriers on North Brother Island, the city began building the final and grandest of Riverside's buildings—a $1.2 million tuberculosis pavilion. Construction of the 150-bed facility was frequently stalled during World War II as the government shifted priorities and redirected supplies. The facility was completed in 1943 but was never used as a tuberculosis hospital, because the Riverside complex had deteriorated and fallen into disuse.

In 1946, North Brother Island was resuscitated with an influx of healthy boarders. The GI Bill had caused a rush at colleges as well as dormitory shortages at City College, Columbia, and Fordham Universities. So New York State leased the island from the city and turned the new pavilion and several other buildings into veteran-student housing, from which it ferried the students to school each day. One pupil, Evan Hunter, later wrote the novel *Blackboard Jungle*, the screenplay for Alfred Hitchcock's *The Birds*,

Historical Detour: Island Exile

Mary Mallon was an unknown, hardworking immigrant, and the picture of health: robust, agile, and powerful. She was also a walking plague feared by every citizen in New York. Confined to North Brother Island for nearly three decades until her death in 1938, Mallon achieved eternal notoriety as Typhoid Mary.

Typhoid fever, an acute, highly infectious disease, was a grave and perplexing problem in New York at the turn of the twentieth century. Many experts believed it spread through polluted water or milk or through the sewers, but could neither establish a source nor halt its deadly march. In 1906, there were 3,467 cases and 639 deaths from typhoid.

That August, an epidemiologist named George Soper investigated an outbreak of typhoid in a family whose cook, Mary Mallon, had just moved on to another job. Soper, who believed the disease was transmitted by people, not pollutants, traced Mallon's career back to 1900 and discovered that seven other typhoid epidemics—resulting in at least twenty-five illnesses and one death—had originated in households where she had cooked.

In early 1907, Soper contacted Mallon to tell her she was spreading typhoid when she handled food. Mallon rejected Soper's request for an examination by attacking him with a carving knife. Soper went to New York's health department and arranged for police protection. When Soper visited Mallon again, she escaped through the back of her house, climbed a fence, and led the cops on a lengthy chase that ended with Mallon barricading herself behind several barrels. Finally trapped and apprehended, Typhoid Mary was sent to Riverside Hospital on North Brother Island.

Soper described Mallon, age thirty-seven, as having blond hair, blue eyes, healthy color, a masculine gait, and "a determined mouth and jaw." The five-foot-six-inch Mallon was fairly heavy but was in good health; she carried typhoid yet was wholly unaffected by it.

On North Brother Island, Mallon was given a small bungalow set on the riverbank. Although not in prison, Mallon loathed the forced isolation. A native of Ireland, she had no visitors, and no family in the area. Nurses left food at the door and hurried off. Except for a dog, Mallon was utterly alone.

Mallon stubbornly dismissed the diagnosis, pointing to her hardy condition as proof of her well-being. Instead, she filed a writ of habeas corpus in 1909, suing the city for detaining her without due process. But several doctors and Soper—who had become a local hero after Mallon's capture—persuaded a judge that she was a danger to the community.

Mallon was released a year later on the conditions that she refrain from cooking or handling other people's food and that she check in regularly with city officials. When Mallon couldn't find work, the city got her a job as a laundress. Mallon, who felt unjustly persecuted, was not satisfied. In 1911, she threatened to sue the city and health department for $50,000. Then she abruptly changed her mind, and rather than pursue the suit before a critical public, simply disappeared.

For more than two years, Mallon eluded city investigators by working in hotels and restaurants under aliases like Marie Breshof and Mrs. Brown. Then twenty-five people—mostly doctors and nurses at Sloane Maternity Hospital where "Mrs. Brown" was working—contracted typhoid; two died. Officials discovered that Mrs. Brown was actually Mallon and traced her whereabouts to Corona, Queens. There they had to climb through a second-story window to apprehend her. In March 1915, the board of health declared Mallon a public menace to be held indefinitely on North Brother Island.

Mallon never tried to flee, although occasional rumors of her escape often put the city on edge. She kept to herself, but this time the Riverside Hospital staff reached out to Mallon, providing her with a job in the hospital's laboratory, and a cottage. Eventually, officials even allowed her to take day trips to the mainland. In 1932, Mallon suffered a stroke. She never walked again, spending her last years in the hospital.

Mallon wasn't the only typhoid carrier in New York, just the most infamous. While some modern writers argue that Mallon was singled out unfairly because she was a lower-class, immigrant woman, when she died at age sixty-nine on November 11,

1938, there were six other carriers in isolation, and 350 more registered with the city's department of health who were checked on regularly. But it was Mallon's case that inspired compulsory health exams for, and licensing of, all food handlers in the city, and it was Mallon who was studied by high school health classes and medical schools. Mallon even found her way into the English language. Anyone called a Typhoid Mary is "a person from whom something undesirable or deadly spreads to those nearby," according to the dictionary.

Even in death, Mallon couldn't shake the stigma. Only nine people attended her funeral, and none would identify himself to a local reporter who covered the service.

and a short story called "Happy New Year, Herbie" set on North Brother Island.

The city reclaimed the island in 1952, returning Riverside Hospital to its historic purpose of isolating undesirables. A 152-bed rehabilitation center for adolescent drug addicts opened in the old tuberculosis pavilion and several other buildings. Financed jointly by the city and state, the ambitious project was the first of its kind. It had a full-time staff of 306, including psychiatrists, teachers, and social workers who provided vocational guidance, schooling, family therapy, and follow-up care. Some patients were referred by hospitals, but most were arrested on drug charges and sentenced to the island as an alternative to jail.

At the time Governor Thomas Dewey and Mayor Vince Impellitteri predicted the facility would eliminate teenage drug addiction as a serious local problem in five years. Six months later, Hospitals Commissioner Dr. Marcus Kogel told the *New York Times* he had "serious doubts" about the program.

Riverside had expected well-behaved and malleable adolescents but mainly received hard-core heroin addicts, two-thirds of whom were between nineteen and twenty-one. The program was haunted by both a high recidivism rate (one patient returned seventeen times) and constant escapes. Some patients drowned during their exodus, but most deserters were picked up by police waiting on shore.

In 1956, the city considered moving the program to City Hospital at the southern end of Welfare Island (now Roosevelt Island) and relocating the

Women's House of Detention in Greenwich Village to North Brother Island. The idea was kicked around for years as Riverside's program became widely viewed as a failure by the city and the media.

"It was just too corrupt," says Frank Lima, a former addict treated on the island several times following arrests in the late 1950s and early 1960s. While the facilities were clean and the food was decent, prostitution and bribery kept the island awash with drugs, says Lima, now a published poet and a teacher at the New York Restaurant School. "We did anything we wanted, whenever we wanted."

Herbert Walcoe, a social worker there, recalls a prison culture in which white, black, and Puerto Rican patients segregated themselves, infusing the island with the racial tension of the streets. Guards and aides were "ripe for making an extra buck" while professionals averted their gaze, he says. A civil service mentality pervaded even the psychiatric staff. "They were going through the motions," says Walcoe.

"It was a depressing island," he adds. "There wasn't really much of an effort to cheer it up. The grounds were weedy and unkempt. The subtext was that this was a hopeless situation."

Riverside Hospital finally closed in 1963, putting an end to North Brother's institutional history (women's detention went to Rikers instead). But the island had one moment of notoriety remaining—it stepped into the Broadway footlights and helped launch actor Al Pacino's career. *Does the Tiger Wear a Necktie?* starring Hal Holbrook and the twenty-eight-year-old Pacino opened in 1969 at the Belasco Theater. Written by former Riverside teacher Don Petersen, the play examined the relationship between one educator and his troubled students. It was a commercial flop, closing after thirty-nine performances; *Newsweek* panned it as "woefully weak in structure" with "all the standard blackboard jungle types." But Pacino's Broadway debut as a young tough on the edge won rave reviews and the Tony for Best Supporting Actor, bringing him bigger offers that soon took him beyond his decrepit fifth-floor walk-up on East Fourteenth Street.

North Brother Island inspired dreamers again in 1970, when the city offered the abandoned island and its dilapidated buildings for sale, asking for an opening bid of $1.1 million. Entrepreneurs came out of the woodwork. Proposals included an amusement park, power plant, movie studio, casino with convention center and hotel (dubbed the Las Vegas of the East), and an integrated urban village connected to the city by monorail.

The cost of construction, transportation to the island, and installing a sewage system—not to mention the airplane noise from nearby La Guardia

Airport—discouraged investors. And finally, the notion of selling North Brother Island was swallowed by red tape when Bronx Borough President Bob Abrams decided the city shouldn't relinquish this "irreplaceable resource" to commercial developers. Abrams, who envisioned an environmental-monitoring facility and park there, repeatedly rallied the board of estimate to block any sale. In 1976, the board approved a plan to lease the island, but there were no bids.

The city continued trying to get North Brother Island onto the tax rolls, but the only serious offer came from the state, when Governor Mario Cuomo considered building a prison for a thousand inmates there in the 1980s. What was touted as an $82 million project in September 1983 became a $125 million undertaking by March 1984, when Cuomo approved the plan. (Riverside's TB pavilion was the only building that wouldn't be razed.) The plan was abandoned in 1985 after Cuomo, conceding that meeting environmental requirements and repairing the island's seawall would drive the price tag above $200 million, decided to build the prison in upstate New York.

Throughout the decade, plans for the island surfaced and sank quickly. Mayor Ed Koch's 1988 promise to ship the homeless to Hart and North Brother Islands was attacked in editorials and by advocates for the homeless, who vehemently objected to the revival of nineteenth-century thinking. Robert Hayes, counsel for the Coalition for the Homeless, called Koch's plan "the gulag mentality of social welfare."

While plans for jails and shelters were being bandied about, North Brother Island was quietly evolving into a true companion to its sibling. A rookery was discovered amid the overgrowth on South Brother Island in 1978, with cattle egrets, snowy egrets, and black-crowned night herons. By 1983, double-crested cormorants had joined the colony. When the smaller island grew crowded, the birds, like people, started looking for more space. By 1989, the birds had discovered North Brother Island next door. These islands are now informally part of the Harbor Herons Project, which started with three islands (Prall's Island, Shooter's Island, and Isle of Meadow) in Staten Island. The project is dedicated to protecting the birds' habitats.

In 2000, North Brother Island was home to nearly two hundred nesting pairs of waders, mostly black-crowned night herons (up nearly one-third from 1994). The Urban Park Rangers, hoping to both diversify and double the population, are looking to reintroduce more native vegetation while removing invasive species like Norway maple as well as leftover fencing and some other man-made structures.

South Brother Island, the harbor's second-most-popular nesting spot, was home in 2000 to twice as many waders, featuring a mix of black-crowned night herons, great and snowy egrets, and glossy ibis. South Brother's total is down by nearly a third from 1994, however; Paul Kerlinger, consulting biologist for the New York City Audubon Society, blames the decrease on a growing number of cormorants on the island. The cormorants' acidic feces destroy habitat for other birds. He recommends actions ranging from oiling the cormorants' eggs to keep their population in check to allowing those birds to be classified as game and hunted, a notion rejected by many environmental groups, including Audubon. "There'll be gridlock until all the waders are gone from here," says a frustrated Kerlinger. "If we're not proactive, we can watch everything go down the tubes."

While South Brother Island today bears no sign of human history, North Brother Island's mortal past proclaims itself in the hollow remains of Riverside Hospital—from the institutional brick morgue to the ruins of the old hospital pavilions and staff residences. They are all being choked by prolific vines and forests that grow denser every year. A tumbledown ferry slip near the water is the only thing not smothered by foliage. The grounds bear other haunting testimony to the island's former identity: a lone shoe, a bedpan, and rotting hospital cots pushed up against the wall of the barracklike buildings. A long brick chimney that has somehow endured the island's years of neglect emerges through the trees as a faithful reminder of North Brother's past.

Historical Detour: The Darkest Hour

It never should have happened. "Limp, charred bodies were laid out in long rows on the grass," *Munsey's Magazine* wrote in 1904. "This was not murder, it was massacre. By midnight, six hundred and eleven lay on the lawn and four hundred more were still in the river."

The families aboard the ill-fated *General Slocum* excursion steamer should have been picnicking on Long Island, not laid out in groups of corpses on North Brother Island: six Gresses, eleven Rheinfranks . . . The island, long a place for healing the ill, had become a gruesome, makeshift morgue for tallying the dead.

Few tragedies seem as reprehensible, as criminal, as the burning of the *General Slocum* on June 15, 1904. The second worst maritime fire in history, it is a saga of negligence aggravated by incompetence, and a tale of an unsuspecting community that chartered a ship and was annihilated in a single afternoon.

On a sunny Wednesday morning, 1,358 members of St.
Mark's Lutheran Evangelical Church in Little Germany on the
Lower East Side clambered aboard the *General Slocum* for their
seventeenth annual picnic in bucolic Huntington, Long Island.
The passengers were primarily German immigrants who could
neither speak English nor swim, and most of those on this week-
day sojourn were women and children—fewer than one hundred
men were on board.

On the surface, the *Slocum* looked superb. The 264-foot vessel, named for Civil War general and Brooklyn congressman
Henry Warner Slocum, was constructed of locust, white oak, and
yellow pine. She featured mahogany interiors, ornate carvings, and
wicker furniture with red velvet. The three decks had recently
been repainted white. The ship's flags whipped in the wind,
bands played, and revelers enjoyed ice cream and fried clams.

While the *Slocum* had been extraordinarily popular when
she first took to the water in 1891, a slew of accidents, break-
downs, and groundings—all with Captain William Van Schaick
at the helm—eroded her appeal. By 1904, the ship was having
trouble getting business. The tightfisted Knickerbocker
Steamboat Company left Van Schaick, sixty-seven, in charge of
an unseasoned crew who worked cheap. The hired hands were
unemployed ironworkers and dockmen with minimal experience
running a rig.

After departing from the Third Street Pier that fateful day,
the *Slocum* headed up the East River. Shortly before passing
Ward's Island, children on board started complaining about a
smoky smell, but their warnings went unheeded. When Lillie
Mannheimer declared the boat was on fire, her aunt shushed her
and a neighbor said it was clam chowder burning. One boy
rushed to the pilothouse, yelling, "Hey mister, the boat's on fire."
Van Schaick, not wanting to be distracted by what he thought was
a prank at Hell Gate—the journey's most arduous stretch—
snapped, "You shut your trap. Get out of here." Finally, another
boy dragged deckhand John Coakley away from his free beer and
toward the smoldering storeroom.

The previous night a deckhand had helped church members
unpack glasses in the bar. He had stuffed hay from the crates in

the storeroom, despite fire regulations prohibiting its presence on board. The danger was heightened since the hay was jammed in with inflammables like wooden furniture, hemp line, and three barrels of oil.

Upon seeing black fumes seeping out from under the door, Coakley foolishly yanked the door open. Then he grabbed whatever was nearby to smother the fire, which happened to be a bag of charcoal. "That did no good," Coakley admitted at the inquest in a masterful display of understatement.

Just past Sunken Meadow Island (now connected to Randall's Island), the smoldering hay exploded into flames. When Van Schaick received word of the emergency, he ordered full speed ahead for North Brother Island, about one mile north. Afterward, most people condemned Van Schaick's decision to bypass piers just three hundred feet away in Queens and the Bronx. But Claude Rust, who wrote *The Burning of the General Slocum* and whose grandmother had died in the disaster, felt that with lumberyards and oil tanks dotting the shoreline, Van Schaick had made the only move possible. And move he did: The ship's acceleration combined with strong winds to fan the flames; tugs coming to her rescue couldn't keep up with the blazing inferno.

En route to North Brother Island, the crisis quickly evolved into a full-fledged catastrophe, revealing an insidious chain of negligence. Rotten fire hoses quickly burst when used; lifeboats were nailed or lashed to the boat. Despite a law requiring weekly fire drills, the crew had never executed one, and crew members helped out only haphazardly; most abandoned ship. After passengers finally got a lifeboat in the water, a frenzied crew member leaped in, capsizing it.

Additionally, 90 percent of the ship's life preservers were thirteen years old, five years over their normal life span. The cork inside them had dried, and many preservers disintegrated upon hitting the water. (Subsequent investigations revealed that Knickerbocker executives had altered invoices to make it seem as if they'd ordered new ones.) To meet weight specifications, some preservers were even stuffed with cast iron instead of buoyant cork because iron was cheaper per pound at the time. A man named John Kircher later testified that after he put his seven-year-old daughter Elsie into a Kahnweiler Neversink preserver, she "sunk as though a stone were tied to her."

Panic tore into the passengers. As the *Slocum* voyaged north, women who couldn't swim clutched their babies and jumped overboard to escape the flames. One boy was sucked into the boat's paddle wheel.

At the last minute, Van Schaick considered the Bronx, before making a sharp turn toward the North Brother ferry slip. The maneuver proved deadly, sending passengers on the upper deck hurtling into the rail, which collapsed, toppling everyone into the now boiling river. The current was rapid and powerful; five hundred people were swept into the river's deeper midchannel. Non-swimmers clutched onto swimmers, dragging them under.

By the time fireboats and police arrived, the *Slocum* was already beached. But the nightmare had just begun. As in any disaster, the fire brought out the best and worst in human behavior.

Ghoulish scavengers rowed out to the wreck and robbed corpses. Others dove for pocketbooks and shoved survivors away from boats if they had no money. One unconscious floater came to and found a man leaning out of a tug, calmly removing her locket and chain. She had to plead before he'd take her ashore.

But one Good Samaritan, a Brooklynite named Samuel Berg, rowed out from 144th Street in the Bronx and saved two women and a child. Reserve policeman Thomas Cooney saved eleven people, then drowned going for a twelfth. Tug captain John Wade risked his livelihood, guiding his rig *Wade* up against the flaming *Slocum* and rescuing more than one hundred passengers.

On North Brother Island, doctors and nurses from the island's Riverside Hospital set up first-aid stations. Patients and kitchen staff pitched in. A convalescent patient named Mary McCann rescued twenty children before collapsing. Even inmates from nearby Rikers escaped their prison briefly to help out.

As the burning ship collapsed, she was towed away to prevent the island's buildings from catching fire. Left behind were many grisly reminders of what had transpired—rescue workers found four dead women with their hands desperately clamped to a railing.

"My mother was burned up and down her left side," says ninety-seven-year-old Adella Wotherspoon, who was only six months old when she, her parents, and two sisters boarded the *Slocum.* "She carried those scars her whole life." Adella's father also survived, but her sisters Anna and Helen did not; Helen's body was never recovered. It is believed that she is buried among the unidentified dead in the Lutheran All Faith's Cemetery in Middle Village, Queens.

The public and the press were outraged. *The New York American* called it "the usual story of such events in this country, where . . . love of money deadens the conscience."

Van Schaick, partly blinded and with a fractured leg, was hidden by police to prevent his lynching. He, the unlicensed first mate, Knickerbocker Steamboat Company officials, and inspector Henry Lundberg, who had certified the boat during inspection the previous month, were found guilty during an inquest and faced criminal charges in federal court.

When no action had been taken by December, the public outcry escalated. In *Munsey's Magazine*, a writer named Herbert Casson warned that disdain for ethical behavior would continue unless "irresponsible directors are taken from their corporate pedestals and treated like ordinary breakers of the law. In short, this aristocracy of crime must be destroyed."

Several inspectors were dismissed, and ships subsequently came under stricter scrutiny. In 1906, Van Schaick received a ten-year sentence for manslaughter. The others went free, including four employees from Nonpareil Cork Works charged with having put iron in the preservers. Some observers felt Van Schaick was made the scapegoat, but most believed he was justly punished and were only angry the others had not been convicted, too.

Van Schaick served less than four years before 250,000 sympathizers petitioned President William Howard Taft for his release. Despite protests, Taft pardoned Van Schaick, who bought a farm upstate with funds donated by supporters and lived there until the age of ninety.

While the legal farce played itself out, the East Sixth Street congregation and the Little Germany community mourned and, ultimately, fell apart. Of the 1,358 people on board the *Slocum* (some accounts say 1,331), 1,021 died. Six hundred families lost a loved one, and one hundred people committed suicide in the fire's aftermath.

"My father walked the streets for days and visited every morgue and every possible place looking for my sister Helen," says Wotherspoon. "I think the disaster had a great deal to do with his declining health." He died six years later, at age thirty-six, of tuberculosis.

The toll was felt most acutely in the schools. Thirty-nine of the fifty-one children in the church's kindergarten program had died. P.S. 25 lost 100 students, then 150 more when bereaved families fled the neighborhood in an effort to put the horror behind them.

The *Slocum* crashed on North Brother Island, but her impact was felt for generations throughout the city—especially in areas like Yorkville and Astoria, where new, smaller German communities were suddenly founded, and on the Lower East Side, where a society disappeared. Today, the *Slocum*'s victims are memorialized by two monuments. One, in Lutheran All Faith's Cemetery in Middle Village, Queens, remembers the sixty-one unidentified dead. The monument was unveiled in 1905 by Wotherspoon, who was the youngest *Slocum* survivor. (She and another woman are the only known survivors alive today.) Each year, to mark the tragedy's anniversary, the Organization of the General Slocum Survivors—made up mostly of Slocum descendants and historians—keeps the memory of the *Slocum* alive by holding a graveside memorial service. The other monument is on the Lower East Side in Tompkins Square Park. It is dedicated to the children who died aboard the *Slocum* and simply states: THEY WERE THE EARTH'S PUREST CHILDREN, YOUNG AND FAIR.

15. Forgotten Islands of the East River

U Thant Island • Mill Rock Island • Furman's Island

Forgotten Islands of the East River

U Thant Island

The smallest island in the East River has a most unusual name, and it's a moniker associated with diplomacy, leadership, and spirituality. A mere one hundred by two hundred feet, U Thant (oo-tant) Island was built on Man-o'-War Reef opposite the United Nations. In the 1890s, the reef was enlarged with rocks and soil excavated from a tunnel being built by piano manufacturer William Steinway, who wanted to bring trolleys from Queens into Manhattan. Steinway died in 1896, leaving his Steinway Tunnel unfinished. During the next decade, financier August Belmont completed the project for his then privately owned Interborough Rapid Transit subway line. Excavated material once again augmented the tiny isle.

For the next seventy years, the island was called Belmont Island. In 1976, some UN employees who meditated with spiritual leader Sri Chinmoy leased the island from New York State. They planted flowers, bushes, and trees, and dedicated the island to the memory of U Thant (1909–1974), a Burmese diplomat who was UN secretary-general from 1961 through 1971. U Thant ascribed to the same beliefs regarding peace and spirituality advocated by his good friend Chinmoy. The group has occasionally held functions on U Thant Island and has erected a thirty-foot-high peace arch made from silver steel tubing. A time capsule buried there includes some of U Thant's speeches, photos, and personal effects, such as his favorite tie clasp. The island was never formally renamed; many maps still call it Belmont Island.

Mill Rock Island

On October 10, 1885, some three hundred thousand pounds of explosives produced on Great Mill Rock and Little Mill Rock Islands were detonated in the East River, producing the largest intentional explosion prior to the atomic bomb. This wasn't war, this was business—the army was removing Flood Rock, the river's most hellish obstacle, to make the waters safe for ship traffic.

The shipping industry had suffered for years from the reefs and rock islands in this part of the river, which had caused hundreds of wrecks and prevented larger vessels from venturing through. The Dutch called the area Hellegat, meaning "bright passage" or "beautiful pass" (although they may have been referring to the entire East River). The English corrupted the name to Hell Gate, since it perfectly described this treacherous portion of the East River.

The War Department first took on Mother Nature in 1851 and, over the next seventy years, blasted some of the most colorfully named islets in the city out of the water: Hen and Chickens; Hog's Back; Frying Pan; Bread and Cheese; and Bald Headed Billy.

Toward the end of the century, the army set up a base for mixing explosives on Great Mill Rock and Little Mill Rock Islands, located a thousand feet off Ninety-sixth Street in Manhattan. Here, the army developed its newest invention, "rack-a-rock," an explosive stew made from a black oil called nitrobenzole that was poured over chlorate of potash and mixed with wooden hoes.

On that fateful day in 1885 when nine-acre Flood Rock was annihilated, the *New York Times* wrote of the Mill Rocks: "People looked at these rugged brown spots with feelings that were deeper than respect."

The hyperbole was understandable considering the buildup. Planning began in 1875, but unsteady financial support from Congress caused endless delays. Finally, engineers constructed a temporary island around Flood Rock's perimeter, from which workmen prepared for its explosion. A week before the 1885 detonation, newspapers were filled with reports of the gradual dismantling of the peripheral island's machinery and houses. Articles also recommended vantage points from which to view the imminent spectacle.

On October 10, approximately a hundred thousand spectators planted themselves on the East River's banks, scaled trees and lampposts, and boarded tugs and rowboats circling the Mill Rocks and Flood Rock. Even patients housed in asylums on Blackwell's and Ward's Islands poured out to watch.

At 11:14 AM, the moment of truth arrived. According to the *Times*, there was "a deep rumble then a dull boom. Up, up and still up into the frightened air soared a great ghastly writhing wall of white and silver and gray." The blast created some fifty geysers, with three fountains spewing water two hundred feet high, then plummeting down "with a wild hissing as if

10,000 huge steam valves had been opened." The river transformed into a boiling mass of white foam covered by a gaseous cloud that turned yellow, green, and blue before dissipating.

Shocks from the blast were felt as far away as Princeton, New Jersey. The *Times,* which devoted its entire front page to the event, declared the blast "another triumph of human skill over the resistance of nature."

Fragments of Flood Rock were used to fill in the area between Great Mill Rock and Little Mill Rock, and by 1890, a new 8.6-acre, key-shaped island—Mill Rock Island—was formed. The army continued using Mill Rock Island until 1949 as a base for surveying and blasting operations and for repairing boats and buoys.

Great Mill Rock and Little Mill Rock were sold in 1664 by Native Americans to Dutchman William Hallett, who snapped up much of the land in the area. Great Mill Rock was first developed between 1701 and 1707, when John Marsh built the tidal mill there that gave both the islands their names. During the War of 1812, the army built a blockhouse with cannons on the island to deter the British from making their way from Long Island Sound. The blockhouse burned down in 1821. In 1850, John Clark claimed squatter's rights to Great Mill Rock and began selling food and booze to passing boats. A decade later, he sold the island for $40 to Sandy Gibson, who moved his entire household there, right down to the cows and chickens. Three years later, Gibson sold the land to a Charles Leland for $300, but stayed on for several more years as a tenant, catching eels and flounder for food.

Gibson's story has often been distorted by good mythmakers and bad fact checkers. A 1938 *New Yorker* article said Gibson lived on Great Mill Rock from 1840 until 1898, when he was evicted by soldiers who were "just starting the job of clearing the reefs out of Hell Gate . . . Nobody knows where he went with his cow and his chickens after fifty-eight years." This fabrication errs at both ends of the timeline, since Gibson arrived in 1860 and had to be gone well before the 1885 explosion. Yet it was repeated in a 1951 *New York Herald Tribune* article and other publications through the years, giving it the aura of fact.

Once the army retired Mill Rock, Parks Commissioner Robert Moses— claiming that commercial interests might develop the abandoned island— had the federal government deed Mill Rock to his department in 1953. When money finally became available in 1967, Moses razed all the buildings on Mill Rock, planting willow and poplar trees in their place. The island wasn't used as a park until the 1980s, when Asphalt Green, an Upper East Side not-for-profit group, offered leadership training for young teens there. The group even tried camping out once, but after dark the island swarmed with rats. "The kids loved it," says art coordinator Dave Mosher. "They got to stay up all night with flashlights and brickbats beating bushes and making noise. But it was not an experience we cared to repeat."

Mill Rock Island has been out of reach for Asphalt Green since the nor'easters of 1992 and 1993 demolished their dock at Ninetieth Street—repairs are too costly for their budget. Since then, the island that captured the city's attention when it helped rock the East River has sat neglected and silent.

Furman's Island

Once surrounded by beautiful freshwater wetlands, the island known as Furman's Island experienced a crude transformation early in the twentieth century when progress stitched it to the mainland. Today warehouses, like the enormous New York City Transit Authority storage facility, blight this once green haven with gray.

The island in Newtown Creek, which flows from the East River and divides Queens and Brooklyn, was called Arnhem in 1638 when it became one of the first settlements in Queens. Located just west of Maspeth and separated from the mainland on its eastern side by the slim, marshy Shanty Creek, this Dutch hamlet of quaint gabled cottages and a church coexisted for a time with Native American wigwams. In 1643, Native Americans destroyed the village in retaliation for Dutch hostilities elsewhere, and colonists fled to Fort Amsterdam in what is now Manhattan.

In 1815, Judge Garrit Furman bought the land south of Newtown Creek, including Furman's Island, and on these fifty-four acres built a mansion where he entertained many New York City millionaires. The pastoral setting also offered Furman great fishing and hunting and inspiration for poetry. One collection, *The Maspeth Poems*, published in 1837, includes a selection titled "Petition of the Shell-Fish, on Maspeth Island, for Protection Against the Turnpike-Makers, That Are Working the Williamsburg Turnpike." In it, the shellfish of Newtown Creek solicit Jove to take pity on their fate—one, ironically, orchestrated by Furman.

For, despite his love of nature, Furman entered into a partnership with the builders of a toll road and bridge (The Maspeth Avenue and Toll

Bridge Company) that crossed his island and provided a direct route from Williamsburg and Bushwick to Maspeth, Newtown, and Flushing. The road, which appears on some maps as Maspeth Avenue, was no more than twenty feet wide and operated until 1866. It then lay abandoned for ten years, and the toll bridge built over marshy Newtown Creek gradually became dangerous for traveling. In 1876, the town of Newtown replaced the old road with Grand Avenue, a new thoroughfare a quarter mile south of the old turnpike.

In 1855, four bone-boiling plants occupied Furman Island. These facilities made boneblack—roasted bones that were used in ink production and sugar refining—and used fat from animal bones to make soap. Eventually, manure and horse-rendering plants also opened on the island, an ideal spot for foul-smelling businesses since there were no residential neighbors.

By 1870, formerly pristine Newtown Creek had become polluted by raw sewage and refinery oil. The Furman estate was sold in 1899 to a Manhattan business syndicate that planned to build an industrial park in the area. While the project never materialized, it's likely that the entrepreneurs began filling in Shanty Creek to join the island to the rest of their property, says Queens historian Vincent F. Seyfried. No one knows exactly when Furman's Island ceased to be an island. "'Who cares?' was probably the sentiment," says Seyfried.

Part V

Jamaica Bay

BROAD CHANNEL • FORGOTTEN ISLANDS OF
JAMAICA BAY AND THE ROCKAWAYS

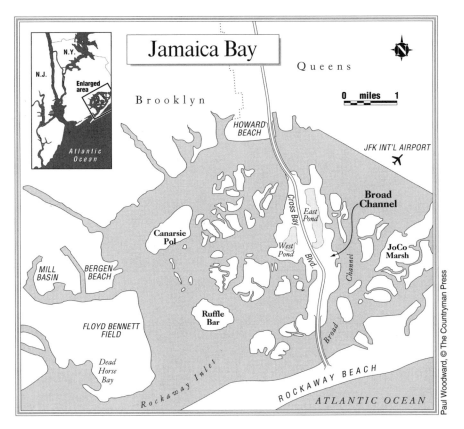

*Secluded from the Atlantic Ocean by the slender Rockaway Peninsula,
Jamaica Bay has lost much of its area to landfill. The bay, about eighteen
square miles in Brooklyn and Queens, is dotted with more than a dozen
islands, some as large as three square miles, others tiny marshy flats that
disappear with the tide.*

16. Broad Channel

"It's the type of place you drive through. I don't think anybody even notices that there is a community there. It is a curious backwater, an unearthly, unworldly place."

—VINCENT F. SEYFRIED, QUEENS HISTORIAN

Broad Channel

THE HOUSES ARE BUILT along canals and on stilts in the water. Boats are parked on narrow streets like cars. No gas station, no pharmacy, no movie theater in this town. Can't get your shoes repaired or your pants pressed here, and if you're trying to find the post office, look for the counter at the back of O'Mac's, a small market on Cross Bay Boulevard.

Broad Channel is a peculiar outpost within the confines of New York City, and the only inhabited island in Jamaica Bay. At first glance, this tiny island neighborhood—a mile long and four blocks wide—seems nothing more than a whistle-stop between mainland Queens and the Rockaway Peninsula. But Channelites, who relish the isolation and anonymity of their close-knit community, consider Broad Channel the Venice of New York City.

Nobody in town owns a gondola, but many of Broad Channel's twenty-five hundred residents have modest boats and spend hours fishing, crabbing, or lazing on Jamaica Bay. When the bay freezes in winter, children skate or ice-sail across its glassy surface in homemade buggies fashioned from ordinary sleds and canvas material.

"Our kids don't care about the tallest building in the world," says Kieran Martin, who retired in 1994 after twenty-six years as pastor of the island's St. Virgilius Roman Catholic Church. "Everything they really want is here. It's fishing, boating, the beach. That kind of thing."

When evening seduces the sun beneath the distant Manhattan skyline, Broad Channel appears worlds away from the city to which it belongs. But belying the island's peaceful exterior is a rough-and-tumble history—from its days as a primitive fishing village to Prohibition-era rum-running—and a philosophy that you *can* fight city hall.

Situated just west of the channel from which it derives its name, the Queens community inhabits the island's southern half, whereas the Jamaica Bay Wildlife Refuge occupies the northern portion. The entire island mass—approximately twelve hundred acres in size—was once a group of small islands (including Big Egg Marsh, The Raunt, Goose Creek, Black Bank

Marsh, and Ruler's Bar Hassock) when the Jameco and Canarsie tribes and, later, Dutch colonists hunted and fished the bay region.

The bay's fishing tradition prospered after the Civil War, when ferries carried vacationers from Canarsie, Brooklyn, to beaches on the nearby Rockaway Peninsula. A handful of oystermen, clamdiggers, and fishermen like Joe, Ben, and Bill Shaw lived in shacks on Big Egg Marsh during summer, providing boats and bait to visitors for $3 a day.

The bay islands remained sparsely populated until 1880, when the New York, Woodhaven, and Rockaway Railroad erected a 4.8-mile-long wooden trestle across Jamaica Bay. The line, which connected mainland Queens to Rockaway, made four stops—Goose Creek, The Raunt, Broad Channel, and Beach Channel—and accommodated far more passengers than the ferries.

Within four years, as many as eighty-seven crowded trains chugged through the Jamaica Bay islands each summer day. The route was sold in 1887 to the Long Island Railroad, and by 1895, the trains carried a million and a half passengers. In 1902, three and a half million fun-seekers rode the line.

Transportation put Jamaica Bay on the map. Tiny fishing shacks, boathouses, fishing clubs, and small hotels—many built on stilts—rose near the railroad trestle. Goose Creek became known for its weakfishing and had a fleet's worth of boats ready for hire, with colorful old-timers like Sebastian "Bas" Hesbach as guides. The Raunt became popular for its rod-and-gun clubs, and Broad Channel had elegant hotels that attracted wealthy fishermen and visitors.

The bay developed a reputation for its shellfishing, with the Rockaway oyster being especially popular. In 1906, an estimated 450,000 tons of oysters and clams, valued at $2 million, were harvested from the bay.

The Jamaica Bay islands were a homesteader's paradise during the late nineteenth century. The town of Jamaica had jurisdiction, but did not exercise title or collect taxes, encouraging squatters to settle there. That changed in the 1890s, when an enterprising and corrupt town supervisor, Frederick Dunton, arranged for the land to be leased for the next hundred years to his business cronies.

Dunton and a developer named Patrick Flynn had ambitious plans for the remote area. Dunton leased some of the land he then controlled to Flynn and supported Flynn's plan to build a trolley line across Jamaica Bay to compete with the railroad. The project, which included a bicycle path and lane for carriage drivers, angered executives of the Long Island Railroad, which held a monopoly in the region.

While costly lawsuits were waged by the Long Island Railroad, New York City (which Queens joined in 1898), and others against the Flynn-Dunton interests, a route was designed, land dredged, trestle spiles erected, trolley cars ordered, and tenants thrown out of their homes. The project was halted in 1902 after New York had the Dunton leases invalidated in court. Title to the land and water eventually reverted to the city.

Flynn lost about $1 million and abandoned several miles of newly constructed roadway and embankments. Twenty years later, the city used them to build Jamaica Bay Boulevard, later named Cross Bay Boulevard, the major thoroughfare that begins in Queens and bisects Broad Channel.

The city then issued permits to anyone who wanted to live in, or develop, the bay area. Broad Channel, unlike the patchwork communities on The Raunt or Goose Creek, grew into a thriving community. By 1908, there were stores, a church, a volunteer fire department with 185 firemen, and four hundred houses, each paying an average of $25 rent to the city's dock department.

In 1915, the city leased a five-hundred-acre parcel of Broad Channel to real-estate developer Pierre Noel with the condition that the land be improved. Noel sublet the lease to the Broad Channel Corporation, which built roads, provided running water and electric light, and subdivided about 150 acres into lots one hundred feet by twenty-five feet. The corporation rented each parcel for about $116 a year to anyone wanting to build a summer home. Broad Channel prospered as a summer resort, offering bungalows and boating to weary city folk in search of respite. People were soon receiving postcards from friends celebrating the lazy life in fashionable Broad Channel.

Grandiose plans were also afloat to transform Jamaica Bay into a commercial port unrivaled by any in the world. Beginning in 1906, an array of private developers and government planners took to the task. The state endorsed the plan three years later, with Congress authorizing $7.4 million for the project if New York City built the docks and basins. The city kicked in $1 million, and in 1913 the bay was partially dredged by the federal government. The project picked up steam during the next decade, when a massive dredging and landfill undertaking thoroughly altered the bay. Channels were deepened in anticipation of the arrival of large boats, and landfill connected some of the islands and eliminated marshes and creeks. But lack of rail freight service and poor coordination at various levels of government doomed the project in the 1920s.

The bay nonetheless felt the negative effects of growing industrialization and New York's burgeoning population. In 1912, seafood caught in Jamaica Bay was blamed for a typhoid scare in Brooklyn and Queens. The U.S. Department of Agriculture temporarily banned commercial fishing in the bay—jeopardizing five thousand jobs—rather than investigate the deluge of untreated sewage pouring into the bay. By 1917, plants in Queens and Brooklyn were discharging fifty million gallons of inadequately treated waste into the bay daily, poisoning clams, oysters, and ultimately people. The water became so polluted that in 1921 the department of health abolished shellfishing in Jamaica Bay altogether, destroying both a major industry and a way of life.

Despite the demise of the long-established fishing industry and the collapse of plans for the harbor, Broad Channel flourished, albeit illegally. During Prohibition, the island, too remote for police raids, proved the perfect venue for rum-running. This sleepy island getaway suddenly became a notorious nightspot. Yacht clubs, speakeasies, and lodgings like the Enterprise Hotel sprang up on what became known as Little Cuba, a homegrown Havana tucked away in New York City.

"The yacht clubs would put on regattas," says eighty-seven-year-old Joe Carey, whose grandparents came to Broad Channel in 1897. "You would be in your glory—you could watch the races and get drunk."

Broad Channel's popularity increased when Cross Bay Boulevard was finished in 1923. Motorists in dandy new cars now zipped to the island at whim, free from train-schedule constraints. The road also paved the way for Broad Channel's growth as a year-round community, a change ushered in by the Great Depression and the need for cheap housing. Bungalows were winterized and many summer residents moved in permanently.

Eventually hard times befell the Broad Channel Corporation, and it went bankrupt in 1939. Suddenly, New York City found itself landlord to a thousand tenants. Residents negotiated with the city to purchase the land under their homes, but were rejected. The citizens of Broad Channel were stuck as permanent renters, a situation that pitted residents against city government for more than forty years.

While Broad Channel continued developing as a community, the islands and marshlands to the north—a wilderness virtually ignored up until the 1930s—were eyed for another purpose. In 1938, Parks Commissioner Robert Moses maneuvered to have Jamaica Bay placed under his jurisdiction, protecting it both from sanitation department attempts to dump refuse there and from new developers, whom he dismissed as "crackpot industrial theorists."

More than 325 bird species have been recorded at the Jamaica Bay Wildlife Refuge.

Jamaica Bay was to be Moses' crown jewel, providing him with a legacy rivaling that of Frederick Law Olmsted and his Prospect and Central Parks. Moses dreamed of a tremendous recreational area along the bay's shore and a wildlife refuge on the islands. Like city officials for decades to come, Moses was indifferent to the plight of Broad Channel, calling the community "a slum" whose four thousand residents should be removed.

After World War II, Moses enlisted wildlife management specialists to help design a bird sanctuary for the Jamaica Bay region. But the project, which included construction of two freshwater ponds, was too expensive. The plan remained unimplemented until 1950, when a fire destroyed much of the wooden Long Island Railroad trestle spanning the bay. When the company abandoned operations, the Metropolitan Transportation Authority (MTA) asked the city for permission to build a subway line in its place. The MTA needed Moses' approval to dredge within the parks system; Moses consented, provided that the MTA build the two ponds.

During construction, the MTA filled in the waters between Broad Channel, The Raunt, Goose Creek, and Ruler's Bar Hassock. The MTA displaced an informal community living without gas or fresh water on The Raunt, and created the single twelve-hundred-acre island, which lies between the North Channel and Cross Bay Veterans Memorial Bridges. Today, the A train and shuttle to Rockaway Beach run along the MTA line, and the hundred-acre East and forty-five-acre West Ponds are the cornerstones of the Jamaica Bay Wildlife Refuge. (No one, however, bothered giving the merged landmass a formal name. Most residents, city officials, and cartographers refer to the entire island as Broad Channel, although some nautical maps and refuge officials still call the northern half Ruler's Bar Hassock.)

The 9,155-acre refuge was opened by the city department of parks in 1953, with Herbert Johnson, the department's turf grass specialist, in charge. While Johnson was not a wildlife expert, his background in botany and his creative planning were instrumental in planting the proper vegetation to attract birds to the ponds. Within five years, 208 species of birds were identified, and today more than 325 species have been recorded.

Johnson retired in 1972, the same year the city, which had never had the money to fully staff or fund projects there, turned the refuge over to the U.S. Department of the Interior and the newly created Gateway National Recreation Area. Since then, it has gained international renown as one of the country's most important urban wildlife refuges.

While the northern end of the island flowered, the town of Broad Channel became ensnared in bureaucratic red tape that incessantly threatened its very right to exist. Throughout its history, islanders have had to battle the government for acknowledgment, respect, and standard city services. In 1948, the board of estimate proposed canceling all homesite leases, which would have fulfilled Moses' desire to clear out the area, but after eight hundred residents marched on city hall, the idea was dropped.

Channelites were again threatened with eviction in 1967, when Mayor John Lindsay called the community a health hazard. He cited the overflow of raw sewage from residents' septic tanks into Jamaica Bay as a source of infectious hepatitis in Queens. Again, the solution was to remove the community, rather than to install a sewer system—a basic amenity in modern cities. In typical Broad Channel fashion, the community retained its own health expert, disputed the city's contention, and forced Lindsay to retreat. The city finally installed a sewer system in 1988, but residents were required to install their own sewer pumps and pay to hook up to the main line (a cost of about $2,000).

Islanders were almost uprooted again in 1968, when the Port Authority of New York and New Jersey proposed extending two runways at John F. Kennedy International Airport—already only one mile away—into Jamaica

Bay and toward island residences. The mayor's office said it would be impossible to maintain the community if the project was granted. Although the city's planning commission had long supported phasing out Broad Channel, the project was rejected because it would damage the quality of life for birds in the refuge.

Lindsay also tried casting the community adrift in the early 1970s by subsuming Broad Channel under Gateway National Park legislation, which would have meant clearing the island of all residents and buildings. Thousands of residents marched in protest, and again the city backed down. The threat of eviction finally ended in 1982, when Mayor Ed Koch passed special legislation enabling residents to purchase their lots "as is," at a cost of $500 for land under water and up to $2,500 for land on a canal. (When the city's board of estimate, which was selling the land, was abolished in 1990, more than a hundred homeowners were forced to resume their battle. The remaining land did not become available until 1995.)

Property ownership hasn't dampened the feistiness of the people of Broad Channel. Unlike many communities where apathy reigns, Channelites remain passionately involved in issues close to home. In 1991, the island's civic association successfully sued the city, blocking its inexplicable attempt to shift 162 of the 2,500 residents from Congressional District 32 to District 31 as part of a citywide redistricting plan. For a community as cohesive as Broad Channel, losing some of its family was unfathomable. The city gave in, redrawing the district line on the opposite side of the train tracks, where no one was living.

The following year the state department of environmental conservation shocked residents when inspectors issued dozens of fines—up to $10,000 each—citing a slew of decks, docks, and bulkheads in violation of the 1974 Tidal Wetlands Act. Residents sued, complaining that the fines were outrageously high, especially since the government hadn't told them permits were required. In fact, it had taken the state eighteen years to notice the illegal improvements. The state eventually lifted or reduced most of the fines, allowing all but the most flagrant violations to remain intact.

For years, islanders were at loggerheads with the city over the toll on the Cross Bay Veterans Memorial Bridge, the island's gangplank to the Rockaways, where vital city services are stationed. A toll across the bridge and back—to shop in the nearest supermarket, pick up certified mail, or attend community board meetings—costs $1.75. Finally, in 1998, EZ Pass customers in both the Rockaways and Broad Channel were permitted to use the bridge for free.

Though the tiny community appears vulnerable, most Broad Channel residents zealously safeguard their small-town way of life and would do almost anything to keep outside influences at bay. "All we have to do is go up and down the blocks in the fire truck and call people to action," says Frank Harnisher, past president of the Broad Channel Civic Association. "We're not afraid to fight. We'd blow up both bridges if we had to."

Broad Channel is the black swan in a city where image and formality are often preoccupations. The only things stilted about the Channel are some of its houses. It's a casual place where islanders feel comfortable popping into a store in their pajamas. They know their neighbors, and are bound by a common history and sense of place often missing in a world on the move. "We don't think in terms of years or decades," says Dan Tubridy, a community leader whose family counts four generations on the island. "We think in generations."

That sense of community cohesion is perhaps personified by the all-volunteer Broad Channel Fire Department, headquartered in a frame house at 15 Noel Road. Established in 1900, the department has about forty-five active members—some of whom have been involved for decades—and is only one of a handful of volunteer companies remaining in the city. There is no paid rescue service on the island. Even the police have a minor presence—the 100th Precinct is stationed across the bridge in Rockaway. Crime is low, however, and misdeeds are often handled the old-fashioned way, with residents straightening things out on their own.

Most Broad Channel residents are white, middle-class Catholics of Irish or German descent, with high school diplomas. Many work as craftsmen or have jobs in the civil service. The 1990 U.S. census counted only 2 blacks, 11 Asians, and 41 Hispanics among the island's 2,483 residents.

The island is an exceptionally stable community, where Broad Channel boys often marry Broad Channel girls. In 1990, more than 60 percent of the 854 households were married couples with children, and the median household income was more than $39,000. There are two churches, St. Virgilius Roman Catholic Church and Christ Presbyterian Church-by-the-Sea; and two elementary schools, St. Virgilius and P.S. 47. Junior and senior high school kids cross the bridge to Rockaway schools.

While most residents savor the *Mayberry R.F.D.* spirit of their town, the climate can also breed conformity and insularity. In this neighborhood, gossip is a serious pastime. Not surprisingly, given their experience, residents are occasionally suspicious of outsiders. There are few rental apart-

ments, and homes are rarely advertised outside the community. Most sales
are through word of mouth.

That insularity revealed an ugly side in 1998, when the island's Labor
Day parade featured a racist float, with white men dressed in blackface
throwing watermelon slices and fried chicken while bouncing basketballs.
Even worse, one man was dragged along behind the truck in a sick "par-
ody" of a Texas lynching of a black man that had occurred earlier in the
summer. Local newscasts showed video footage, and newspapers reported
that in past years Channelites had voted floats like "Hasidic Park" and
"Gooks of Hazzard" as the year's "funniest."

Some residents were angry at outsiders for judging them—particularly
when Mayor Rudolph Giuliani fired the city police officer and two firefighters involved in the float, and then revoked money from the volunteer fire
department that had sponsored the parade. Other residents, however, made
a public act of contrition. When the Reverend Al Sharpton marched with
protesters into Broad Channel, some citizens—including Tubridy and his
brother—greeted them with lemonade, crumb cake, and a warm welcome—a far cry from the response Sharpton has received in other predom-
inantly white neighborhoods like Bensonhurst, Brooklyn.

Even with the Manhattan skyline in the distance and the wildlife refuge
down the road, many residents prefer staying home, especially these days,
when Broad Channel has finally secured the amenities many communities
take for granted.

In 1990, the town got its own satellite library and a much-needed building extension for P.S. 47 that includes the island's first elevator. In 1993,
after twenty years of waiting, Broad Channel Community Park was built.

While many island homes are small, weathered bungalows left over from
the days of the Broad Channel Corporation, property ownership has given
the community a new lease on life. The 1990s saw many residents secure
home improvement loans for the first time. On weekends, the sounds of
buzzing saws and banging hammers now join the chorus of gulls flying over-
head. Some homes boast new additions; others have been knocked down in
pairs to make way for larger, more modern homes. Still others have been
raised off the ground, especially after the tumultuous nor'easter of 1992
flooded bottom floors. According to Tubridy, homes go for $150,000 to
$200,000, and more and more are selling for $300,000-plus. "Homes down
here are steadily going up in value," he says.

One incongruous addition to Broad Channel is Charles Howard's new $1 million home on Channel Road, on the east side of the island. Howard is a fourth-generation islander who made it big in the portable toilet business. Rather than move away, he chose to build his mega-mansion of imported marble and mahogany on Broad Channel soil, despite groans from some of his neighbors. "Broad Channel is getting better and better," he says. "I couldn't think of anywhere better to build."

Land ownership and the willingness of banks to finance loans have also allowed the community's commercial district to make a modest comeback. Broad Channel may never reclaim its heyday, when it flaunted a bar on every block, seven gas stations, barbershops, butchers, and fourteen restaurants, but some of the empty storefronts along Cross Bay Boulevard have been filled, mostly with everyday businesses like a laundromat, bagel shop, and pizzeria.

But don't expect a Gap on every corner or a mall in the marina. Broad Channel's limited size and out-of-the-way location deter invasion by retail giants like Wal-mart, Home Depot, and modern-day Pierre Noels. And most islanders like it that way.

Broad Channel may be an urban outpost, an inconvenient place to live within the grand scheme of New York City, but its residents are rooted here by tradition and love of the bay. Each day the sunrise and sunset stretch out unobstructed across the horizon. The subway chugs along like a rinky-dink railroad through brown reeds and russet meadows and past tiny box houses that fly Old Glory every day—not just on Flag Day. Everything changes slowly on Broad Channel, or not at all. It's a city neighborhood clinging to its small-town soul.

Exploring the Island

The **Jamaica Bay Wildlife Refuge,** (718) 318-4340, is truly a respite from the push and shove of urban life. More than 325 species have been spotted in this ornithological melting pot along the Atlantic Flyway. Within this gorgeous avian mosaic are black-bellied plovers, American oyster-catchers, marbled godwits, white-rumped sandpipers, short-billed dow-itchers, Wilson's phalaropes, egrets, black-crowned night herons, and others.

This refuge is not just for the birds, however, even though it was created with their flight paths in mind. Rangers have introduced plants that attract butterflies, like the tiger swallowtail, painted lady, and question mark; reptiles, like the painted turtle; and amphibians, like the spring peeper and gray tree frog. The fragrance and nectar of buddleia seduce butterflies, while blackhaw appeals to pheasants and cardinals. Warblers and mockingbirds like northern bayberry, and long-eared owls roost in Japanese black pine.

East Pond and **West Pond** are the two main areas for bird lovers and nature enthusiasts; trail maps are available at the visitors center. (The refuge is free.) The 1.75-mile **West Pond Trail** begins at the visitors center, wraps around the forty-five-acre pond, and offers little shade from the sun much of the way. The more popular trail, it is accessible year-round and offers views of the city juxtaposed against the marshland of Jamaica Bay with its ducks, geese, and the occasional beached boat. An auxiliary terrapin trail along this walk is closed in June and July, when diamondback terrapins lay their eggs. At West Pond, there are benches where you can quietly observe the everyday routines of the sanctuary's waders and waterfowl or maybe even see a peregrine falcon playfully swoop down on a flock of gulls. The final stretch, or **Upland Trail,** heading away from the pond and back toward the visitors center, is markedly different in ambience. **The North and South Gardens** are populated by a wide array of trees and shrubs: autumn olive, gray birch, red maple, willow oak, and Japanese black pine trees, along with salt-spray rose shrubs, yucca, and even prickly pear cactus. You'll hear an ensemble of chirps, caws, and whistles as the birds whoosh past you from one thicket to another.

Those inclined toward an even more secluded, Waldenesque experience may prefer the primitive **East Pond Trail** across the street from the visitors center. It's well worth the dash across six lanes of traffic on Cross Bay Boulevard—just wait for a break in the flow of cars. To create mudflats for migrating shorebirds, the water level is lowered in summer. Because much of the three-mile trail rings the hundred-acre pond, it's frequently a mucky trek, so wear duck shoes or boots. The rewards to those who proceed undaunted are solitude and lots of wildlife. On especially muddy days— mostly in spring and winter—portions of the trail are closed.

Highlights of the trail include a four-person blind looking out onto a window of life at half-acre **Big John's Pond.** Named for a bulldozer operator who helped create the pool in 1983, the pond offers plenty of action: Painted turtles bask in the sun; glossy ibis pluck insects from the water's surface with their long, slender beaks; and dragonflies move about as if their darts and dives were choreographed. By the time you reach East Pond, the din of Cross Bay Boulevard has faded. All is quiet except for the occasional wingbeats of majestic swans or flutter of small ducks sailing on the pond, and the periodic whoosh of a nearby subway train.

The ideal seasons to visit the sanctuary are spring and fall, although more and more people are braving the cold to view the increased number of wintering birds here. Spring features the greening of the salt marsh, the blooming of wildflowers, and the arrival of songbirds. In summer, the refuge is a hot spot for waders like egrets and herons. (Unfortunately, flies, poison ivy, and ticks also summer here, so bring insect repellent and dress appropriately.) Autumn finds the area populated by shorebirds and hawks, while saw-whet, long-eared, and snowy owls, along with snow geese and bufflehead ducks, all drop by in winter.

Park rangers offer dozens of free programs and tours throughout the year; choose from the quirky—everything you ever wanted to know about the horseshoe crab—to the seasonal—harvest moon and migratory shorebird walks. Popular programs may require reservations.

About a half mile farther down Cross Bay Boulevard from the sanctuary is the community of **Broad Channel.** While there are no historic sites or museums, you can get a feel for this unique neighborhood by strolling the side streets. Many old bungalows and houses on stilts are still around, although home ownership has inspired some modernization.

You can rent boats for crabbing and sight-seeing in the bay, or drop a fishing line off the Cross Bay Veterans Memorial Bridge and catch weakfish, porgies, and fluke. Founded in 1938, **Smitty's Boat Rental,** 301 East Ninth Road, (718) 945-2642, rents sixteen-foot skiffs with outboard motors and carries a full line of bait and tackle from spring through fall.

Where to Eat

Broad Channel has little to offer the hungry visitor. For a quick bite and some local flavor, try the counter at **Coogan's Luncheonette,** 724 Cross Bay Boulevard, (718) 474-8335.

Island Hopping

🚗 *By car:* Take the Belt Parkway east to exit 17, make a right onto Cross Bay Boulevard, through Howard Beach and over the North Channel Bridge. Continue about one mile to the Jamaica Bay Wildlife Refuge—the visitors center is on the right side—or continue straight into the community of Broad Channel.

🚆 *By subway:* The A train stops right in Broad Channel. To get to the

refuge, walk west to Cross Bay Boulevard, then make a right and continue a half mile. The visitors center is on your left.

🚌 *By bus:* The Q53 express bus from Roosevelt Avenue, Jackson
Heights; the Q21 from Woodhaven and Queens Boulevards, or Liberty
Avenue and Cross Bay Boulevard; and the Q21A from the New Lots
Avenue subway station all stop in Broad Channel. Walk a half mile back
along Cross Bay Boulevard to the refuge visitors center.

17. Forgotten Islands of Jamaica Bay and the Rockaways

Ruffle Bar • Barren Island • Bergen and Mill Islands • Hog Island

Forgotten Islands of Jamaica Bay and the Rockaways

Ruffle Bar

While many islets in Jamaica Bay were home to squatters' fishing huts in the late nineteenth and early twentieth centuries, Ruffle Bar came the closest to rivaling Broad Channel as a full-fledged community. Located just over the Brooklyn border in the bay, Ruffle Bar gained popularity after the Civil War as a ferry stop for tourists traveling from Canarsie to Rockaway. By the 1880s, a group known as the Windward Club sponsored boat races at Ruffle Bar; in the 1890s, the town of Flatlands leased lots on the 150-acre island, and the Skidmore House hotel opened.

Ruffle Bar got another boost around 1914, when Pierre Noel founded the Ruffle Bar Association and began developing the island. By 1926, landfill helped the marshy island accommodate forty buildings including one housing the Certified Oyster Company. Children rowed to the Rockaways for school. But the Depression decimated the community, and by the 1940s only a handful of squatters remained. The island is abandoned today, with broken dishes, coal stoves, and building foundations the only vestiges of a lost community.

Barren Island

For centuries, Barren Island maintained a low-profile, pastoral serenity. But as New York struggled with industrial-age growing pains, the island emerged as a site so crucial to urban life that it could no longer be ignored. In fact, after its factories arrived, nearby residents denounced Barren Island as the most noxious and noisome of neighbors.

Today, Barren Island is no longer an island. It's part of the Gateway National Recreation Area's Floyd Bennett Field at the southern end of Brooklyn's Flatbush Avenue. Until landfill connected it to the mainland in 1926, Barren Island was a triangular-shaped isle at the western edge of Jamaica Bay. One of the area's largest landmasses, it contained seventy acres of salt marsh that were submerged in spring and thirty acres of uplands that featured forests of cedar trees fringed by white sand beaches. Barren Island lay among dozens of islets large and small, though only a few, like Riches Meadow, Plum Island, and Big Slop Marsh, were individually named. Native Americans called the area Equindito, or "broken lands."

Europeans arrived around 1625, starting with the Dutch West India Company. The Dutch called it Beeren Eylant, prompting the English variants Bear Island, Barn Island, and Barren Island. At low tide, the water was shallow enough for livestock and men to wade from the mainland to the island, where rich salt-hay pastures were grazed and harvested. But nobody settled on Barren Island until the early nineteenth century.

The first resident was a man named Dooley, who built a house on the eastern end and operated an inn for sportsmen and fishermen. John Johnson took over Dooley's business in 1830 (see *Historical Detour: Fools and Gold*), by which time three or four families lived on the island.

Still, the island remained essentially barren until the late 1850s, when entrepreneurs found its location—isolated, yet easily accessible by boat through the Rockaway inlet—ideal for industry. From 1859 through 1933, more than two dozen companies set up shop at different times, virtually all of them in the fertilizer, fish-oil, or garbage disposal businesses.

The first two businesses were fertilizer plants that focused on horse rendering. One was owned by William B. Reynolds, who had a municipal contract to remove dead animals, butcher's blood, and other refuse from the streets of New York. In one month, Reynolds collected 500 horses and cows, 100 to 220 dogs, cats, other small animals, and quantities of blood, offal, and bones, all for the handsome sum of $1,500. The island's western bay soon changed from Dooley's Bay to Dead Horse Bay.

The plants, including Reynolds's, transformed this goulash into glue, bone dust, and fertilizer, which was sold throughout the world, even to grape growers in Europe's Rhine Valley. The two original fertilizer companies didn't last long, but horse rendering remained an important ingredient in Barren Island industry until 1921.

Fish-oil plants were the next arrivals, opening in the late 1860s, after large schools of menhaden were discovered in the nearby Long Island waters. Menhaden oil was used for tanning leather and mixing paints; the fish scraps were used in fertilizer. By 1883, the fish-oil plants employed ten steamships and 350 men. The laborers, most of them single, were southern blacks and European immigrants. They lived in segregated dorms and usually worked separately, too.

The island earned an unsavory reputation as a site of filth, squalor, and nasty odors. And with nearby Coney Island, the Rockaways, and Jamaica Bay developing into havens for tourists, residents, and fishermen, a conflict was inevitable. In 1890, when several government investigations castigated

Historical Detour: Fools and Gold

In November 1830, Captain William Thornby brought two new workers—seaman Charles Gibbs and steward Thomas Walmsley—aboard *The Vineyard* for a run from New Orleans to Philadelphia. What should have been a routine venture for a brig laden with staples of the South evolved into a sordid tale of murder, greed, and misfortune on the islands of New York.

The Vineyard's cargo consisted of cotton, molasses, sugar . . . and $54,000 in Mexican currency. Unbeknownst to Thornby, Gibbs and Walmsley had just fled Cuba and nasty reputations as ruthless pirates. When they discovered the cash, they hatched a mutinous plot, enlisting seamen Aaron Church and Henry Atwell and cabin boy Robert Dawes. Gibbs and Walmsley bludgeoned the captain to death and threw his corpse overboard. Church and Atwell badly wounded mate William Roberts and, when he begged for mercy, tossed him into the deep.

Then the pirates made their own fatal misjudgment: They let the remaining seamen James Talbot and John Brownrigg live, promising each of them a cut of the cash if they'd keep their mouths shut.

Instead of steering toward the City of Brotherly Love, *The Vineyard* headed for Long Island. With land in sight, the crew burned and sank the ship, split the booty, and escaped in two small boats. But their glorious plans quickly went awry when they were overwhelmed by fierce gale winds near Rockaway Bar: Church, Talbot, Atwell, and $23,000 were lost at sea; Gibbs, Walmsley, Brownrigg, and Dawes dumped all but $5,000 to lighten their load.

The survivors pushed on to Barren Island's Pelican Beach, where they buried the remaining treasure. They told a tragic tale of shipwreck to resident Nicholas Williams (in some accounts William Johnson), who sent them to his brother-in-law, John Johnson, proprietor of Dooley's, the local inn.

That night, while the others slept, Brownrigg confessed the misdeed to Johnson. Rather than confront the criminals, Johnson took them to Sheepshead Bay to arrange for transport to Manhattan. Then he and Williams raced to the spot Brownrigg had mentioned, dug up the loot, and re-hid it. Meanwhile, as Gibbs negotiated for a ride to the city, Brownrigg confessed to the authorities. This time they all ended up in jail.

Brownrigg and Dawes turned state's evidence, and the pirates were scheduled for execution. Gibbs admitted to killing over a hundred men and women in his brutal career, and the hanging became a major event. On April 23, 1831, hundreds of boats filled with spectators turned out to see Gibbs and Walmsley hanged at Ellis Island.

On Barren Island, the tale was far from finished. Johnson went behind his brother-in-law's back and stashed the booty in two places along the beach. When Williams learned he'd been duped, he tattled to the ship's insurers, who sued Johnson. No evidence was found and Johnson was acquitted of theft. He retrieved one bag, but the other, containing $1,600 in silver, had been swept away by the tides. Local lore has it that a decade later, in 1842, a storm washed Johnson's lost loot onto the shore, but the water pulled most of the coins away before residents could snatch them up.

the Barren Island businesses for leaving thousands of dead fish on the docks, company officials pledged to clean up their act. It was a promise Barren Island businesses would make, and fail to keep, continually for the next thirty years.

Part of the problem was resolved after a national depression and menhaden shortage, between 1890 and 1894, wiped out most of the fish-oil factories. But a new generation of fertilizer and horse-rendering factories flourished—in one blistering five-day stretch in August 1896, one company hauled in 1,256 dead horses.

The smells got worse that year when New York, after ending its policy of dumping garbage in the ocean, awarded a lucrative garbage disposal contract to Barren Island's newest tenant, the New York Sanitary Utilization Company. The city had tried burying garbage on Rikers Island, but the odors were discernible in Manhattan and Queens. Barren Island was considered ideal, because it was so remote that "few New Yorkers would know how to find it," wrote the *New York Times*.

For the first time, existing laws about separating trash into different categories were enforced; garbage went to Barren Island, while old rags and paper were separately collected and sold by the city. Ashes were still sent to Rikers Island. The Sanitary Utilization Company transformed garbage into fertilizer as well as grease for soap and candles. (During World War I, the raw product was sold to the government for making glycerine in bombs.) The company's vice president was Thomas White; he and his brother Andrew were the barons of Barren Island. They owned most of the island, including a rendering company, and were already collecting garbage from New York hotels.

The New York Sanitary Utilization Company, along with the other refuse disposal and fertilizer factories on the island, was a major headache for politicians. In 1897, Brooklynites as far as four miles away testified before the board of health that they had to close their windows when the wind was blowing. But once again, the companies were merely warned to abate the nuisances.

Tired of holding their noses, the Anti–Barren Island League extracted election-year promises in 1898 from state legislators of both parties to shut down the Sanitary Utilization Company. After a heated battle with plant proponents Mayor Robert Van Wyck and Governor Theodore Roosevelt, the legislature overrode the governor's veto and abolished the garbage reduction process in Brooklyn.

But in an era ruled by big-business interests, the courts declared the bill unconstitutional, saying the legislature had overstepped its authority by disregarding the city's autonomy and the private property of the Sanitary Utilization Company. So the company kept churning along, with a thousand tons of garbage arriving daily on Barren Island.

The prosperous rendering and processing industries gave birth to a true community of barbers, butchers, hotels, and saloons along Main Street, the island's only thoroughfare. A small boat, *Fannie McKane*, ferried residents to and from Canarsie twice daily. The population, which had grown to eight hundred by the mid-1890s, peaked at fifteen hundred, with Poles and Italians adding to the ethnic mix. In 1900, a second church, St. Andrew's Catholic Church, opened. Families now outnumbered single male inhabitants. In 1901, P.S. 120, with six classrooms and a playground, replaced the old one-room school.

When the bay froze and stranded residents, they lived off their livestock and homemade German bologna. Other hardships were less bearable— besides being scorned by their Brooklyn neighbors, these lower-class residents were shortchanged by the government and battered by Mother

Nature. They had no public water supply and no sewage system, there was no fire department, and medical care was limited. It took three hours to reach a hospital in bad weather.

Worst of all, Barren Island itself was literally falling apart. During thirteen terrifying minutes in November 1905, a four-hundred-by-two-hundred-foot chunk of the island's southeast corner was sucked into the bay, taking a two-story warehouse with it. Only six months later, a fire wiped out sixteen Sanitary Utilization buildings, causing more than $1 million in damage and forcing the evacuation of six hundred families. Then, in April 1907, two of the company's new buildings and a pier were swept away as the island ruptured again.

The company survived the disasters, only to encounter more dangerous foes in the next decade: budget-conscious politicians and outraged citizens. The escalating controversies eventually doomed the community.

In 1912, city officials proposed selling the rights to collect New York's garbage, rather than to continue paying the Sanitary Utilization Company an average of $200,000 a year for the chore, since the company was reaping nearly $1 million annually from its postreduction products. Nothing changed, but the issue would come back to haunt politicians.

Despite improvements made to minimize the smell, complaints from nearby homeowners' associations inspired investigations by the city's health department over the next three years. The plants were forced to close occasionally in the summer due to the stench. Then, in 1916, Mayor John Mitchel's administration announced that a modern processing facility would be built on Staten Island, with a new by-products company paying for its construction and the right to collect the city's garbage.

Staten Island, which had its own disposal plant, angrily opposed hosting the rest of the city's garbage. Swinburne Island was considered, but was dismissed as too small, while others suggested building an island on Romer Shoals in the Lower Bay. Despite the fury of Staten Islanders, construction began in the now notorious Fresh Kills area.

Garbage disposal became a major issue in the vicious campaigns of 1917. By this time, the new Metropolitan By-Products Company on Staten Island was functioning at 50 percent. Complaints poured into city hall, but the Mitchel administration defended the plant, blaming the offending stink on nearby New Jersey factories. Ironically, Tammany Hall Democrats cried corruption, claiming that Mitchel, a Republican, was in cahoots with real-estate developers seeking to protect ventures in the Rockaways by investing in Metropolitan By-Products. They also accused Mitchel of promising the company a payoff if Staten Islanders blocked the project. Democratic mayoral challenger John Hylan promised Staten Islanders he'd repeal the contract, although he avoided detailing alternative sites for the garbage.

After defeating Mitchel, Hylan investigated the Metropolitan By-Products Company and threatened to revoke its contract if health issues weren't resolved. Hylan then had fifteen barges of city garbage dumped in the ocean rather than use the facility. The refuse washed up on Coney Island, and at the same time, the Metropolitan By-Products Company defaulted on its contract. After long denying rumors about reviving Barren Island as the city's wastebasket, Hylan acknowledged he had nowhere else to turn.

Brooklynites protested the return of the New York Sanitary Utilization Company, and Hylan took political heat for his financial fiasco—the city was to pay the company $1,000 a day to process the garbage. But in 1919 the mayor "solved" the dilemma by reverting to the city's unsanitary but politically palatable policy of dumping garbage at sea. The Sanitary Utilization Company dismantled its facilities in 1921, with one small processing company staying on until 1933.

In the meantime, the advent of cars killed off the horse-rendering industry. By 1918, Barren Island was bringing in only six hundred carcasses a year, the number previously averaged in twelve days. The last plant closed in 1921, and the island became an economic has-been.

While industry and opportunity faded, a newcomer to Barren Island inspired hope in the community. Jane Shaw, a teacher transferred to the island's P.S. 120 in 1919, became known as the Angel of Barren Island. Devoted to her students and their families, Shaw taught English to immigrant parents in the evenings, and on Sundays showed movies in the school. When the island's doctor left after the factories closed and population declined, residents turned to Shaw for treatment of minor ailments.

Shaw eventually became principal of the school and successfully lobbied Senator Robert Wagner to assign official names to the island's anonymous streets and change the community's name to South Flatlands to lessen residents' isolation from the rest of Brooklyn. In 1930, Shaw took on the Census Bureau after it omitted this urban outback, and forced the bureau to send an inspector to the community to count the remaining 416 residents.

By this time, however, Barren Island had lost its island status. In the 1920s, Brooklyn was extended by landfill into Riches Meadow and finally out to Barren Island to accommodate the rapidly developing borough. A young Brooklyn pilot named Paul Rizzo then established Barren Island

Airport, which caught the eye of city planners looking for a municipal airport site. But to accommodate New York's first airport, the city needed more room than tiny Barren Island could supply. New York added nearly eight hundred acres of landfill and renamed the area Floyd Bennett Field (for Admiral Richard Byrd's copilot on his Arctic flights).

More than twenty-five thousand visitors witnessed a defense display by an aerial armada of 597 planes (one flown by Charles Lindbergh) when the airport was dedicated on May 23, 1931. Two years later, Wiley Post took off from there on the first solo flight around the world. While Floyd Bennett Field failed commercially, it was an important military airfield during World War II.

During these developments some residents held steadfast to their homeland, living as tenants on city-owned property. In 1935, Robert Moses decided to expand Brooklyn's nearby Marine Park and ordered the residents to leave by the following year. A few diehards, who still called themselves islanders, were unwilling to relinquish their world, and moved onto a fifty-one-acre tract still owned by the White family. In 1942, the federal government bought the White tract to expand the air base. The tenacious community, which had lived amid the stench of garbage and horse flesh, and had survived decades of hostile attacks by nature and neighbors, faded into oblivion.

Exploring the Island

Gateway National Recreation Area offers an impressive array of free activities at **Floyd Bennett Field,** (718) 338-3338, so call for a seasonal calendar. Outings focus on the area's unsung flora and fauna and aviation history rather than on its pungent Barren Island days. Activities include walking tours of Dead Horse Bay and hangar row (where you'll see historic planes like a 1940s Indiana National Guard relic), and seining in Jamaica Bay. The field also hosts art exhibitions and cultural and ethnic festivals. (Many activities require reservations.)

But the old airfield's most unique asset is that it offers Brooklyn's only camping site: yes, camping out in the Brooklyn wilderness. The site, which can be reserved for a single tent but is large enough to accommodate several, is relatively tame, like a huge backyard with picnic tables—except that you might spot possums, rabbits, herons, and even falcons. You can also fish in Jamaica Bay, which is only two hundred yards away, stroll along its banks, or walk the nearby two-mile nature trail. The campsite is open from April to November. There is a second campsite area for groups, which features six wheelchair-accessible platform tents.

The **Gateway Sports Center,** 3200 Flatbush Avenue across from Floyd Bennett Field, (718) 253-6816, features a batting range, driving range, tennis courts, and miniature golf.

Island Hopping

By car: Take Flatbush Avenue south to the end, or the Belt Parkway to exit 11-S, then take Flatbush Avenue south to Gateway.

By bus: Take the Q35 from Flatbush and Nostrand Avenues to Gateway.

By train: Catch the 2 or 5 to Flatbush Avenue, and transfer to the Q35 bus.

Bergen and Mill Islands

Long before Wall Street became America's financial capital, moneymakers of the land converged on Bergen and Mill Islands in the northwest corner of Jamaica Bay. The currency wasn't coins or dollars, it was clams—and their abundance made the islands integral to the Native American wampum industry of the day.

Other nearby sites were also wampum producers, but these Brooklyn isles offered one major advantage—their geography discouraged intruders. For enemy Mohawks to attack Bergen Island, they had to cross a creek and open meadows, while the Canarsies who lived there fired at them from the shelter of the forest.

When white pioneers arrived, Mill was two small bits of arable upland and Bergen was sixty acres of uplands and meadows. During peaceful times, many tribes and European settlers, who acknowledged the currency's legitimacy, visited the islands for white wampum and dark or blue wampum—called Indian's gold by settlers. But once New Amsterdam was well established, Bergen and Mill lost their strategic value for the Native inhabitants; soon after, the whites took over the islands.

Aside from nearby Barren Island, these were the only two islands in the region inhabited by Europeans during the colonial period. Mill Island derives its name from a gristmill built there around 1666, which operated until the 1880s. In 1675, Jan Martense Schenck bought the island; his descendants owned it for a century and a half. In the late nineteenth century, Robert Crooke transformed the pastoral island into an industrial site, building a lead-smelting plant. He later sold the island to oil refineries and smelting companies.

Bergen Island was the subject of bitter feuds from the seventeenth through the nineteenth centuries, as litigious descendants of the original settlers squabbled over deeds and titles. The fracas spawned an identity crisis for the island, which donned a variety of names, including Meutelaers, Bestevaers, and Omities Island. By the 1850s, it had begun appearing on maps as Bergen Island, named for Cornelius Bergen, who lived there with his wife and son.

Little changed until the 1890s, when chewing gum manufacturer Thomas Adams bought the land and, together with Percy Williams (who later became a vaudeville theater magnate), established the Percy Williams Amusement Park. It featured musical extravaganzas in the casino and a castle-shaped roller skating rink, as well as free vaudeville acts on the pier near the Grand Esplanade.

On opening day of the 1905 season, thirty thousand fun-seekers reveled in the attractions, which also included a Ferris wheel, a 150-foot slide called the Slippery Slip, and stuntman Professor Jakob, who set himself afire before diving 90 feet into a pool of water.

Over the next decade, the masses came by trolley and ferry to play at what was called Bergen Beach. Two more amusement parks opened, and entertainers built homes on the island, making it a fashionable place to live. The sensation, however, was short-lived. By 1920, pollution in Jamaica Bay, declining trolley service, and the overwhelming popularity of nearby Coney Island put an end to the merrymaking.

Bergen and Mill Islands were incorporated into Brooklyn as part of a plan to create a commercial harbor in Jamaica Bay. Landfill restructured Mill Island into Mill Basin by 1922; today it's a middle-class neighborhood. According to some maps, Bergen Island was connected to the mainland as early as 1911; others record it as autonomous until 1918. Bergen Island once extended northwest as far as Avenue T and Island Avenue, which is now Veteran Avenue. Today the former island is shared by the community of Bergen Beach and the Gateway National Recreation Area.

Island Bonus

The two-room clapboard house Jan Martense Schenck built in 1675 stood on Mill Island/Mill Basin until 1952, when it was moved to the **Brooklyn Museum,** 200 Eastern Parkway, (718) 638-5000, for preservation. The one-and-a-half-story house—with a loft for sleeping and grain storage—appears as it might have in 1730. Dutch touches include an open hearth and a large, ornate bureau called a *kas.*

Hog Island

A tiny island. A brief existence. For nearly a century, Hog Island was the missing island in the story of New York's archipelago.

This barrier island rose from the waters just south of the Rockaways during the 1860s, growing by the next decade to be one mile long. Like many of the small Jamaica Bay isles nearby, Hog Island attracted summertime visitors and entrepreneurs, who built bathing houses and restaurants. But in August 1893, one of the most devastating hurricanes to ever hit New

York demolished the island, causing $80,000 worth of damage, wiping out pavilions, restaurants, and cabins. Although the island resurfaced several times in the next decade, another round of storms finished it off in 1902.

Hog Island vanished from memory, too, until coastal geologist and Queens College professor Nicholas Coch and his students—looking into erosion of the Rockaways—discovered artifacts that tipped them off to the existence of a long-gone island. Archival research turned up further details, leading to a 1997 *New York Times* feature on Hog Island, which once again found itself in the spotlight for but a moment.

Part VI

South Brooklyn Waters

CONEY ISLAND • FORGOTTEN ISLANDS OF SOUTH BROOKLYN

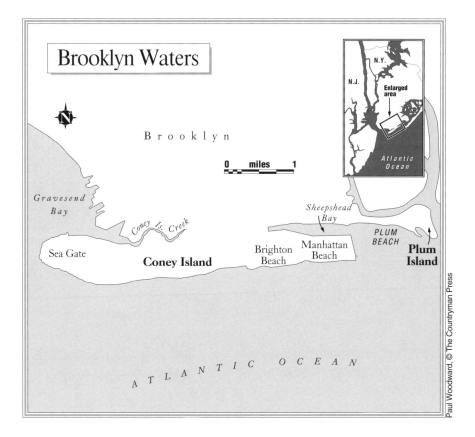

Coney Island Creek is now just an inlet off Gravesend Bay and is separated from Sheepshead Bay by landfill. The creek once ran the length of Coney Island, dividing the island from the Brooklyn mainland.

18. Coney Island

"Like the mad Russian monk Rasputin, Coney Island has been stabbed, shot, poisoned, clubbed, and has still survived."
—MARIO PUZO, *NEW YORK MAGAZINE*, SEPTEMBER 3, 1979

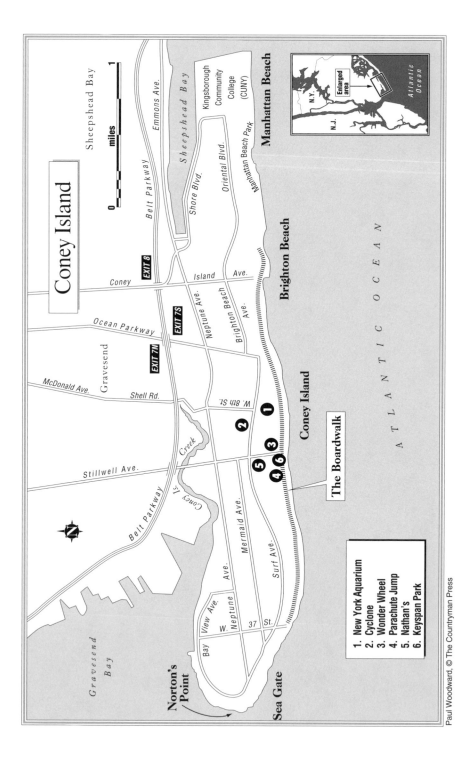

Coney Island

Sheepshead Bay

miles
0   1

Sheepshead Bay

Belt Parkway

Emmons Ave.

Shore Blvd.

Oriental Blvd.

Manhattan Beach Park

Kingsborough Community College (CUNY)

Manhattan Beach

EXIT 8

Coney   Island   Ave.

Neptune Ave.

Brighton Beach Ave.

Brighton Beach

EXIT 7S

Ocean Parkway

Gravesend

EXIT 7N

McDonald Ave.

Shell Rd.

W. 8th St.

Stillwell Ave.

Mermaid Ave.

Surf Ave.

Coney I. Creek

Belt Parkway

Bay View Ave.

Neptune Ave.

W.   37   St.

Coney Island

The Boardwalk

Sea Gate

Norton's Point

Gravesend Bay

N

A T L A N T I C   O C E A N

2
1
3
5
4 **6**

1. New York Aquarium
2. Cyclone
3. Wonder Wheel
4. Parachute Jump
5. Nathan's
6. Keyspan Park

N.Y.

N.J.

Enlarged area

Atlantic Ocean

Paul Woodward, © The Countryman Press

Coney Island

STEP RIGHT UP, CHECK IT OUT—it's the ultimate sideshow, ladies and gentleman, take a peek! We've got death-defying rides and bearded ladies, tall tales of political hooliganism and ripping yarns about entrepreneurial flimflammery, all guaranteed to be 100 percent tru . . . ly amazing!

This is Coney Island. It's an eternally evolving fable in which Erich Weiss polished his act in the 1890s before achieving international fame as Harry Houdini. A decade later, Israel Baline (Irving Berlin) performed at the local cabarets, while the next generation saw Archibald Leach (Cary Grant) work as a stiltwalker at Steeplechase Park.

This is Coney Island. It's the home of hype and hucksterism, where every story must be taken with a grain of salt. The owners of Steeplechase Park advertised its size as fifteen, then twenty-one, then twenty-five acres, although it hadn't grown an inch—the numbers just increased with their ambition. And the hot dog's origins are so distorted that Coney Islanders held a fiftieth anniversary fir it in 1939 and a one hundredth anniversary in 1967.

Even basic geography gets taken for a ride at New York City's playground. Once three islands collectively called Coney Island, they were later fused together by storms into a single five-mile strip. Around 1918, however, the island itself was physically joined to southern Brooklyn. When New Yorkers speak of Coney Island today, they refer only to the amusement area, formerly known as West Brighton. Actually the island-turned-peninsula also encompasses the communities of Manhattan Beach, Brighton Beach, and Sea Gate.

While the appellation Coney Island is internationally renowned, its origins are a conundrum. The name, which first appeared on a map in 1670, was most likely conceived by European colonists, who found coneys (rabbits) running wild on the islands. But Coney may also be a corruption of John Coleman, an officer on Henry Hudson's *Half Moon,* who was killed on the island by Canarsie Indians in 1609. A more improbable tale involves an early resident named Cooney, who went insane after his wife, child, and crude hut were swept away by a tidal wave.

Coney Island's documented history starts in the 1640s, and from the beginning it was an unconventional place. In 1644, the Dutch government granted an eighty-eight-acre island—the middle island of Coney's triad—to settler Guysbert Op Dyck. Yet the following year, the government also granted the town of Gravesend—which included all three islands—to Lady Deborah Moody, a wealthy, liberal Englishwoman fleeing religious persecution in Massachusetts. This was the only grant ever made to a woman, and Gravesend was the only part of Brooklyn settled first by the English.

Guysbert's Island was sandwiched between Piney Island to the east and Sedge Bank to the west. The islands were separated from Gravesend (now part of Brooklyn) by what is today called Coney Island Creek, a tidal creek that ran from Gravesend and Sheepshead Bays.

In about 1661, Op Dyck transferred the title for Guysbert's Island to Dirck de Wolfe, a Dutchman who established a salt production plant there. De Wolfe's business lasted until he tried to stop English Gravesend farmers from grazing cattle on his island and the confrontation turned ugly. The Gravesenders retaliated by destroying de Wolfe's garden and burning his fences, beginning what was to become a tradition of Coney conflagrations. They even threatened to throw de Wolfe into the fire, which nearly sparked an armed confrontation between the Dutch government and the English settlers. In 1662, the court awarded the English the rights to the island.

For the next 160 years, the islands remained uninhabited and were used primarily for hunting and grazing. Lumber was harvested from their cedar groves. The lone entrepreneurial development came from Thomas Stillwell, a descendant of Nicholas Stillwell, one of Gravesend's original settlers. In 1734, Stillwell deepened Coney Island Creek and turned it into a canal he hoped would provide a shorter, safer route for boats traveling from Jamaica Bay to New York Harbor. But the idea never caught on. Big changes came to the islands in the second half of the eighteenth century, when storms leveled the islands' high sand ridges, filling in the narrow inlet between Sedge Bank and Guysbert's Island. Coney Island remained two islands until January 1839, when a tremendous gale filled the remaining inlet, leaving one long island in its wake.

Coney Island was first developed in the 1820s by enterprising Gravesenders, who formed the Coney Island Road and Bridge Company. They constructed a toll road surfaced with shells leading from Gravesend to Coney Island, where they built an inn called the Coney Island House. Traffic on Shell Road was initially limited to a handful of wealthy New

Yorkers headed for this remote resort, which because of its isolation grew in fits and starts.

One early venture was the Coney Island Pavilion, opened in 1844 by two New Yorkers named Eddy and Hart, who sold tasty clams and rented bathing suits to beachgoers. Churches throughout Brooklyn tried to dissuade people from frolicking at Coney's shore on the Sabbath, but had little luck, especially as the beach gradually became more accessible. Steamboat service from Manhattan began in 1847, and three years later, Coney Island Plank Road (now Coney Island Avenue) was laid. The guest list at the Coney Island House by then included Washington Irving, Herman Melville, Henry Clay, Daniel Webster, P. T. Barnum, and Jenny Lind.

But still, according to Walt Whitman, who swam naked there, Coney Island remained a "long, bare unfrequented shore, which I had all to myself, and where I loved after bathing, to race up and down the hard sand, and declaim Homer and Shakespeare to the surf and seagulls by the hour."

While Coney Island's growth was tempered by inconvenient and unreliable transportation—boats ran infrequently and carriage rides were even more arduous than trains with their many connections—the surf and sun were too seductive to ignore. By 1865, Coney Island had numerous chowder stands, bathhouses, a dozen hotels, and a growing reputation. "We know a sand-bank where a wild time may be had for a very small outlay of money," the *New York Times* wrote in 1868.

In the early 1870s, weekend crowds soared to thirty thousand people, even though many establishments served mediocre food in ramshackle shanties, and often rented towels and bathing suits still wet from the previous customer.

Meanwhile, as Democratic boss William Marcy Tweed's men ruled and plundered New York, an air of lawlessness invaded Coney Island. The most notorious section was the West End, soon called Norton's Point after Mike Norton, a Tweed crony who opened the Point Comfort Hotel with loot he'd earned doing political favors for the Boss. Three-card-monte players brazenly set up shop along the beach, while pickpockets initiated weight-guessing games with gullible tourists who were patted down and subsequently freed from their wallets. Norton went bankrupt in the 1880s, and the den of thieves shifted toward West Brighton, where superior transportation was delivering daily doses of potential victims.

Indeed, transportation had significantly improved in 1875, when Andrew Culver united several small rail lines into the Prospect Park and Coney Island Railroad. That first year, the line transported one million vis-

itors to West Brighton's beaches and Charles Feltman's new Ocean Pavilion, which fast became the area's most popular and influential institution,
where the hot dog was invented . . . or so the story goes (see *Historical
Detour: A Dog's Tale*).

The new rail was an astonishing success—two million people rode it the
following year. To attract more tourists, Culver purchased the country's
tallest structure—the three-hundred-foot-high Observation Tower—and
brought it to Coney Island from the Centennial Exhibition in Philadelphia.
The year 1876 also marked the completion of elegant Ocean Parkway,
which stretched across Brooklyn to Coney Island.

The development of Coney Island then pushed eastward again, with
Austin Corbin paving the way in 1877 with his magnificent Manhattan
Beach Hotel. Corbin had stayed at the Coney Island House with his family
in 1874 after doctors prescribed ocean air for his ailing son. A restless
businessman, Corbin roamed the island and decided to build a luxury
resort on the vacant eastern portion.

He bribed William Stillwell, Gravesend's surveyor, to help him illegally
purchase the parcels needed. (Stillwell similarly abetted a man named
William Engeman, who developed Brighton Beach.)

President Ulysses S. Grant presided at the opening of Corbin's resort,
which catered to New York's moneyed society. One of the world's largest
hotels, it staged plays and operas in its theater, reenacted historic battles
under a fireworks-filled sky in its two-thousand-seat amphitheater, and
each day served twenty thousand elegant meals in its lavish dining rooms.
John Philip Sousa and his band performed there often; Sousa even penned
a tune called "Manhattan Beach March."

Corbin provided convenient transportation via his New York and Manhattan Beach Railway, which made the trip from city to hotel in only an hour.
Exclusivity ruled at Manhattan Beach, where Corbin, a ruthless aristocrat,
had the private beach fenced in and patrolled by detectives. In 1879, the
New Hampshire–born banker banned Jews from Manhattan Beach, stating,
"We do not like the Jews as a class. As a rule, they make themselves offensive to the kind of people who patronize our road and hotel."

Suddenly, everyone wanted a piece of the action at Coney Island.
Corbin's elitist hotel was soon followed by two other colossal resorts: the
Oriental Hotel, which featured circular towers surmounted by minarets,
and the Brighton Beach Hotel—described in 1899 by *Appleton's Dictionary
of Greater New York* as "a resort for Brooklyn people. It differs from Manhattan Beach much as Brooklyn does from Manhattan borough . . . there is

a little less of elegance . . . and more of a family and comfort-taking aspect."
(The hotel did, however, serve draft champagne.)

In 1878, the Iron Steamboat Company began delivering visitors to its
new Iron Pier in West Brighton, which was lined with saloons and ball-
rooms. A year later, the Brighton Beach Racetrack opened, joining nearby
racetracks in Sheepshead Bay and Gravesend and turning the region into
America's racing capital. By 1884, six railroads stopped at Coney Island,
and three additional lines ran shuttles from end to end.

The action, however, also had a sinister side. West of Ocean Parkway, a
thriving brothel business and a dangerous slum called the Gut flourished
under the intentionally averted gaze of nefarious Police Chief John Y.
McKane, who once testified that "houses of prostitution are a necessity on
Coney Island." (See *Historical Detour: The Chief.*) The Gut's most infamous
destination was the Elephant Hotel. Built in 1884, this unusual pachy-
derm-shaped building was 122 feet high, with tin "skin" and four-foot-tall
glass eyes that glittered at night. By the time the hotel burned down in
1896, the phrase *seeing the elephant* in Coney Island parlance meant
"being up to no good."

But it was another creature, which also arrived in 1884, that revolution-
ized Coney Island. The world's first roller coaster, the Switchback Railway,
was erected on West Tenth Street by thirty-six-year-old Ohioan L. A.
Thompson. The gravity-based ride traveled a mere six miles per hour (compared with today's eighty-mile-per-hour coasters) and was so primitive that
passengers had to get out while workers pushed the cars up to the second
peak. When two competitors advanced the technology, Thompson shot
back with two new coasters, the Scenic Railway and Pike's Peak, each of
which combined exotic scenery with a thrilling ride.

As America careened into the technological age, Thompson's invention
inspired several generations of Coney coasters and scenic railways, among
them Dragon's Gorge, Mile High Sky Chaser, Drop the Dip, Over the Great
Divide, and Roosevelt's Rough Riders (the site of Coney's worst coaster
accident in 1910, when seventeen people were thrown from a height of
thirty feet, and three died). Thunderbolt, built in 1926, had a small house
attached to the ride's frame where the owners lived; the ride was immortal-
ized as Alvy Singer's childhood home in the Woody Allen film *Annie Hall.*
The coaster closed in 1983 and deteriorated until it was demolished, amid
mild protests, in 2000. However, the most beloved roller coaster of all, the
Cyclone, is still active and is even an official New York City landmark.

The roller coaster wasn't Coney Island's only invention. William Mangels, a German immigrant who owned a carousel manufacturing company, designed several rides, including the Whip, a kiddie favorite featuring small cars that whipped around the bends of an oval track.

Coney's next major innovation, however, was not a technical feat. It was a marketing ploy. The enclosed amusement park, which debuted in 1895, was pioneered by Captain Paul Boyton, who had gained international fame in 1875 when he crossed the English Channel in a thirty-five-pound rubber suit he had invented. Dressed in his creation, Boyton later kicked his way down the Rhine, Seine, Danube, and Missouri Rivers.

The aquatically inclined Boyton opened Sea Lion Park between Surf and Neptune Avenues, offering attractions like juggling sea lions and a new water ride called Shoot-the-Chutes. However, Boyton failed with Flip-Flap, the first roller coaster to loop the loop; imperfectly engineered, it left riders with aching necks.

Boyton's amusement park concept sparked the imagination of George C. Tilyou, who had already proved himself one of the shrewdest entrepreneurs in West Brighton. Tilyou was three years old in 1865 when his father, Peter, opened Tilyou's Surf House restaurant and hotel on Coney Island. By fourteen, George was showing signs of Barnumesque salesmanship: He took bottles and cigar boxes from his dad, filled the bottles with salt water and the boxes with sand, and sold them to souvenir-hungry tourists. In 1882, he opened Tilyou's Surf Theater, but five years later he and his father were forced out of business after the younger Tilyou testified in a state investigation against Chief McKane.

It wasn't until he witnessed the awesome debut, in 1893, of the Ferris wheel while honeymooning at the World Columbian Exposition in Chicago that Tilyou entertained visions of a Coney comeback. Unable to purchase the original Ferris wheel, Tilyou built a smaller version at Coney Island, which he audaciously touted as "the world's largest Ferris wheel." Four years later, he mimicked Boyton's park idea by building Steeplechase Park, which set bold new standards in amusement park size and style. Tilyou also introduced the combination ticket, which allowed customers to enjoy a mélange of amusements for one price, and later built Steeplechase Pier to funnel people straight from boats into his park.

Tilyou capitalized on the popularity of Brooklyn racetracks by making a mechanical horse race the centerpiece of Steeplechase. People jeered, cheered, and even bet on the "horses," which were double-saddled with paying customers who accelerated and braked their way around the entire park via an iron rail, from Surf Avenue to the beach and from West Six-

Historical Detour: A Dog's Tale

In 1867, or 1871, 1874, or 1889—depending on the story—Charles Feltman, hoping to supplement his business of selling pies from a wagon, supposedly slapped a sausage in a bun and invented the frankfurter. While Coney Islanders relish this myth, neither an 1884 Feltman profile nor his 1910 obituaries mustered a single mention of the hot dog's tale, celebrating instead Feltman's rags-to-riches life and his pioneering role in establishing Coney Island as a seaside resort.

Born in Hanover, Germany, in 1841, Charles Feltman came to Brooklyn alone at age fourteen and, after surviving the winter of 1857 on stale bread and water, worked in bakeries for a decade before opening his own business.

In 1871, Feltman's bakery began selling bread and pastries to Coney Island restaurants. Three years later, he opened Feltman's Ocean Pavilion and, while others chortled, persuaded Andrew Culver to include evening trains on Culver's new railroad line, enabling beachgoers to stay for dinner. In his beer gardens at Surf Avenue and West Tenth Street, Feltman served seafood dinners, while the hot dogs at his stand soon replaced the clam as Coney Island's most famous food. Feltman's also became Coney's first restaurant with music—courtesy of Wannemacher's Seventy-first Regiment Band—and, so his obits proclaimed, the first to have Tyrolean yodelers. He hired orchestras and costumed Bavarian folksingers, built a lavishly decorated three-story ballroom (supposedly the world's largest), installed Coney Island's first merry-go-round, and later added roller coasters and movies.

Feltman's, which survived until 1954, drew two hundred thousand customers annually in the 1880s, and peaked in 1923 with 5.2 million patrons. Whether Charles Feltman invented the hot dog is debatable, but he certainly served a lot of them.

teenth to West Eighteenth Street. Although the ride cost $37,000 to build (a $600,000 value today), it held true to the simple themes that enabled Steeplechase to outlast its competitors, Luna Park and Dreamland. Both parks, built in the next decade, relied heavily on lavish spectacle, whereas at Steeplechase the customers themselves were the entertainment; giggling couples particularly enjoyed clutching onto and tumbling into one another on Tilyou's circuit of thrills.

Steeplechase classics included the Barrel of Love, the Human Roulette Wheel, and the Down and Out—a dark, steep, screw-shaped chute that dumped participants onto the spinning disks of the Human Pool Table. Visitors were also thrust onto the park's public stage, complete with falling scenery, moving floors, and skirt-blowing air, providing laughs for a seated audience. (By the time Steeplechase had run its course in 1964, modern social mores had rendered these semi-illicit thrills archaic.) Steeplechase's unforgettable logo was a garish face with leering grin and an improbable forty-four teeth. Hired hands marched around the Funny Place, as the park was known, in animal costumes, an idea Walt Disney later copied.

Tilyou's marketing know-how even enabled him to make disaster profitable. In 1907, while leaving church, Tilyou learned his beloved park had been destroyed by fire. Unfazed, he calmly instructed his men to wait until the fire cooled, then erect a fence and put up a sign advertising "Admission to the burning ruins 10 cents." Tilyou earned enough money to rebuild Steeplechase Park, a large section of which he enclosed to offer entertainment in any weather. Tilyou died in 1914, but his three sons kept drawing customers for another half century, adding attractions like the 1939 World's Fair Parachute Jump.

In his lifetime, Tilyou was not only savvy but also greedy. Steeplechase charged an entry fee to the beach behind the park; the practice was deemed illegal several years after his death. What's more, it was Tilyou's avarice that provoked the establishment of Steeplechase's greatest rival—Luna Park. At the 1901 Pan-American Exposition in Buffalo, Tilyou had persuaded Fred Thompson and Elmer Dundy to bring their new ride, Trip to the Moon, to Steeplechase. The ride was a smash in 1902, yet Tilyou wanted to cut the duo's share from 60 to 40 percent. Thompson and Dundy quit Steeplechase and took their ride down the block. The following summer, they opened Luna Park.

Dundy handled business matters, and named the park for his sister Luna back in Des Moines. Thompson, a Tennessean who had studied architecture, was the park's creative force, juxtaposing incongruous styles and tossing tradition aside. One must "dare to decorate a minaret with renaissance detail or to jumble romanesque with l'art nouveau," he wrote.

What they concocted was an "electric Eden," a fantasyland of candy-colored towers, trellises, domes, and spires illuminated by 250,000 electric lights—a spectacular sight in an era before electricity was a basic amenity. (Decades after the park was gone, budget-conscious New Yorkers reprimanded children who left lights on by saying, "What do you think this is, Luna Park?")

Built on the former site of Sea Lion Park, Luna Park drew forty thousand people on opening night and cleared $600,000 in profits its rookie year. Dundy and Thompson built a scenic railway called Trip to the North Pole and a romantic water ride called Canals of Venice, adding them to Boyton's Shoot-the-Chutes, which remained there. Other new attractions included Hagenbeck's Wild Animals, the Monkey Theater, a candy deli that sold confections shaped like hot dogs and fried oysters, and reenactment spectacles like Fire and Sword, which promised "realistic massacre together with many other features of real warfare at close quarters."

Anyone who believes that daytime talk shows and tragedy-of-the-week movies have reduced Americans to tasteless and morbid voyeurs has forgotten Coney's steady stream of macabre and popular exhibits, like the reenactment of the 1889 Johnstown Flood. Run independently of the big parks, its advertisements boasted, "Where the morning before had stood a noble town filled with prosperous and happy people, now all was desolation and death . . . The Johnstown Flood appeals to all young and old and should be seen by every visitor to the island."

For sheer voyeurism, nothing topped Luna's Infant Incubators, where twenty-five cents bought a glimpse of premature babies. The infants received expert medical care and mothers willingly offered them up to receive the free treatment. Dreamland lured the incubator exhibit away in 1904, but it returned to Luna Park for good in 1911.

In 1912, however, five years after Dundy's untimely death, the hard-drinking Thompson lost Luna Park in bankruptcy. The new owner, Baron Collier, kept Thompson on as manager until he died in 1919. But Collier wasn't innovative, and new technologies like talkies and radio eventually rendered Luna's wonders passé. The Heart of Coney Island slowly declined, and in 1946, after two fires in three years, the lights went out on Luna Park.

Coney Island's last big park, Dreamland, was opened in 1904 by former senator William H. Reynolds, whose Tammany Hall friends provided a sweet deal for property at Surf Avenue and West Eighth Street. Based on the Luna model, the grander, more elaborate Dreamland promised to be the greatest amusement park of all. Its imperial design cost $3.5 million and included one million lights (four times as many as Luna's), a 375-foot-tall main tower with a beacon that shone fifty miles out to sea, and baroque-style columns, arches, gargoyles, and griffins so sophisticated they were analyzed by architecture critics.

But Dreamland's extravagant facade couldn't mask its obvious similarity to Luna Park. Dreamland's attractions were either derivative (scenic railways like Coasting Through Switzerland, spectacle shows like Fall of Pompeii and Fighting the Flames) or outright copies (Shoot-the-Chutes and Canals of Venice). Although dazzling, Dreamland lacked the boisterousness and whimsy of Luna Park, and never gripped the public's imagination the same way . . . until the day it burned to the ground seven years later.

At 1:30 AM on May 27, 1911—the season's opening day—a fire started in the wiring of Dreamland's turbulent water ride, Hell Gate. While Coney Island had experienced ten multi-alarm fires in eighteen years, this was by far the worst. As forty-four hundred firemen struggled against the inferno, Manhattanites could see the flames licking the night sky. Dreamland was left in ashes and nearby restaurants, bathhouses, and attractions like Thompson's Scenic Railway and the Observation Tower were destroyed. Nobody died, but a lion named Black Prince from the wild-animal show staggered, bleeding and burning, onto Surf Avenue, before climbing the tracks of the Rocky Road to Dublin roller coaster, where he was shot. Scavengers armed with pliers yanked out Black Prince's teeth for souvenirs, and the next day, crowds paid ten cents to view his corpse.

Samuel Gumpertz, who had risen from managing Dreamland's Lilliputian Village—occupied by three hundred midgets—to managing the entire park, quickly built his own Dreamland Circus Sideshow on the old park's ruins. But with Dreamland's destruction coming on the heels of a reform that had closed the Brighton Beach Racetrack, many observers predicted the demise of Coney Island. Indeed, an era of elegance was ending—in the next decade, the Manhattan Beach, Brighton Beach, and Oriental Hotels were razed, making way for urban residential housing. But the experts were wrong. Coney Island wasn't dying, it was simply taking on a new flavor . . . and it was about to become more popular than ever before.

Between 1915 and 1920, three subway lines arrived at Coney Island, and suddenly every New Yorker could reach the beach for only a nickel. With Nathan's, which had opened in 1916, asking only another nickel for a hot dog or a milk shake, Coney Island became the Nickel Empire—truly a summer resort for the masses, who would often sleep on the beach on Saturday nights rather than return to their sweltering tenements.

A million revelers, or 18 percent of the city's populace, visited Coney Island on a typical summer Sunday in 1920, a vast increase over 1900, when a hundred thousand people, or 3 percent of the city residents, made the same pilgrimage. To accommodate the throngs, Coney Island opened an eighty-foot-wide boardwalk along the beach in 1923, officially named Riegelman's Walk after former Brooklyn borough president Harold Riegelman. The 1920s also gave birth to Thunderbolt, the Cyclone, and Wonder Wheel. By 1938, Coney Island boasted thirteen carousels, eleven roller coasters, twenty shooting galleries, three freak shows, and two hundred eateries. In Coney Island's peak years just after World War II, the Coney Island Chamber of Commerce seems to have gleefully exaggerated attendance figures—newspaper reports of 36 million visitors in 1946 and 2.5 million on a single Sunday in 1947 sound mathematically improbable— but on hot summer days, the workingman's resort appeared packed with every man, woman, and child in the city.

In subsequent decades, the record crowds gradually dissipated as home air conditioners and car travel gave New Yorkers other summer options, amusement areas elsewhere became more sophisticated, and the misguided deeds of Robert Moses and the government transformed Coney Island's identity. In 1949, the fun-hating parks commissioner—who had previously banned everything from fishing to flying kites at Coney Island— stunned local merchants by denouncing Coney Island as "an over-commercialized mistake." He then began rezoning the amusement area for passive recreation. The influential *New York Times* supported Moses' endeavor, parroting his pronouncements that people preferred retreats like Jones Beach (a Moses creation) to "gadget resorts" like Coney.

Moses later changed course, however, and in his dual role as city construction coordinator and parks commissioner announced at the 1958 groundbreaking for the Luna Park high-rise apartments that Coney Island should instead be rebuilt as a residential community. Between 1960 and 1973, fifteen large housing projects and apartment buildings were erected on Coney Island. After Steeplechase Park closed in the 1960s, Fred Trump (Donald Trump's father) demolished it, planning to build four thirty-story towers there that were never realized. Neighborhood shops and houses were also razed in anticipation of federal financing for more buildings, but President Richard Nixon cut off the funds, leaving this once dynamic area pockmarked with rubble-filled lots and forbidding housing projects. Jobs and commerce vanished as banks, small businesses, and movie theaters closed—all a chilling tribute to the destructive powers of poor urban planning. Although no longer an island, the government's neglect of Coney Island left it as isolated as if it were out at sea.

Historical Detour: The Chief

In 1869, John Y. McKane, an unknown, uneducated builder from Sheepshead Bay, was elected one of Gravesend's three town commissioners and authorized to lease the town's common land, which included parts of Coney Island. By the 1880s, McKane had metamorphosed from this low-profile administrator into the grand pooh-bah of Coney Island, a ruthless and dictatorial political boss whose powers stretched from the Elephant Hotel to the White House.

Born in 1841 in Ireland's County Antrim, McKane came to Brooklyn as an infant. In his teens, he worked as a carpenter's apprentice, later opening his own business and shrewdly capitalizing on the rapid development of Coney Island by building its bathhouses and beer halls. This thickset, ruddy-faced man didn't drink, smoke, or gamble and soon became superintendent of his local Sunday school.

A scrupulous and highly productive town commissioner, McKane more than doubled the town's leasing revenue in his first two years. But power seduced McKane, who soon subverted his principles in an effort to garner the post of Gravesend supervisor. Toward that end, McKane built support and made powerful friends by leasing land to them at a fraction of its worth. Austin Corbin, the developer of Manhattan Beach, paid $1,500 for land valued at one hundred times that amount. A similar bargain was afforded Paul Bauer, with McKane building Bauer's West Brighton Hotel and Casino. Developers often returned the favor by hiring McKane's company to do construction work.

McKane's shady deals paid off. In the late 1870s, he was the first working-class man elected to Gravesend supervisor. He convinced the state legislature to allow him to replace Brooklyn police with his own Coney Island force, and made himself police commissioner. As head of the town board, board of health, and water board, he wrote local laws and audited contracts. He also began giving land away to influential cronies. The Chief, as McKane was called, ran Coney Island as he saw fit, creating what the *New York Times* later called "Sodom-by-the Sea." He employed pickpockets for "detective" work, licensed the era's leading bank robbers to run saloons, allowed the notorious Gut district to prosper down the road from police headquarters, and crushed anyone who opposed him.

McKane's netherworld prompted an investigation by the state assembly in 1887. The *Times* wrote that his see-no-evil policy "largely turned Coney into a nest of dives, disreputable houses, gambling hells and cheap and nasty shows." McKane's brazen defense was "I do not make inquiries." In other words, unless he stumbled upon an illegal activity, he would not investigate.

The assembly committee called for McKane's indictment, but his comrades in Albany buried the report. McKane promptly retaliated against George Tilyou—the only islander to name names during the hearings—by forcing Tilyou and his father out of business. That summer, a thousand McKane disciples held a gala for the Chief at Bauer's Casino, where a massive portrait of McKane draped with the Stars and Stripes hung above the entrance. McKane was given a gold shield featuring a diamond star—surrounded by emeralds and more diamonds—worth $1,500 (more than $22,000 today).

McKane effected his greatest abuse of power on Election Day. In the 1884 presidential election, when New York State went Democrat by 1,047 votes, McKane's control of local voting booths was widely credited with helping put the reform-minded Grover Cleveland over the top in a crucial state. After a quarrel with Brooklyn's Democratic boss, Hugh McLaughlin, however, McKane switched parties. In 1888, McKane fixed the Gravesend vote, helping Republican Benjamin Harrison defeat Cleveland.

McKane's arrogance and unfettered authority ultimately proved his undoing. In 1893, reform candidates in Brooklyn tired of McKane's election shenanigans, and called for a fair count in Gravesend. While the town had only 1,700 legal voters, McKane had tallied 2,547 votes in 1891 and claimed 6,218 registrants in 1893. Reformers who confronted McKane were beaten up and jailed, and when a second group arrived with an injunction on Election Day, McKane had them roughed up, boasting, "Injunctions don't go here."

McKane's despotic declaration was played up in the local press, prompting a trial that brought national attention. He was found guilty of election fraud and misuse of public funds, and served four years upstate in Sing Sing. McKane returned to Brooklyn in 1898 and, after a series of strokes, died in September 1899.

Not all of the former island was written off, however. Manhattan Beach, with its stable upper-middle-class neighborhood and Kingsborough Community College, has remained unchanged for decades, and in the last twenty years, a tremendous influx of Russian immigrants has remade Brighton Beach into a Little Odessa. On the west end is the walled-in and increasingly pricey Sea Gate community, which has a growing Russian Jewish and ultra-Orthodox population. Ironically, Sea Gate was enclosed in the 1890s partially to keep out Jews, while today there are murmurs that the strict religious Hasidic Jews use the boundaries to exclude other ethnic groups.

In the late 1980s and early 1990s, medical waste washing up on Brighton Beach and Coney Island's beaches, and violent teenage crime in Coney Island, once again prompted cries of the region's demise. But shouts of imminent self-destruction date back to the nineteenth century. In the 1880s, muggers drizzled knockout drops into the drinks of unsuspecting saloon patrons; in the early 1900s, child prostitution was epidemic; and in the 1930s and 1940s, sewage stained the beaches.

In recent years, Coney Island has, however, begun the arduous climb back toward prosperity—thanks to the government's reversal on anti-recreation zoning, the perseverance of community groups and merchants, and the enduring appeal of the beach, boardwalk, and remaining amusement area. In the mid-1990s, the city improved police patrols and repaved streets while the federal government rehabilitated the eroded beaches. The subway station is now being renovated. The Astella Corporation, a not-for-profit housing organization, has built nearly one thousand private homes in the last fifteen years, says director Judi Orlando, adding a new wave of working-class residents—mainly Asian and Egyptian immigrants—to the ethnic stew of African American, Latino, and longtime Italian residents. Astella has also played a role in reviving commercial development, along with ANCHOR, a state- and city-funded program that targets specific neighborhoods for residential and commercial revitalization. Formerly empty lots on Mermaid Avenue now feature a Rite Aid, a Pioneer Supermarket, and numerous mom-and-pop stores.

Although Coney Island is always awash in nostalgia for the good ol' days, it is showing signs of reinventing itself yet again as a new generation of entrepreneurs revives and replaces the hulks of abandoned rides. And after three decades of broken plans, even Steeplechase Park is again inhabited. The Brooklyn Cyclones, a single-A minor league affiliate of the New York Mets, made their debut on this historic site in a brand-new stadium in 2001. "It has brought new energy to the area," Orlando says.

The stadium—initially controversial—displaced the long-planned-for Sportsplex amateur athletics complex, which was to be funded by various government agencies and would have featured a twelve-thousand-seat arena, gyms, and training centers. Whereas the complex would have provided year-round recreation and jobs, the new ball club is seasonal, playing only thirty-eight home games. The stadium, however, will be made available for high school or college games in the future, and a Little League field for the community will be built on the property.

After much political posturing by Mayor Rudolph Giuliani and Brooklyn Borough President Howard Golden, the city agreed to provide $30 million to help fund the Sportsplex on another site in Coney Island; the Brooklyn Sports Foundation, which had spent years planning the complex, agreed to relinquish control to a newly created local development corporation. The Sportsplex could be operational by 2003. The city also earmarked an extra $30 million for other physical improvements in Coney Island.

"Coney Island has really gotten its act together," says Dick Zigun, who operates Sideshows-by-the-Seashore, a long-running freak show.

Each summer, more than five million subway riders and countless carloads of visitors still carouse in Coney Island's sand and surf or brave the frenzy of the amusement rides. From the ageless Cyclone to the brand-new ballpark, Coney Island seems to have a future after all.

Exploring the Island

Coney's island days are long gone, but the peninsula remains a cherished destination for anyone pursuing simple, often hedonistic, pleasures. The major attractions are the beach and two neighborhoods—Coney Island and Brighton Beach. Sea Gate, on the western end, has guards that keep outsiders at bay. Manhattan Beach, on the eastern end, has a public beach but minimal public parking, which helps it retain the air of exclusivity developed in the nineteenth century. (There is one parking lot on Oriental Boulevard.)

To fully embrace Coney Island, cast off your inhibitions, disregard decorum, and celebrate the tacky. (Call ahead between Labor Day and Memorial Day. Many rides close down or operate only on weekends during the off-season.)

When the **Cyclone** opened in 1927 on Surf Avenue and West Tenth Street, its 110-second ride over nine hills rocked the senses in unforgettable style. It still does. One of the few wooden-track roller coasters around, the rattling Cyclone—with its first drop of eighty-five feet at a sixty-degree angle—nearly jolts you out of your body. According to legend, a man who lost his voice due to trauma in World War II rode the Cyclone five years later and staggered off saying, "I feel sick." From then on, he could speak. (Don't worry, the rickety feel is merely part of the ambience—the tracks are all periodically replaced.)

The Cyclone is owned by New York City and operated by **Astroland,** (718) 266-3434, the largest pay-one-price amusement park in Coney Island today. Astroland offers thirty-five rides including the spinning ride Break Dance, and a log flume as well as some geared toward kids; as a sign of the times, Astroland is making the largest single investment in its history in new rides and attractions.

Deno's Wonder Wheel Park, (718) 372-2592, is next to Astroland. The **Wonder Wheel,** a twenty-four-car Ferris wheel weighing two hundred tons and standing 150 feet high, is the park's centerpiece. Opened as an independent ride in 1920, this New York City landmark has since carried thirty-one million customers around and around and around. Deno's has twenty-five other rides as well, including go-carts and the Spook-A-Rama haunted house as well as a kiddie park featuring the Sea Serpent, a family-oriented roller coaster. Deno's sponsors fireworks every Friday night at 9 PM in-season. Coney Island also has independent operators with other rides and attractions.

Bumper cars are as much fun as you remember at **El Dorado Bumper Disco,** 1216 Surf Avenue off West Twelfth Street, (718) 946-6642. Outside, the prerecorded barker invites passersby to "bump, bump, bump yo' ass off." Inside, blasting music, flashing lights, and slamming cars bring you to the zenith of mindless merriment on which Coney Island has built its reputation.

Down the block is the **Sideshows-by-the-Sea** freak show run by a modern-day George Tilyou named Dick Zigun and his not-for-profit group, **Coney Island USA,** 1208 Surf Avenue, (718) 372-5159. (The entrance is on West Twelfth Street.) Although the delightfully gauche barker lays it on thick, this is less of an excursion into seamy voyeurism than its predecessors since societal changes have shifted the emphasis from people with deformities, like Pinhead Boy, to stupid human tricks. One performer chews glass, another swallows swords, and a third lies on a bed of nails while audience members stand on him. The crassness has a peculiar charm, although the poor pacing and self-consciously amateur style soon wear thin. (Scattered throughout Coney are other "freaks," like the living Decapitated Woman—someone in a skimpy bikini whose head is skillfully obscured by black cloth and bright lights.)

Upstairs is the organization's overlooked **Coney Island Museum.** Although the showroom isn't the full-fledged museum Coney deserves, the displays are charming. There are tributes to the old parks—a Steeplechase horse with a TWO ON A HORSE sign, and sheet music for John Philip Sousa's Luna theme song, "I've Made Plans for the Summer"—as well as reminders of the area's less respectable side—a wooden milk bottle from an impossible-to-win midway game, and photos of early freaks like Seal Boy.

Coney Island USA also sponsors several cultural events, including a tattoo show each September and concerts each Friday night in summer. The highlight is the **Mermaid Parade,** which has inaugurated each summer since 1983 on the season's first Saturday. The parade is more intimate and homey than its larger cousins on Thanksgiving and St. Patrick's Day, but is raucous and flamboyant in grand Coney Island tradition. Almost everyone marching along Surf Avenue and the boardwalk is costumed as a mermaid or King Neptune, yet it never gets boring. One year, the tentacled, silver Mermaids from Mars were followed by an S&M mermaid, a sea maiden outfitted in torn newspapers, and even a dachshund dressed as a mermaid. The parade's most regal Neptune is crowned king and presented with a cardboard thermometer to turn up the temperature and usher in summer. Neptune and Zigun then plunge, fully clad, into the ocean and declare the season open.

On the former home of Steeplechase Park, Surf Avenue at West Fifteenth Street, is the new sixty-five-hundred-seat ballpark, Keyspan Park, erected for the **Brooklyn Cyclones'** debut in 2001, (718) 449-8497. Many fans will have an ocean view. Those sitting along the first-base line will look out onto the Cyclone and Wonder Wheel and Astroland's new tower ride, while spectators along the third-base side will see the Parachute Jump just beyond the stadium's walls. The Jump, closed in 1963, had been slowly deteriorating and was to be dismantled by the city until locals fought for its preservation. Affectionately called the Eiffel Tower of Brooklyn, it has a fresh coat of paint, brightly colored base panels . . . and national landmark status. A concourse connects the stadium directly to the boardwalk.

Mermaids From Mars make a terrestrial visit to Coney Island's annual Mermaid Parade, where kookiness is the order of the day.

Just beyond the Jump at West Twentieth Street and the boardwalk is the **Abe Stark Skating Rink,** (718) 946-6536, open for ice skating and hockey during Coney Island's off-season.

Despite its proximity to the ocean, the **New York Aquarium,** Surf Avenue and West Eighth Street, (718) 265-FISH, seems out of place here.

Coney's atmosphere is brassy and boisterous; the gliding creatures in the aquarium's tanks and seascapes are graceful and soothing. The amusement area is all about fun; the aquarium aims to educate while it entertains. Yet the aquarium, which moved to Coney Island in 1957, is finally acclimating to its environs. The traditional stars are still here: beluga whales, penguins, and an array of sharks. But in the last decade, several jazzy new exhibits have opened, including Discovery Cove, which uses creatures like the leaf fish, an expert in camouflage, to teach wildlife survival techniques; Sea Cliffs, a Pacific Coast replica, where you'll learn that sea otters eat the human equivalent of eighty hamburgers a day; Sensational Seahorses; and Alien Stingers, featuring jellyfish.

Where to Eat

A Coney Island parable tells of a couple of starving cabaret performers who, in 1916, complained to a Feltman's delivery man/roll slicer about the frankfurter's ten-cent price tag. Heeding the cries of these struggling entertainers—Jimmy Durante and Eddie Cantor—young Nathan Handwerker took his $300 life savings and opened a stand selling hot dogs for a nickel.

Another myth: To quell public fears concerning the quality of these cheap dogs, Handwerker gave free hot dogs to doctors, who chomped away while clad in their reassuring white coats and stethoscopes. Some say Handwerker actually hired bums and dressed them up as physicians.

A fact: The spiced-meat formula devised by Nathan's wife, Ida, had sold a hundred million hot dogs by 1955 and still sells nearly a million a year from this site alone.

Nathan's, 1310 Surf Avenue, (718) 946-2202, serves corn, barbecued chicken, and fried seafood (including frog legs), but its hot dogs and fries remain the quintessential Coney dining experience.

According to legend, Babe Ruth once consumed twenty-four Nathan's franks and two gallons of lemonade in a single sitting. But for the record books, Nathan's sponsors a hot-dog-eating contest every July 4. The twelve-minute record—reestablished several times in recent years—stands at twenty-five and one-eighth hot dogs (with buns); it was set in 2000 by Kazu-toyo Arai, Japan's sushi- and noodle-eating champion.

Tops among the other food stands—which offer similar menus of corn dogs, clam strips, knishes, Jamaican beef patties, and beer—is **Ruby's,** on the boardwalk off Stillwell Avenue. This joint's got no name out front—the signs just say BAR and RESTAURANT. But it's got character; it dates to the teens and its walls are covered with photos of Coney Island, then and now.

William's Candy Shoppe, 1318 Surf Avenue, (718) 372-0302, opened in 1926 and seems oblivious to these health-conscious times: jelly apples, cotton candy, giant swirl lollipops, and candied marshmallows whisper sweet nothings from large storefront windows.

Another old-time candy store, **Philip's Confections,** (718) 372-8783, has made chocolates, candies, shakes, and egg creams since 1928. Long located in a small booth in the Coney Island subway terminal, the shop is being forced to move sometime in 2001 due to Transit Authority renovations. Co-owner John Dorman, who has been with the shop since 1948, vows to stay in Coney Island.

Don't worry, Coney Island also has food your mother would let you eat. In 1965, after buying fifty-eight-year-old **Gargiulo's,** 2911 West 15th Street, (718) 266-4891, three Russo brothers revived its flagging reputation. Thirty years later, with a second generation of Russos at the helm, Gargiulo's remains one of Brooklyn's most popular Italian restaurants (with space for private parties of twenty to four hundred people). It has a simple yet tasteful decor; dishes are moderately priced and made with exquisite ingredients—one of the Russos makes fresh mozzarella each morning. From the *pennette pasquiline* to the creamy chocolate mousse cake, the food will have you sighing softly in appreciation. And you'll be squealing with excitement when they bring the lottery shaker to your table afterward—if you guess the right number, the meal is on the house.

Carolina's, 1409 Mermaid Avenue, (718) 714-1294, greets you with a glass of sweet vermouth and fresh, warm bread. Save some bread for dipping in the zesty sauces accompanying dishes like hot antipasto, fried ravioli, and veal rollatini. While the food is excellent and the prices moderate, the atmosphere might make you think you've stumbled into a bad bar mitzvah—catering-hall decor and a tacky synthesizer player banging out everything from "My Way" to "Havah Nagila." You know it wasn't like this when the restaurant opened in 1928.

One place that doesn't change is **Totonno's,** 1524 Neptune Avenue, (718) 372-8606. Opened in 1924 by Totonno Pero, who had worked in Lombardi's (New York's first pizzeria), the coal-fired brick ovens are in good hands with the third generation of the Pero family. They make fresh dough daily and turn out some of the city's finest pies.

A taste of old Brighton Beach survives at 1001 Brighton Beach Avenue, where **Mrs. Stahl's,** (718) 648-0210, has sold knishes since 1935. (Before that, Mrs. Stahl baked them at home and sold them on the beach.) Today,

Mrs. Stahl's has been relegated to the storefront's back corner, and a Russian fast-food joint has taken over the rest of the space. Still, the variety of doughy pockets boggles the mind—broccoli, sweet potato, kasha, mushroom barley, and pineapple cheese, to name a few.

The best Russian food in Brighton Beach is not in the restaurants but in the shops, particularly **M & I International Foods,** 249 Brighton Beach Avenue, (718) 615-1011; **White Acacia Supermarket,** 283 Brighton Beach Avenue, (800) 834-1836; and **Exclusive Deli,** 411 Brighton Beach Avenue, (718) 368-3001.

With a main dining room seating 450 people, **National,** 273 Brighton Beach Avenue, (718) 646-1225, is among the largest of new Brighton Beach's Russian supper clubs, offering a prix fixe, multi-course meal and live entertainment. A cross between a wedding celebration and Disneyland's It's a Small World ride, a night at this club is not so much a true Russian experience as it is a Russian interpretation of American self-indulgence and European glamour. So get a group of friends together, dress up, and prepare for a surreal night of partying.

Some of the food here is traditional Russian fare, but the emphasis is more on excess than ethnicity. At National, dinner includes seventeen cold appetizers (herring, jellied chicken, and grilled vegetables, to name a few); six hot appetizers (including mussels and barbecued ribs); a main-course platter of chicken, beef, and lamb; and dessert. A bottle of vodka is included, and you are allowed to bring your own alcohol, too.

After gorging yourself with food, it's time to dance. A live band performs everything from traditional Russian music to "Hotel California" to the hora, while futuristic videos and camera shots spotlighting the cavorting crowd fill a big screen. The dancing goes until 3 AM, breaking only for the wackiest cabaret show imaginable: a broad, colorful spectacle with acts that include a multi-colored, long-necked, Sesame Street–type bird lip-synching "Putting on the Ritz."

Other well-established clubs offering similar romps include **Odessa,** 1113 Brighton Beach Avenue, (718) 332-3223; and **Primorski,** 282B Brighton Beach Avenue, (718) 891-3111.

Along the boardwalk in Brighton Beach are several hybrid Russian eateries, most offering sushi and hamburgers along with chicken Kiev and *kostiza moldavien* (marinated pork chops). Their food is better than the nightclubs' fare, but the emphasis at the outdoor cafés is on vodka, cigarettes, and vibrant conversation. They're also ideal places for people-watching, since the boardwalk is a veritable mob scene on summer nights—people of all ages chat in a babel of languages (mostly Russian and Brooklynese) as they drink or stroll or simply relax on benches. Unlike Manhattan, where everyone is rushing to some distant destination, in Brighton Beach there is a sense that nothing much is needed beyond the boardwalk, the cool breeze, the stars in the sky, and the waves shimmering in the moonlight.

Island Hopping

By bus: Many buses travel to Coney Island. The B29, B36, B64, B74, and X29 all go to the western half, while the B1, B36, B68, and B49 all go to the eastern portion.

By train: The B, D, F, and N trains all stop in Coney Island. The D and Q stop in Brighton Beach.

By car: Take Coney Island Avenue or Ocean Parkway south to the peninsula or take the Belt Parkway to exit 7 and get on Ocean Parkway.

19. Forgotten Islands of South Brooklyn

Plum Island • White Island

Forgotten Islands of South Brooklyn

Plum Island

LONG BEFORE THE UNITED STATES invaded Grenada, Panama, or Haiti, American troops were called in to protect vital interests and establish order at a troublesome spot much closer to home.

The brief story of Plum Island is one of the stranger chapters in New York history, in which this 150-acre strip just east of Coney Island was invaded twice within a year by the U.S. Army.

Plum (or Plumb) Island blossomed after the United States purchased a portion of it in 1891 to build a fort. When the plans fell through, enterprising Brooklynites set up tent camps and shacks and, later, bars and inns on this federal land since alcohol and tobacco could be sold without local excise taxes. By 1907 there was a five-cent ferry to Sheepshead Bay and nearly a hundred homes in this poor man's resort, including one owned by sixty-six-year-old John Greenwood, who had grown up on Plum Island when it supported nothing but three shacks. (His father helped capture the notorious pirate Charles Gibbs.)

Anxious to turn a profit from the land, the federal government dispatched army troops in May 1908 to clear out the squatters, and leased the property to Winfield Overton, a former judge. When the Plum Island squatters returned, Overton allowed them to stay, but began acting as if he were the czar of Plum Island. He established his own police force, and in August nearly provoked an armed confrontation with New York police by declaring that during an upcoming carnival he would hold boxing matches—illegal in New York at the time—and would use force to defend his federal land rights.

Overton eventually backed down, but in April 1909 the government revoked his lease, organized the Plum Island Association, and put new leaders in power. When rumors of Overton's return circulated, the army sent in soldiers, this time to defend residents from the ruler the government had originally installed.

Overton never returned and islanders lived in peace for nearly three decades. Even after New York City bought the island from the federal government in 1924, hundreds of Brooklynites summered there, with grocery peddlers and icemen bringing supplies across at low tide.

A new overlord, Robert Moses, arrived in 1937, kicking out the last squatters and shutting down the beach so he could build the Belt Parkway over the land. By 1940, landfill linked what had become Plum Beach to Brooklyn. Moses, who had cut off the residents from their local swimming spot, opened a picnic area there for Belt Parkway drivers. Today this forgotten chunk of land, east of exit 9B, is part of the Gateway National Recreation Area.

White Island

The name White Island rarely shows up on city maps. Local residents, fishermen, and employees at the Marine Park Golf Course don't even refer to this seventy-three-acre hump by its proper name—they call it Mau-Mau, Golf Course, or Gilligan's Island (the latter for a recent squatter). But now, thanks to a new nature trail that features views of the island, White Island is being properly recognized.

It was named for Alfred T. White, who in 1917, along with Frederick B. Pratt, donated 150 Brooklyn acres to the city to be set aside as parkland. The borough was developing rapidly, and the men wanted to preserve the area's waterfront property and rich marshland. The land was so valuable that businessmen pressured the city not to accept the offer; it took the city seven years to embrace the deal. At that time, White Island didn't exist.

Then, in 1934, the Supreme Court ordered New York to stop dumping garbage in the ocean, so Parks Commissioner Robert Moses used waste to fill in marshes and create Marine Park. Over the next quarter century, White Island too grew out of several marshy islands and household trash— it is, at its core, a collection of old banana peels, ash, concrete debris, and newspapers referring to President Dwight D. Eisenhower.

There were plans to build an executive golf course on the island, but by the time funds were raised to build a bridge to the island, White Island had come under the protection of the National Park Service. Except for the occasional squatter or fisherman who would row past the carcasses of dozens of wrecked boats to try his luck from the island's edge, White Island sat undisturbed until 1995. That year, it enjoyed an environmental makeover thanks to a law that forced builders of a nearby development that destroyed eighty acres of wetland to make up that land elsewhere. The project involved removing derelict boats and debris and restoring the island with plantings, thus helping to fulfill the legacy of the man for whom it is named.

Exploring the Island

White Island may be inaccessible, but it can easily be seen from a gravel trail at the new **Salt Marsh Nature Center at Marine Park,** (718) 421-2021, which opened in spring 2000. The one-mile loop begins at the back of the nature center, meandering through a protected salt-marsh environment, much like what Alfred T. White wanted preserved. The trail, rich with salt-marsh hay, salt-marsh cordgrass, and the wildlife that calls this ecosystem home, features several viewing spots along the way. Lookout Hill offers an excellent chance to see the marsh and White Island from a perch perspective. The view of the island is even better once you round the bend en route back to the nature center. These days, nature has claimed the island, so there is little resemblance to its landfill past.

The Urban Park Rangers offer free guided tours at 1 and 3 PM on Saturdays and Sundays, along with periodic lectures. The nature center is closed Wednesdays. An exhibit describes the qualities of a salt marsh and how it fits into the bigger ecological picture as well as a bit of history about the Marine Park area.

Island Hopping

By car: Take the Belt Parkway east to exit 11-N. Take Flatbush Avenue to Avenue U and turn left. Take Avenue U to East Thirty-third Street. Parking is across from the nature center.

By subway: Take the D train to Avenue U, then transfer for the B3 bus toward Kings Plaza, getting off at East Thirty-third Street.

By bus: The B3 bus stops right by the nature center on Avenue U at East Thirty-third Street.

Part VII

The Kills

PRALL'S ISLAND • SHOOTER'S ISLAND • ISLE OF MEADOW

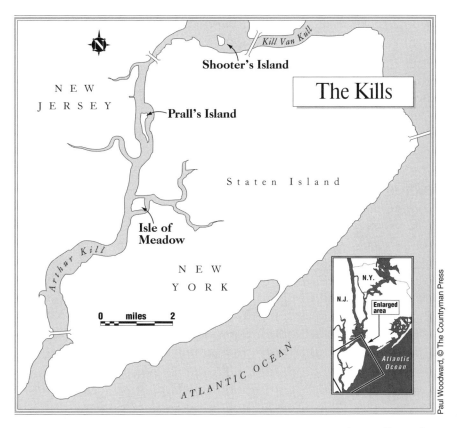

The Kills separate Staten Island from New Jersey. The Arthur Kill winds its way up Staten Island's western shore, while the Kill Van Kull wends between Staten Island's northern shore and Bayonne, New Jersey, before flowing into Upper New York Bay.

20. Prall's Island, Shooter's Island, and Isle of Meadow

"They're in the middle of some of the most commercial insults foisted on civilization, from the hell on earth that's called the Elizabeth and Linden oil refineries to the massive ship traffic that goes up and down the Kill."

—MARC MATSIL, DIRECTOR OF NATURAL RESOURCES,
NEW YORK CITY PARKS DEPARTMENT

Prall's Island, Shooter's Island, and Isle of Meadow

SOME CALL IT A MIRACLE. Others say it just goes to prove the resilience of nature. From March to September each year, more than fifteen hundred nesting pairs of herons, egrets, and ibis build nests and nurture their young amid the green patches of New York's islands that exist along the periphery of this concrete jungle.

New York City lies along the Atlantic Flyway, one of four North American migration routes. While this rookery—the most significant for waterbirds in the state—has spread over time to include islands in Lower New York Bay, the East River, and the Hutchinson River, it all started in the Arthur Kill and Kill Van Kull, with Prall's Island (80 acres), Shooter's Island (43 acres), and Isle of Meadow (101 acres). Waders first arrived on Shooter's Island in 1974, branching out to Prall's Island four years later and Isle of Meadow in 1988.

The Kills, which border northwest Staten Island, have since the 1880s been home to heavy industry and more ship traffic than the Panama Canal. By the late 1960s they had become so polluted that the water couldn't sustain the fish and other marine life that many of the birds eat. The Clean Water Act of 1972, however, improved conditions enough to support some aquatic life, which, in turn, attracted to the islands glossy ibis, black-crowned night herons, yellow-crowned night herons, snowy egrets, great egrets, and cattle egrets.

"The birds are there because the fish are there," says Marc Matsil, director of natural resources for the New York City Parks Department, which, together with the New York City Audubon Society and state and city agencies, is working to enhance and protect the birds' fragile wetlands habitat through a plan called the Harbor Herons Project.

Despite ecosystem improvements, this extraordinary avian haven is still extremely vulnerable. In 1990, a series of spills dumped nearly 1.6 million gallons of oil into the harbor's waterways and wetlands. The gravest peril came in January when Exxon's underwater pipeline between Linden and Bayonne burst, pouring 567,000 gallons of fuel oil into the Arthur Kill. About seven hundred waterfowl and gulls died (the waders had gone south for the winter) and nearly two hundred acres of salt marsh were damaged, killing the organisms at the bottom of the food chain.

Nesting patterns for the waders suffered for several years, with snowy egrets and glossy ibis—dependent on the salt marshes and tidal mudflats for food—reproducing less and losing many chicks in infancy. Exxon pleaded guilty to criminal charges and paid $15 million in criminal and civil penalties to an array of city, state, and federal government agencies. That money was spent on cleanup and research into the effects of the spill as well as rehabilitating the contaminated areas by hand-planting salt-marsh cordgrass and other native plants.

While the birds' presence in New York City is reason for optimism, their continued survival is threatened by pollution and chronic habitat destruction. Blanchard says the most ominous threat is the "supposedly limitless growth of Staten Island," which has prompted the government to consider expanding the Goethals Bridge and Staten Island Expressway. "Decisions about accommodating traffic are destroying our natural areas," he says, particularly Staten Island's Old Place Creek and other wetlands and hummocks central to the birds' ecosystem and foraging grounds.

In recent years, other seemingly less dramatic threats have driven thousands of birds from Prall's and Shooter's Islands, both of which belong to the parks department. (Isle of Meadow, which belongs to the department of sanitation, retains the city's biggest bird population; in 2000, it hosted 596 of the city's 1,500 pairs of nesting waders.) On Prall's Island, the problem seems to be a decline in the tree canopy and the presence of raccoons and red-tailed hawks. In 2000, the parks department's natural resources group (NRG) received $410,000 in city and state money to begin restoring the habitat.

"I'd give the tree canopy a D," says NRG restoration ecologist Carl Alderson, pointing to the sudden and sharp decline in gray birch and the explosion of the invasive ailanthus tree, which provides unsuitable "branch architecture" for herons and egrets. After a survey, Alderson expects to remove the ailanthus and plant suitable, durable trees like the post oak and chestnut oak, creating a maritime forest botanical reserve. He will also recommend trapping and removing the raccoons. "We'll have to take an active role in controlling the predators," he says.

The aggressors on Shooter's Island are of a different species: "Young, male humans," says Paul Kerlinger, a biologist and consultant for New York City Audubon. He cites the presence of campfires, an American flag, and wine bottles as evidence. "They are driving the birds out," he adds.

Historical Detour: Ruthless People

Nothing much ever happened on Prall's Island. The quiet salt
meadow once fed livestock that sloshed over from Staten Island.
In 1910, it was a depository for dredge spoils scooped from the
Arthur Kill. That was about it.

Then, in 1916, the city proposed building a garbage facility
there. Virtually overnight, Prall's became the subject of a bitter
debate over its ownership, prompting opposing interests to seize
the island with little regard for the law.

While Staten Island and Queens processed their own gar-
bage, refuse from other boroughs was treated on Brooklyn's
Barren Island, until complaints from Brooklynites forced Mayor
John Mitchel to close the plant. Without any public notice,
Mitchel won approval for a new garbage facility on Staten Island
at a special board of estimate meeting on April 10.

Needless to say, Staten Islanders were not happy. "The Garbage War" dominated the front pages of the *Staten Islander* and
Staten Island Register, inspired formation of the Staten Island
Vigilance Committee and the Women's Anti-Garbage League,
and provoked thousands of Staten Islanders to denounce Mitchel
at city-hall protests.

When Prall's Island, just off Staten Island's west shore, was
selected as the plant site, the island's ownership quickly became
a matter of dispute. As Manhattan real-estate man J. Sterling
Drake prepared to sell Prall's to the plant's builders, Edward P.
Doyle, a leader of the anti-garbage movement and a real-estate
man himself, claimed he held the title.

Doyle secured the island with a barbed-wire fence, built a
shack, and hired twin seventy-one-year-old watchmen, James
and William Farmer, to keep the contractors out. On May 18,
under cover of darkness, fifteen men raided Prall's Island, kid-
napped the lookouts, and confiscated the controversial land. The
Farmers were taken by launch to Brooklyn, where they were
freed but warned that returning to Prall's Island might result in
death. The old men notified the police, who stormed the island
and arrested the group, found huddled around the shack's stove.
The island-snatchers had been employed by Drake, who was

later indicted for the kidnapping.

Two days later, Edward Doyle took out a full-page ad in the *Staten Islander,* defending the validity of his title and stating that in order to stop the plant he would take possession of any site by "any title available and by any means necessary." Doyle claimed to own not only Prall's Island but also other local properties delineated in a land grant made in the early eighteenth century by Queen Anne. Drake countered that his title had been undisputed for a century and that Doyle's claim would destroy the local real-estate market. Drake even said he worked on Prall's Island, cutting salt hay.

When the plant's builders became frustrated by Drake's inability to sell them Prall's Island, they took possession of a marshy hummock near the Fresh Kills called Lake's Island. The city approved the relocation, but the facility operated for less than two years before being abandoned. Lake's Island later became home to the city's notorious landfill, while Prall's Island slipped back into anonymity.

Visitors have even torn down NO TRESPASSING signs explaining the presence of nesting birds, in flagrant disregard for their survival. Enforcement is being stepped up.

Despite the birds' absence, Kerlinger, Alderson, and Peter Blanchard, a naturalist for the Trust for Public Land, say past experience shows that the birds will return to the islands over time if the habitat is improved and the aggressors are removed. (Kerlinger adds that birds sometimes rotate their locales after a buildup of nest parasites.) In the meantime, the overall number of birds in the harbor suggests that they may simply be inhabiting some of the city's other islands. "They were not wiped out, they just shifted sites," says Kerlinger.

In fact, today there are more birds on the harbor islands than there were in 1994. The new "in" neighborhoods for herons and egrets include Hoffman Island in Lower New York Bay, Goose Island in the Hutchinson River, and Canarsie Pol in Jamaica Bay. Says Blanchard, "I'm constantly encouraged."

While the islands are now often referred to collectively as the Harbor Herons Project, each possesses a distinct history.

Situated in the Kill Van Kull across from Mariner's Harbor on the north shore of Staten Island, Shooter's Island was a popular colonial hunting preserve. During the Revolution, agents for General George Washington used the island as a drop-off point for delivering messages.

Until industry arrived in the mid-nineteenth century, the area surrounding Shooter's Island was known for its thick, tasty oysters. In the early 1860s, David Decker—whose ancestors were among the earliest Dutch settlers on Staten Island—had a small shipyard on what was then an eleven-acre island. The Shooter's Island Petroleum Refining & Storage Company bought the island in 1865 and added a new dock and huge buildings. At the turn of the twentieth century, the Townsend-Downey Shipbuilding Company built cruising and racing yachts there.

The island's most spectacular event occurred on February 25, 1902, when two thousand invited guests, including President Theodore Roosevelt, witnessed the launching of *Meteor III*, a magnificent racing yacht built for the emperor of Germany, Kaiser Wilhelm II. The *New York Times* called the affair "the most distinguished gathering ever assembled to witness the naming of a vessel in American waters." The yacht featured a majestic eagle figurehead on its prow; a main saloon with fireplace, grand piano, and mahogany bar with silver handrails; and a dining table that seated twenty-four.

Mostly, however, the workers at Shooter's Island toiled on projects with more grit than glamour. During World War I, the Standard Shipbuilding Company employed nine thousand men who churned out steel cargo ships for the war effort. When operations ended in 1920, the island became a dumping ground for derelict vessels. Today, the landscape is littered with rotting dry docks, piers, and pilings.

It was during the shipbuilding days that about thirty acres of fill were added to Shooter's Island to accommodate the massive shipyards. Most of the expansion was on the island's north side, enlarging it beyond its New York border and into New Jersey. Today, Shooter's Island is forty-three acres, thirty-four of them in New York City. Two New Jersey cities— Bayonne, which owns seven and a half acres, and Elizabeth, which owns one and a half acres—have granted New York conservation easements, allowing it to manage the entire island as a wildlife refuge. If the island is not used for this purpose, the properties revert back to New Jersey.

Throughout the 1960s and 1970s, Representative John Murphy, a Staten Island Democrat, spearheaded an effort to blow Shooter's Island out of the water. He claimed that removing this obstacle would make navigation easier for ship traffic and create jobs in the region. But much to the delight of environmentalists, a study by the Army Corps of Engineers concluded that Shooter's Island was not hazardous to navigation and recommended against spending $60 million to obliterate it.

Prall's Island, in the Arthur Kill just south of the Goethals Bridge, has minimal documented history. It was known as Dongan's Island when New York governor Thomas Dongan took title in 1688. The name was later corrupted to Duncan's Island. The name Prall's Island, which took hold in the late nineteenth century, is likely derived from a prominent local family who lived on Staten Island just across from the marshy island.

During the two world wars, surplus ships anchored off the island's shores were dubbed the Prall's Island Fleet by locals, who often rowed out to investigate the military leftovers. Through the centuries, however, Prall's Island was generally ignored—until 1978, when exotic herons, egrets, and ibis were discovered nesting there.

Isle of Meadow, less than two miles south of Prall's Island and at the intersection of the Arthur Kill and the Fresh Kills, was dubbed Dead Man's Island in the eighteenth century after a deadly accident occurred there. A ferry crossing the Arthur Kill was blown off-course in 1768, forcing ashore nine men, two slaves, and a boy. A sharp wind and lack of shelter killed one man and the boy; the others lost fingers and toes from frostbite.

Ten years later, three boats with American soldiers landed on the island, catching off-guard British sentries posted there. By the late 1790s, the island was referred to as Ye Island of Meadow or Island of Salt Meadows.

A rickety wooden footbridge connected the island to Staten Island until a storm destroyed it in 1929. The department of sanitation proposed joining the island to the mainland in 1940, but instead developed land east of the island and created the largest landfill in the world. More than seventeen thousand tons of New York City garbage pass the Isle of Meadow and its remarkable bird colony every day.

The Harbor Herons Project seeks to ensure that the entire urban estuary complex is protected from further degradation. Toward that end, Kerlinger has solicited help from numerous agencies and not-for-profits, including the Trust for Public Land, the National Park Service at Gateway, and the Urban Park Rangers. Even citizens have become involved, phoning in from Co-op City windows in the Bronx to report sightings on nearby Goose Island. "My job is to develop a program for New York City Audubon, but also to do the best I can for the herons and the egrets," Kerlinger says. "I'm encouraging this to become bigger so there's less of a chance that some horrible transformation can take place here."

Herons and egrets were almost extinct at the turn of the twentieth century, when their gorgeous feathers were used to decorate women's hats. Now they thrive on islands that have grown wild and glorious despite the surrounding industrial jungle. These islands are beacons of green to birds hungry for sanctuary in an urban environment. And the birds, in turn, are a reminder that not all is lost. "These birds are pioneers," says Katharine C. Parsons, a scientist with the Massachusetts-based Manomet Observatory for Conservation Sciences, a non-profit research organization that launched a study of these birds in the 1980s, "and an incredible symbol of wildness and recovery."

Acknowledgments: No Author Is an Island

For helping with the first edition of this book, we would like to thank the many people quoted herein as well as express our deepest gratitude to all those who helped make the rather tedious task of research relatively smooth sailing. Thanks to the staffs of the New York Public Library, the Brooklyn Public Library, and the Long Island Room of the Queens Public Library, particularly to the folks in the periodical department at the Mid-Manhattan Library, and to Faigi Rosenthal and the *Daily News* research librarians.

We would also like to thank the staffs of the Bronx Historical Society, especially John McNamara; the New-York Historical Society and the Queens Historical Society, particularly Jim Driscoll and Vincent F. Seyfried; the New York City Municipal Reference Library; the Staten Island Institute of Arts and Science, specifically retired archivist Hugh Powell and Curator of History Vincent Sweeney; the National Park Service; the Ellis Island Research Library, particularly Barry Moreno; the Hudson River Foundation; the Harbor Defense Museum; St. Francis College library; the Brooklyn College library; and Norman Brouwer at the South Street Seaport Museum.

We will always remember the wonderful tours of these forever-special islands provided by the following individuals who gave so generously of their time: from the U.S. Coast Guard, Lieutenant Commander Paul Milligan, Chief Adrian Kavanagh, and the crew of the *Cutter Wire*, as well as Lieutenant Pat Ryan and everyone at the Guard's Brooklyn air station; Ed Knapp at WFAN-AM; Don Riepe of the Jamaica Bay Wildlife Refuge; Peter Mott of the New York Audubon Society; Fred M. Kinneary of the U.S. park police; Tom McCarthy of the department of corrections; Niguel Long; Jennifer R. Wynn, managing editor of *Prison Life* magazine; Captain Skippy Lane and historian Tom Nye; April Costentino of the New York City Parks Department; and Rita Mullaly of the Gateway National Recreation Area.

We are also indebted to the following people who helped us dig up hard-to-find tidbits and steered us toward more obscure research sources: Ray

Curran of the Bronx office of the department of city planning; Ben Miller; Steven H. Corey; John Parascondola of the U.S. Public Health Service; Ira Steinberg of the New York City Parks Department; Paul Silver of Silver & Ziskind; Judy Berdy and Eugenie Martin; Katharine C. Parsons of the Manomet Observatory for Conservation Sciences; author Katherine A. Kirkpatrick; island aficionado Andy Engel; Seth Kamil and Big Onion Walking Tours; Sara McPherson, editor of *The Current;* Dan Tubridy; Emil Lucev; and John Gallagher.

Many of the people mentioned above combed the manuscript to help weed out mistakes, but we also relied on a few other expert sets of eyes: Thanks to Russell Gilmore, Stephen Laise, Bill Twomey, Robert Caro, Gerard Wolfe, Joseph Viteritti, Frank Duffy, and John Manbeck.

The second edition of this book would not have been possible without Alan Glazen, who helped us transform the book into a documentary and thus inspired this new edition. Last but not least we would like to thank everybody at The Countryman Press, from Carl Taylor, who believed in our project at the beginning, and Helen Whybrow, who saw us through the first edition, to the folks who made it happen this second time around, beginning with Kermit Hummel, who gave us the green light, as well as managing editor Ann Kraybill, and Jennifer Goneau, who oversaw the spectacular redesign of the book cover.

Selected Bibliography

We wish we could have listed every research source, but that would have doubled the length of the book. What follows, therefore, is a partial bibliography. These books not only provided historical perspective but in many cases also led us to contemporary sources—newspapers, magazines, memoirs, and personal papers (including those of City Island forefather Benjamin Palmer), government reports, maps, and journal articles—that also helped us in the writing of this book. Some newspapers worth mentioning are the *Staten Island Advance, Brooklyn Eagle, Newtown Register,* and City Island's *Island Current.* Not included in this research inventory are those books already cited in the text, such as *The Iconography of Manhattan Island* by I. M. Phelps Stokes and *The Power Broker* by Robert Caro.

Barlow, Elizabeth. *The Forests and Wetlands of New York City.* Boston: Little, Brown, 1971.

Berengarten, Sidney. *Ellis Island.* Unpublished, 1932.

Black, Frederic. *Jamaica Bay: A History.* Washington, D.C.: Gateway National Recreation Area, 1981.

Duffy, Francis J., and William H. Miller. *The New York Harbor Book.* Falmouth, Maine: TBW Books, 1986.

Flood, Allen and Robert Mullen. *City Island: Her Voyage Through History.* City Island: Self-published, 1949.

Gschedler, Andre. *True Light on the Statue of Liberty and Its Creator.* Narberth, Penn.: Livingston Publishing, 1966.

Holliman, Jennie, and Regina Maria Hughes. *The Statue of Liberty,* Parts I and II. Unpublished, 1934.

Homberger, Eric. *The Historical Atlas of New York City.* New York: Henry Holt and Company, 1994.

Kraut, Alan. *Silent Travelers.* New York: Basic Books, 1994.

Kroeger, Brooke. *Nellie Bly: Daredevil, Reporter, Feminist.* New York: Times Books, 1994.

McCullough, Edo. *Good Ol' Coney Island.* New York: Scribner, 1957.

McNamara, John. *History in Asphalt: The Origins of Street and Place Names.* New York: Harbor Hill Books with Bronx Historical Society, 1978.

Payne, Alice. *Tales of the Clam Diggers.* City Island: Self-published, 1969.

Pisciotta, Alexander. *Theory and Practice of the New York House of Refuge.* Thesis, Florida State University, 1979.

Pitkin, Thomas. *Keepers of the Gate: A History of Ellis Island.* New York: New York University Press, 1975.

Reitz, Conrad. *Fort Lafayette: Civil War Prison 1861–1864.* Unpublished, 1962.

Richmond, John. *New York and Its Institutions, 1609–1872.* New York: E. B. Treat, 1872.

Rothman, David. *Discovery of the Asylum: Social Order and Disorder in the New Republic.* Boston: Little, Brown, 1990.

Smith, Thelma E. Knickerbocker. *Scrapbook: The Islands of New York City.* Municipal Reference Library, Notes: Volume XXXVI, Number 6, June 1962.

Stiles, Henry. *The History of Kings County.* Brooklyn: W. W. Munsell and Co., 1884.

Toward North Brother Island. New York: Institute of Man and Science, 1978.

The WPA Guide to New York City. New York City: The Federal Writers' Project, 1939.

Van Wyck, Frederick. *Keskachauge, or the First White Settlement on Long Island.* New York: Putnam, 1924.

Index

The Countryman Press and Backcountry Guides publish numerous other guides to New York, New Jersey, and New England. Here is a small sampling of our books:

Travel
New Jersey's Special Places
New Jersey's Great Gardens
The Best of the Hudson Valley and the Catskill Mountains:
   An Explorer's Guide
Connecticut: An Explorer's Guide

Hiking
50 Hikes in Connecticut
50 Hikes in New Jersey
50 Hikes in the Adirondacks
50 Hikes in Eastern Pennsylvania

Walking
Walks & Rambles in Dutchess and Putnam Counties
Walks & Rambles on Long Island
Walks & Rambles in Westchester and Fairfield Counties
Walks & Rambles in the Western Hudson Valley

Bicycling
25 Bicycle Tours in the Hudson Valley
25 Mountain Bike Tours in the Hudson Valley
30 Bicycle Tours in New Jersey
25 Mountain Bike Tours in New Jersey
Backroad Bicycling in Eastern Pennsylvania
Backroad Bicycling in Connecticut

Fishing
Good Fishing in the Adirondacks
Trout Streams of Southern New England
Trout Streams and Hatches of Pennsylvania
Mid-Atlantic Trout Streams and Their Hatches

We offer many more books on travel, outdoor sports, history, nature, and other subjects. Our books are available at bookstores everywhere. For more information or a free catalog, please call 1-800-245-4151 or write to The Countryman Press, P.O. Box 748, Woodstock, Vermont 05091. You can find descriptions of all our books on the Internet at www. countrymanpress.com.